More Adventures
in Eternity

First published by O Books, 2008
O Books is an imprint of John Hunt Publishing
Ltd., The Bothy, Deershot Lodge, Park Lane,
Ropley, Hants, SO24 0BE, UK
office1@o-books.net
www.o-books.net

Distribution in:

UK and Europe
Orca Book Services
orders@orcabookservices.co.uk
Tel: 01202 665432 Fax: 01202 666219 Int. code
(44)

USA and Canada
NBN
custserv@nbnbooks.com
Tel: 1 800 462 6420 Fax: 1 800 338 4550

Australia and New Zealand
Brumby Books
sales@brumbybooks.com.au
Tel: 61 3 9761 5535 Fax: 61 3 9761 7095

Far East (offices in Singapore, Thailand, Hong
Kong, Taiwan)
Pansing Distribution Pte Ltd
kemal@pansing.com
Tel: 65 6319 9939 Fax: 65 6462 5761

South Africa
Alternative Books
altbook@peterhyde.co.za
Tel: 021 555 4027 Fax: 021 447 1430

Text copyright Gordon Phinn 2008

Design: Stuart Davies

ISBN: 978 1 84694 081 1

A CIP catalogue record for this book is available
from the British Library.

Printed and Bound in the UK

O Books operates a distinctive and ethical publishing philosophy in
all areas of its business, from its global network of authors to
production and worldwide distribution.
This book is produced on FSC certified stock, within ISO14001
standards. The printer plants sufficient trees each year through
the Woodland Trust to absorb the level of emitted carbon in
its production.

More Adventures in Eternity

Gordon Phinn

BOOKS

Winchester, UK
Washington, USA

CONTENTS

INTRODUCTION

While it has become a commonplace in esoteric studies to declare that when *the student is ready the teacher will appear*, it is also pretty much a given that many of those thus subpoenaed by the questing soul might well be residents of planes other than the physical. And although I'd been given several lucid hints throughout the decades that my course of study would be sparked and supervised from, well, to put it simply, *above*, it was not until the winter of 1998 that my convention bound ego finally surrendered to the flow of images deposited by 'Henry' on the mental level of my tiny, cluttered apartment. It was there they had waited, patiently, to be translated into words on a page, words which readers of *A First Hand Account* will likely have by now absorbed.

Doubtlessly, 'Henry' was a teacher, a teacher who had appeared when 'Gordon' was ready. But he had appeared on the *astral** plane. (Later he would *dis*appear, not quite when I felt ready, but that's another story) Previous teachers, such as Cyril Scott, David Spangler, Georges Gurdjieff, Jeddah Krishnamurti, and Dorothy MacLean, to name but a few, whether alive or then passed on, had all been *physical* plane residents at the time of their transmissions. And although I'd been deeply impressed with such discarnates as 'The Tibetan', 'Seth', and 'Emmanuel', I hadn't quite put them on the same level as the others. A slight bit of physical plane snobbishness perhaps?

Well, now I was talking to a dead man, a dead man that no-one else could see, a dead man whose ability to outsmart my attempts at verification were effortless and quite childish in their glee. What on earth would people think? Well, *hey neat* and *pretty cool* were two responses. *Amazing* and *awesome* were two more I heard after folks had read some of the pamphlets I published. If anyone tittered behind my back they did so very discreetly. And once I'd done a little research, especially works like Jon Klimo's *Channeling*, I realized my experience was not so odd. If anything, it was a bit *too* predictable. Channeling your guide and then your Higher Self?

Been there, done that.

Part two, *More Adventures In Eternity*, now in your hand, picks up the stories exactly where part one concluded. In fact, the opening section was transcribed almost immediately after finishing part one. But because of a long delay in finding a suitable publisher I filed my notes, feeling then that to pursue what seemed to be shaping up into a long series without securing a print outlet would be foolish.

However, in those intervening years, I gave many talks and seminars locally, and here in the western suburbs of Toronto, it was not hard to notice the audiences' hunger for more and more details of the deeper, wider consciousness I was experiencing. Even without a publisher I came to see I was on the right track. When Frank DeMarco of Hampton Roads finally declared his delight with the manuscript, I could feel the *full steam ahead* signs popping up. Some months later, with the editing and polishing of *A First Hand Account* completed, and that all-important nod from my editor, I lunged with great enthusiasm into what I then called the 'Afterlife Sequel'.

From September 2003 until the summer of 2004, I spent much of my time in libraries and cafes with a laptop, transcribing fresh 'Henry' material and trawling through what seemed like acres of notes to piece together 'Gordon's' expansion. Both these names are in *inverted commas* because, as one moves gradually through deeper and wider expressions of consciousness, the nametags of both incarnate and discarnate personalities seem less and less significant. Rather than the individual expression, one identifies more with consciousness itself. Individuals seem more like actors than essences. Actors whose performances deserve appreciation and applause, but only in the context of a play whose drama, however compelling, will soon be over. Needless to say, the post-performance cast party *is* the afterlife, where we can all sip, nibble and rehash to our heart's content.

Higher Self/Monad/Disc/Source Self/Atman (take your pick)

Theosophists and others used the term *Monad* to denote that part of the human which was (a) eternal and (b) did not descend into incarnation, but sent tiny sparks of itself into the physical to explore and report back to base. They also stated that *Higher Self* was an aspect of the *Monad*, an aspect existing one level 'lower down'. The entity Seth, as translated by Jane Roberts, spoke of the *Source Self* from which all others were projected. That flowering of Hinduism called Vedanta saw *Atman* as the immortal part of the self, which is eternal, absolute being, bliss and consciousness, and expressed its union with Brahman (the one god) as *tat tvam asi* (thou art that). Bruce Moen experienced his soul source as a *Disc* which included many other souls intimately concerned with the progress of his journey and ultimate transcendence.

Having absorbed all these concepts over the years of my reading and meditation, I now feel most comfortable with the term Higher Self, although I have absolutely no objection to the others. I see it as my source and succor, and feel its existence on the vibrational level just one step down from the ultimate, or god, level. Although it is virtually omniscient, it can only communicate to me, 'physical Gordon' what (a) I am ready to receive, and (b) what my brain has language for. Your Higher Self, by the way, is much the same. Please feel free to continue as you alone see fit.

Although the post-mortem progress of the individual in the general direction of the Higher Self was hinted at on several occasions in part one, I did not then realize that the evocation of Higher Self consciousness was to be one of the main purposes of the trilogy. As pointed out by entities such as Seth and others, Higher Self exists not in time but eternity, and amongst other attributes, experiences its various expressions (incarnations) as simultaneous, and not as the linear cause-and-effect progress implied by past-life regression studies.

However useful and instructive past life regressions are, and I myself am both an experiencer and practitioner, the involution/evolution journey of that 'divine spark from the godhead' discussed by many systems seems quite inoperative from the p.o.v. of the Higher Self. To the reincarnating personality, the relationships, traumas and ecstasies of past lives can all seem too real and relevant to currently experienced situations, and as a therapeutic and educative tool their value to the psyche is unimpeachable. But to the Higher Self such psychic reparations may be little more than timely first aid. Higher Self seems (to me, as of this writing, August 2004) endlessly fascinated with combining and recombining various energies into packets of information which function as psychic templates for incarnate personalities to express their always evolving reactions to the challenges posed by physical plane existence.

In a sentence, Higher Self sees things one way while the incarnate personality sees things another way. Will there be a blending of perspectives? I sure hope so; 'physical Gordon' has been chiseling out his response for years. The progress report looks like this: as the incarnate personality continues to expand, its perceptions overflow their original dimension. What was once defined by space (a body), becomes defined by time (many bodies). What was once defined by physical plane reality (inevitable extinction) becomes redefined by astral plane reality (apparent immortality) and then further refined by Higher Self contact (eternity experienced in a huge variety of self-engineered limitations). And as a result, the one-track mind becomes the multi-dimensional being.

In considering both these multiple incarnation models and how one might possibly merge the two, or at least travel smoothly between them, one gradually arrives at the following understanding: the Higher Self model, with its group soul/source hotel scenario, has the great advantage of allowing one to unload the burden of 'famous' past lives onto the more-than-willing, couldn't-care-less Higher Self. And in doing so, you see that 'you' are not the direct result of any past life. You're related, psychically and energetically, but you are not simply the latest version of whoever appeared to go before. In family terms, you're much more like a cousin than a son or daughter. And as I had come across at least three historically notable characters in my ship of holy fools, none of which I disclosed to any but my most trusted friends, I embraced this knowing with a great relief, a 'relief beyond conceit', as I once termed it.

Some traditions speak of the 'soul-infused personality'. That state is considered the result of the incarnate personality overcoming the relentless pull of his desires and fears long enough to feel 'the still small voice within', that of the soul which seeks to establish a secure knowledge base on the physical plane. Since the soul and its energies are the core emanation from Higher Self into the body of man, such a state is the patient ambition of Higher Self.

Simply put, such experiments have a success rate of varying percentages. But due to the inevitable influence of the economic, political and religious belief systems fashioned throughout history by man, in his denial and ignorance, such soul connections are usually translated into the acceptable frameworks of 'angel', 'deity', 'savior', 'saint', 'demon', 'spirit guide', and 'prophet'. That the beings indicated by such terminologies *really* exist is not to be denied, but on many occasions that 'light of inspiration' is actually one's soul, swinging from the rafters of your current belief system, trying to get your attention.

One thinks of Robert Monroe's 'Inspecs', remarkably wise guides who turned out, much to his shock, to be aspects of his Self on a mission from god. Monroe Institute graduate Bruce Moen has also elaborated on his experience of this phenomenon in his *Exploring The Afterlife* series. Which brings me to www.afterlife-knowledge.com , Bruce's online home. Though *A First Hand Account* was experienced and put together by 'Gordon' before he joined this online community, the experiences and explorations discussed herein were often shared on the conversation board of 'afterlife-knowledge'. As such sharing was of great value to 'Gordon' in his quest, I would like to thank Bruce Moen, Marilyn Traver, Ginny Rankin, David Pierce, Jeff Williams, 'Alisha', 'Rebecca', 'Rosalie', and all the unnamed others for their invaluable contributions to the unfolding of this sweet little mystery

*Astral vs. Mental Body

When reading Robert Monroe's trilogy, beginning with Journeys

Out of The Body, it becomes obvious that his modus operandi is that of the *astral* body. As he rather pointedly avoids mention of any of the traditional teachings of this nature, it is unclear which, if any, he was influenced by. But if one studies the work of esoterists such as Charles Leadbeater, Cyril Scott, and the two works by Hereward Carrington and Sylvan Muldoon, all of which predate Monroe, it is plain that he is, in no uncertain terms, an astral adept. Lesser know works such as *Practical Astral Projection* by 'Yram' and *The Art And Practice of Astral Projection* by 'Ophiel' only confirm this view.

(In fact another couple of out-of-print rarities, both predating Monroe, make for a fascinating comparison. Caroline D. Larsen's 1927 *My Travels In The Spirit World* and Alice Gilbert's 1949 *Philip In The Spheres* are well worth the search. Readers of Monroe's *Far Journeys*, where he moves through time by over a thousand years, will be intrigued to find Gilbert and her deceased son doing much the same while obe at night.)

All of which underscores a fascinating conclusion: Monroe decided *not* to teach astral travel. For the hemi-sync tapes, as I discovered after reading Bruce Moen's first book and purchasing the set *Going Home* for myself, enable a projection of consciousness that is decidedly not *astral*, but is strongly suggestive of *mental* body activity. As recent works by Robert Bruce, Robert Peterson and Preston Dennett attest, astral travel beginners continue to be shocked by loud noises and shuddering vibrations, not to mention threatening apparitions and seductive desires. The experiences are very much *in your face*, as they say, and can, quite easily, be overwhelming, chasing the newbie student right back into his physical body. Hemi-sync, on the other hand, is very subtle in its effects. Those of a paranoiac frame of mind might even say insidious. Events tend to the wispy and telepathic, the emotions and fears/desires of the post-mortem crowd more, shall we say, theatrical than overwhelming, more distanced and easier to deal with.

For those of a basic *trusting* disposition, as Bruce Moen often points out, the problem can often be, not initiating a transcendent series of events as such, but believing that they have *already* occurred. Retrievals and explorations can often be astoundingly easy. This, as you will see, was very often my experience. Very early on I found myself doing retrievals while I thought I was just getting ready to do one. And from the conversation board I found others had much the same experience. My conclusions were twofold: the world of spirit operates at a much faster rate than ours 'here', and one's experiences 'there' seem to just whiz by, and/or the retrievals had been done while obe at night and were merely being replayed by soul so that physical Gordon's brain would get the message and relay it on the conversation board to others.

While I found Bruce Moen to be a very reliable guide in this matter, - *trust is always the first issue* - he would say, I discovered on rereading some of the older (1850onward) esoteric literature, much advice on the wisdom of using the mental body over the astral. In the areas of mediumship, healing and travel, the mental body was definitely the way to go, if only students could be shown how. In one's astral, it was implied, one was prey to all the nasty detritus of that plane, mischievous elementals, manipulative magicians/shamans, the malicious deceased, – but in the mental one was freed from such astral white trash. My puzzle-completing *Aha!* experience came while reading lucid dreamer Robert Moss's *Dreamgates*. A journal entry from 1995 sums it all up rather nicely:

"I enter a sphere of light. My physical body is far below; I look down on it as if I am looking down from an airplane. I see a second body floating above it. I have a sense of liberation from the tug of feelings and desires. I am told 'You are now in your mental body'. Its form is that of a point of light. I am guided through a series of exercises to test the role of Kama, or desire. I descend into the astral body to experience the force of appetites that live within it. I return to a sphere of light that now embraces the whole scene."

Yes, that's what I was doing! Being a point of light and expanding into whatever body and clothing was useful for the situation at hand. A trickster with a divine sense of mission and compassion. Sounds good, doesn't it? Indeed it does, as do the rest of the expanded states I shall describe for you, all of which lead me to believe that using *consciousness* as my tool and *intent* as my motive force, I can be virtually anywhere, do anything, and communicate with everyone, from the highest to the lowest. As can you. The only limitations are the parameters of your current belief system and your level of self-esteem. The entire spectrum of created beings throughout time and space await your calling card, should you so wish to pass it along. For example, a small series of episodes not included in the text.

Some years ago I read in regressionist Bruce Goldberg's *Time Travelers From The Future* that in some discoveries of repeated alien abduction scenarios the guiding presence of tall blond humans from over 1,000 years in the future was inescapable. And not only that, they seemed to be more or less in charge of the Greys and Hybrids doing the legwork. Because of the vast divergence of opinion amongst serious abduction researchers, I shall limit myself to merely pointing out that I was affected by this, and like much of one's reading in the metaphysical and paranormal, it was filed for future reference.

Some time in the middle of the period later referred to as 'Gordon's expansion', I took to meditating in a serene and lovely church garden. As was common for the time I suggested to whomever that I was available for retrieval work. I immediately found myself in the upper bedroom of an old house, with a woman seemingly at the end of her tether: rushing about, tearing at her hair, wailing. Her husband had been lost at sea. I tried to make myself a visible and calming influence, and was soon taken for an angelic presence. A spiritual dialogue conforming to the norms of mid-nineteenth century Protestantism developed. Having grown tired of taking so many notes on retrievals by then, I have none for this and apologize. But I can tell you that over the next couple of months, about every week I would return to the scene of this poor lady's aggravation, to work with her on the themes of (a) abandoning dissolute behavior, and (b) calmly accepting god's ways. She seemed to truly feel that I was an angel, and her sense of being blessed was truly humbling. More than once I had to raise her from my feet. On about visit four, I promised to bring the spirit of her beloved to her. On visit five he appeared, thank god, and I stood back quietly. The joyful, ghostly reunion, perhaps solid evidence of instability to neighbors, seemed to seal her road to recovery. On another visit I tried to explain that I was not an angel but a human from about one hundred years in the future, guided by kindly spirits. She tried to understand, asking about the quality of life in my world. I spoke about telephones, television, cars and planes. Yes, it was a challenge, and I wonder if ultimately such information might have been more upsetting than inspiring. In the months to come I often had psychic visions of her walking the streets of the town, lonely but somehow at peace with her loneliness. And as the area had a well documented history of boat building and seafaring, I assumed I had merely shifted backward in time, perhaps not moving more than a couple of hundred yards from my bench in the garden. And it was not until much later that I recalled Bruce Goldberg's book.

PROLOGUE: FREEDOM IS FUN AND

FUN IS ETERNAL

It is not with any sense of gravity or piety that I stand before you expounding on the joys of eternal life. There is no great system of religious or philosophical thought which determines my attitude. No personal gods or prophets govern my sense of grace. I have graduated from all those binding systems, as you yourselves will do in one or other of your lives. I am now free to explore the ever expanding limits of my freedom. That freedom is fun and that fun is eternal. I shall show you how to enjoy both the freedom and the fun.

Much of what I shall tell you will seem impossible to enact in a physical body, except when out of it at night, but it will give you a sense of what can be accomplished when one is free from the cares of incarnation, which for most of you will not be long. In about forty years many of you reading this text will already be permanent astral residents, not because of any particular disaster scenario, although those dramatic fluctuations in the flexing of nature's muscles will always provide exit visas for those who feel they need them, but because you will have covered as much of your life plan arrangements as your frail form will allow and will have the great good sense to die without a fuss. And as I am sure many of you will agree, that forty years will fly by in a twinkle.

I am Gordon's Higher Self, and I am sending this attitudinal information to his writer's ego in accordance with his life plan desires. He is, like all my consciousness projections, a limited form with unlimited potential. Although he moves through his physical plane relationships within the parameters set by his society, both legal and psychological, and feels the resulting rigors as keenly as any, he knows that one day, as the saying goes on earth, he will curate a planet and people it with life forms of energy projected and perfected.

In this he is no different than any of you there: you are all, in essence, energy projections from Higher Selves, those spheres of light energy which kick around the known universe creating the kind of havoc civilizations are built on. All of you have rejoined your Higher Selves at the end of any of your physical and astral incarnations and experienced that bliss of our life together, but carrying that bliss back into your next incarnation usually proves to be well nigh impossible, and you are left with vague notions of that better life somewhere, that myth which religions are all too anxious to exploit.

At the turn of this second millennium, according to those calculating by the most recent descent of the Christ, such information is no longer a zealously guarded secret, and can be gleaned from any number of "new-age" books, but as it is a message well worth repeating, in any form possible, Gordon has decided to once again give his heart to its propagation, and has only needed the slightest of nudges from me to ensure the task's completion. He knows that one day many of you will be out here, looking back at who you are now and laughing. He wants you to get a sneak preview at that laughter.

That I am the possessor of an eternal life is in no way a matter of doubt. That you are the inheritors of such a condition is perhaps a topic of some consideration amongst you. I shall not enter the debate, for Gordon has convinced me that chipping away at skepticism with airy-fairy theories and anecdotal evidence accomplishes little, if anything, for the effort expended, and that educating the already converted in the almost infinite subtleties of spiritual evolution within this solar system is the only way to go. I shall take him at his word, for while I represent an accumulated wisdom of many life experiences throughout the eons, he is my sharpest and most reliable contact in this current epoch on earth.

In short, he has an accurate perception, unclouded by either false piety or frantic paranoia, of what a certain type of new-age person is ready to think about next. I shall therefore introduce you to a number of beings, in the astral and beyond, who are living and enjoying their slice of eternal life. First up is Gene.

SECTION ONE:

HENRY DOES VIETNAM

GENE DISCOVERS HENRY

Yes I'll be taking over for a bit, and I'd like to point out that the whole idea was Henry's and he cajoled me into it since I was doing this kinda work much more than he was. For no particularly good reason I'd started working with earthside psychics doing retrievals some time back. About ten years, your time, after I'd passed. Henry told me to tell you all the gory details, that you'd lap it up.

Well, I got shot while trying to rob a bank for a radical political group in the early seventies. I wasn't born a violent or greedy man, but we all felt our government was terminally corrupt and that our righteous contempt justified what we thought of as a determined extension of civil disobedience. So I died, as they say, with my boots. Most of my comrades went to hospital and then jail. They're now dentists, social workers and political science professors. And me, I'm an astral helper. Trained by Henry, of course. He found me floating above the robbery scene, not knowing I was dead. He stood beside me, stroking a beard that I thought was his, and said "That's some shoot out down there, huh? Just like the old West."

Not knowing what else to do I agreed with him. I was really too busy trying to cope with the impression that I was floating about one hundred feet above the ground to be bothered arguing with him. And that was strange in itself, as I was never one to back down from a disagreement. Instead I asked him why the old West. Oh, same fierce individualists battling against corrupt authority, he said , absent minded professor like, sure that the very fabric of their lives depended on it. I considered his comparison and found it wanting, but could not be bothered to debate with him. The action below was much too interesting. It engaged my passions much more than any historical comparisons.

Henry told me later that this was because I was vibrating at the astral level, which is all about experiencing and transmuting the emotions, whereas he liked to vibrate at the mental level, which is all about thinking, conceptualizing and considering at one's leisure. He was wise not to try and tell me this at the time, as I was far from being able to accept or understand it. I was too obsessed with the forces of oppression winning out once again. Fascist Amerika followed me around like a pack of bloodthirsty dogs. It had followed me into death and I didn't even realize it, so caught up in the heat of the moment was I.

Henry tried to get me to leave several times, but I was much too fascinated with the action down below to budge. This trait of mine was to be used to great advantage later on, but for the moment Henry seized my hand and dragged me down to ground level. He made me look at the fear and anger of the police as they crouched behind their vehicles, poised for orders. I squirmed and tried to bolt, sure we would be spied. But of course we were ghosts, nevermore to be seen or felt by the living. Henry tried to get me to feel the inner thoughts of one of the cops. Later he told me it was a telepathic trick he had learned from his own guide, but at that point all I knew was that his hand was on my forehead and I could hear the man praying that he would survive and be able to look after his two kids. He prayed to Jesus, he prayed to the Blessed Virgin Mary, and he prayed to his wife, who seemed to have died.

Henry removed his hand and we're suddenly inside the bank looking at my comrades. Sonya was bent over something crying. I was shocked: normally she was tougher than the men in action. When someone lost their nerve it was always Sonya who did the shouting. I looked closer, but still could not make out who she was mourning. I looked up to see Henry, sitting on the floor with his back to a wall, with the kind of look you usually see on a kid watching cartoons. He looked up at me and waved, as if to say "Hey! Pretty neat huh?"

I looked down again and realized the leather jacket on the body below Sonja was mine. Sonja was crying over me! I couldn't believe it. We'd fucked a few times, but it was all part of the revolutionary ethic: women were equal in every way to men and could choose as many lovers as they wished. I never for a moment thought of her as mine or of her loving me as anything more than a respected comrade in the struggle. But she was obviously broken by my death. And that shocked me more than the fact of my death, because, of course, I felt very much alive, more alive than ever in fact, whereas Sonja's pain flooded me like some kind of all over toothache. I tried to comfort her but my arms passed right through her. I tried it two or three times. Still no luck.

Henry was no help: he just sat there grinning, goofy and stoned, just like the helpless hippies we hated for their dopey conformity. I couldn't see through his clown act to his calm in the center of the storm pose. I walked over and asked what the hell was so funny. His smug reply was something about how seriously people took their agendas. I wanted to smack him for making fun of my friends, but just kind of growled instead. He reached out his hand and pulled me down beside him. He did not look like a strong man, but he sure knew how to move me into position. I'll never forget what he said next.

"Don't you get it Gene? You're dead! There's nothing more you can do here."

I must've sounded desperate when I said, "I must help my friends. I must!"

"Well you go down with the ship if you want to, but I've got better things to do." And with that he was off, and I mean gone. Gone in a flash.

GOING DOWN WITH THE SHIP

I made an instant decision: I'd hallucinated after a blow to the head, but I was fine now. I tried to grab the dead man's weapon but couldn't seem to grip it. I tried to shout directions to the others: they seemed to have no coherent plan of action, but my advice was ignored. Dick was badly wounded and wanted to surrender. I was sure we could still make a break for it. Moments before, from above, I'd known there wasn't a hope: the building was completely surrounded, and there were sharpshooters on the roof, but back in the action I somehow forgot all that. Dick and Harv were arguing and had grabbed each other by the lapels. I knew they were wasting their energy and decided to separate them. I got right between them to push them apart. Of course it was hopeless, my hands went straight through. They went right on arguing, faces inches apart. I went to try and talk some sense to the others, but it was hopeless, no one paid me the slightest attention. Even Sonya ignored me.

I found myself in the vault where the employees were locked in. Don't ask me how I got through the door. Then I remembered: it was me who'd herded them in there! They looked so tense and panicked I immediately felt badly for them and tried to tell them everything would be alright soon and the police would let them out. Two of the women were crying uncontrollably and I tried to console them, despite all my earlier failures at communication. I had my arm around one's shoulder when Henry appeared just beside her, grinning at me. He asked if I was getting anyplace. I made a face at him. He shrugged. Then he said, quite calmly, "Watch this."

Standing back a couple of feet, he stared intently at the woman. A sort of glowing golden orange light emanated from him, coming maybe from his chest I wasn't sure, and wafted about her kind of , well, intelligently, enclosing her torso and head in a kind of cloud. A minute passed, maybe more, but she found composure or it found her, I'm not sure, and she turned to the other woman, trying to comfort her. Henry looked at me and said, "See, this is how you help people. With your mind."

And that was about when he had me. I knew I was in the presence of someone pretty special. I didn't take much convincing after that. He took me to the real afterlife, showed me around, and helped me get settled, just as if I'd moved to a new neighborhood on earth.

THE REAL AFTERLIFE

At first he just had me close my eyes. I asked if it was some kind of trick. He said yes, it was, but not the kind I was worried about. I decided to trust him and see where it got me. I knew he was lying about us being dead, but I figured I'd follow along and see just what he had up his sleeve. In no time at all we were standing in what looked liked a five star hotel. People bustled about the lobby pretty much like they always do in those places: preoccupied. We'd arrived unannounced but no one seemed to notice. I was relieved: I'd been the center of attention for a while there and it was nice to have the pressure off. I felt like putting my hands in my pockets and whistling. Henry asked if I wanted a beer. I said sure.

He knew exactly where the bar was. Very classy too. He leaned up against the bar as if he'd been a regular for years. The bartender nodded at him and smiled. Was it to be the usual?   Two glasses of golden brew appeared as if from nowhere. The bartender smiled and asked me how I was doing. I thought about it for a moment. I decided: just fine thanks. The beer tasted unbelievably good. I said as much to Henry and asked what it was. Just some local specialty he said. I thought it was probably just another of his lies, but you couldn't lie about the taste: it was fabulous. I drained it in two gulps and asked for another.

"The man's thirsty," the bartender grinned to Henry, "What you too been up to then? No good I'll bet."

"Not so fast partner. We've been fighting the oppressive state, haven't we Gene? We got God on our side."

I chuckled, but it was just to be sociable. I'd definitely be rearranging his priorities when we got outside. Like all true believers I thought our cause was sacrosanct. But this beer was too good to waste. I held my ground and sipped. Henry and the bartender seemed really tight. Maybe they had some con going.

The bartender asked if Henry was showing me the sights. Two lovely blondes sat down next to us and ordered glasses of white wine. Willowy and radiant would be a good description   The

bartender introduced them as Susan and Angela, telling them I'd
just come to town with Henry. They laughed at that, telling me that
he'd only just brought them a couple of days before. Henry raised
his glass and wished them cheers. I pretended not be puzzled and
asked them how they were enjoying things.

"Too good to be true if you really want to know." That was
Susan. I knew because they each had nametags saying 'Hi my
name is'. Angela nodded, sipping. Yes, absolutely, no question
about it. I'd no sooner thought how nice it would be to be shown
around by these two instead of Henry than he suggested it. He said
he could relax now, knowing that I'd be in safe hands. Draining his
beer, he asked that it be put on his tab, smiled all round and said
goodbye.

Angela and Susan seemed to think he was the greatest and I
certainly wasn't about to start disagreeing. I asked about the hotel.
I hadn't stayed in one for years and was really starting to enjoy all
the capitalist decadence I disdained only hours before. They told
me they had a double but there were plenty of singles available. I
should go to the desk and reserve now. Then we could all go for a
swim in the pool.

That was all I needed to hear. I followed the two of them like a
puppy eager for treats. It was on the way up in the elevator that
they mentioned the beer truck losing its brakes and crushing their
little chev at an intersection. On their way to get their hair done,
the two of them, an upscale salon downtown for a little treat and
look what happened. Live together, dead together, roommates for
all time, they laughed.

I wish I could tell you that was the start of a beautiful
friendship, but I actually only spent my first day or so in their
delightful company. A day in which I firmly put aside all my hang-
ups about women who regularly went to beauty parlours and
actively hustled for husbands in the bars at the edge of the
business district, and in which they, I assume, shelved all their
mainstream paranoia about political radicals ripping up their
treasured American dream. I think they must've found me some
kind of outlaw cute or something because we certainly had fun

together in our orientation day together. That's what Henry called it when he came by the next day, to 'collect' me as he put it.

The hotel itself was absurdly large for the small town it was in. It seemed very much like some well proportioned tourist destination spot somewhere by the ocean in New England. The sort of place that manages to be successful without opening its doors to the world. All the buildings lay in beautifully landscaped grounds. The small, impossibly pretty harbour held any number of smartly bobbing sailboats, and in the bay beyond sailed plenty of the privileged species. I had my usual thoughts about the dispossessed and underprivileged, but suppressed them. I knew it was not the sort of thing Angela and Susan would want to hear about, and for some reason, maybe to do with those old fashioned male thoughts about wanting to get laid, the kind of thoughts I thought I'd ditched on my way into the movement.

We oohed and aahed at every turn. The town was so darn pretty. Normally I'd want to puke at such postcard crap, but somehow that day I was willing to upgrade my normal reactions, maybe for the reason I just mentioned. Then I noticed that there were no cars. Or buses or trucks. And come to think of it I hadn't actually seen a road in a while. The sidewalks were a sort of sturdy rubbery stuff and everywhere else was grass or soil or sand. Angela and Susan had suddenly started to play leapfrog. I called after them "Where are the cars?" A couple nearby, who'd been standing admiring the boats, echoed my query, "Yeah we were wondering that too."

Angela, after jumping over Susan and losing her balance and rolling around laughing, shouted, "It's heaven stupid, there are no cars !" Susan turned back to me and grinned, "Hey Gene, check this out!"

She then floated four or five feet up in the air and waved. I waved back, completely frazzled. What the heck was this? The couple by the sea wall clapped and cheered.. They looked retired; at ease the way those folks do. I asked if they'd ever seen anything like this before. They said "Yes, yesterday in the park, there were kids flying alongside their kites. It was crazy!"

Although they looked like the kind of bonehead republicans you see wintering down south, the kind I always felt I could do without, for some reason I felt I could believe them. Susan called again "Try it Gene. It's easy!" She was still up there, grinning a mile wide. Angela was lying on the grass looking up at her and giggling. I just knew all that stuff about the truck at the intersection was bunk. We'd known for a while the CIA had been using suspected radicals as drug guinea pigs for years, but we'd never known the extent of the program's success. Our arguments about it had spiraled into a lot of ultra paranoid name-calling and we knew we had to call it quits before we destroyed ourselves. We'd seen what they'd done to the Panthers. But what kind of amazingly long lasting high was this? Something new obviously. No side effects though, just pure, uninterrupted hallucination. So, as I thought 'just wait till this hits the streets' I reached up for Susan. That is, I stretched out my right arm in her direction as if she was going to pull me out of a hole. She began some disco dance steps, giving me the old come on. I floated up to her level and began imitating her moves. Angela soon joined us, and we boogied about midair for a few minutes like five year olds chasing balloons at a picnic. I caught a glimpse, mid-gyration, of the retired couple beaming up at us like proud parents. Stranger things have happened, but at that point I couldn't think of any.

After all that shenanigans, we met a couple of guys who wanted to take us for a sail in their yacht.

You know what sailors are like; once they get their hooks into you they won't let you go. Angela and Susan were certainly up for it, and I couldn't see why not, even though the only sailing I'd done was some strictly amateur smuggling from Maine up to Nova Scotia and back. The whole affair was uneventfully pleasant, except for a surprising few minutes where Roberto and Clive enlightened us on the fascinating world of male homosexuals, a kind of ultra-hip Peyton Place of jealous trysts and secret assignations, later to be quite common knowledge, but then quite the revelation, even for a well traveled outlaw like me. God only knows what Susan and Angela thought. I know I'd never heard of poppers before, and I wouldn't again till the age of Aids flooded the astral with sick skinny crippled men, but that's getting ahead of my story.

Back at the hotel, Angela told me to go get dressed for dinner and they'd meet me in half an hour for cocktails. I didn't like to say that I had no change of clothes with me, so I sauntered off hoping that a shower would do the trick. I watched the other guests carefully as I made my way to my room. They seemed genuine enough. A group of grade schoolers passed me in the hall, boys and girls about ten years old, I guessed. One teacher jumped into the elevator with them , laughing at her luck, but the other missed it, and I found myself smiling at her and making small talk. She looked like a small town girl from the mid west. You know, dad sold the farm and bought an implement dealership, and she went to college and got her degree but went back home to teach school and settle down. I'd seen plenty of them on my travels. Of necessity, people like me moved from state to state. Yes, she loved the hotel, and wasn't it so nice that they brought us all here to calm down and get used to things. My paranoid fantasy reasserted itself and I was nodding politely and trying to scrutinize her mask. Then she looked serious for a moment and whispered, "Bus crash on the interstate. Washington for the weekend. I don't think half the kids realize it yet. But I always believed in Jesus, so if it be his will...you know." It was the tweak of her nose as she said "you know" that stuck with me. It was so natural and unaffected I couldn't see it as part of some grand scheme to derange me. Then after a shower I checked the closets on a whim and , guess what, there were clothes hanging up in there. Too weird.

They were all pretty generic conservative, but I found a casual shirt and pants I could stomach and a pair of suede shoes that fit like a glove, and the thought of joining the gorgeous Angela and Susan for dinner swayed me in the direction of guileless forward movement, so I returned downstairs as robotically dapper as they come. Of course, hindsight is miraculous in its definition; at the time I saw myself as cool as Robert Redford.

And did so for quite some time I might add, even after a

dressing down by good old Henry, always reliable when it comes to blowing the accumulated dust off your ego. This he did the next morning when he arrived at my breakfast table and informed me we would be moving on. I was quite indignant: what did he mean by moving on, and who the hell was 'we'? I still hadn't figured out what was going on, but like any true ignoramus, I knew what I liked, and Angela and Susan were just about my two favourite girls in the universe at that point. I didn't know whether to be amused or ashamed about the Playboy fantasy we'd enacted the night before. They were exactly the type of bourgeois women I professed to despise, but I knew now had always been attracted to. I felt like I'd died and gone to heaven.

Henry slid into a chair beside me, and helping himself to a spoonful of my scrambled eggs, said, "That's exactly what I've been trying to tell you my boy. You have died and you have gone to heaven. What about all these people, I wondered out loud, waving my fork.

"They're all dead too. Every last one of them."

"And Angela and Susan?"

"Certified stiffs. Still in the morgue if I'm not mistaken. Mangled almost beyond recognition. Never know it to look at them now, would you?" Henry's jowly face beamed at me, daring me to believe.

I was almost there.

"But I feel so alive, so ...brimming with energy."

Henry grinned. "Feel like you could rob four or five banks, maybe blow up an induction center? I know the feeling. When I first arrived I couldn't get settled. Once I discovered the astral Rockies all I wanted to do was hike and camp out. I became very adept at communing with nature but my social skills took a nosedive."

"Actually all I want is to hang out with the blondes and rediscover the joys of superficiality."

Henry laughed. Apparently I was not to be given the chance. There was work to do.

"And what work might that be?" I queried, suddenly curious.

"Rescuing dead boys from Vietnam. They're so full of anguish and drugs and youthful energy they don't know they're dead, most of them. We need young fellows like you who are good in an action situations. Souls who understand about sex and drugs and rock music in a way that old duffers like me just can't. I was really formed by the fifties and can't quite make the right connection."

Well the altruism and patriotism of the whole enterprise grabbed me right away. We'd been fighting to stop that pointless slaughter for years, and really not getting anyplace fast except ever more confirmed in our righteousness, so the thought that I might be of some real help galvanized me into Henry's agenda.

After explaining a few basic ground rules about travel in this new world and what he called the awesome power of thought, he ushered me out through the lobby, bustling as usual. I noticed he gestured to the desk clerk, who nodded back knowingly. I guessed, quite correctly, as it turned out, that my room was now vacant Angela caught up to us at the door and looked quite excited when Henry told her he was taking me on an adventure. Susan appeared as Henry was explaining the nature of our operation, and joined Angela in immediately shrinking from any possible involvement. Although dead at least three days longer than me, they were obviously still quite naive about many things. Of course, Henry's little pep talk had turned me into an instant expert, and I took pride in explaining that we couldn't really get hurt, as we were just sort of dipping into that dimension to pull out a few survivors, just like you'd dip your hand in a stream to pull out a few little fish.

Henry assured them we'd be back in no time, and suggested they polish up their tennis for our return, as we were planning to whomp them. Apparently Henry had already shown them the tennis club, as they mentioned a coach by name, and thought they might just go over there after a swim that very morning.

Hugs and kisses later we parted laughing, all of us pretending we were not going to war.

GOING TO WAR

At a quiet spot on the edge of town, just behind a line of trees, Henry took my hand and warned me to close my eyes. We were headed to the jungle and it would be a dizzying trip for a neophyte. I took him at his word. Thus began my career as an astral helper. Dead barely a day and I was doing the rounds with an old hand. Of course, mostly I was just learning the ropes, standing back and watching as Henry bluffed his way around a series of dead soldiers in a variety of outfits. That, as much as anything, astonished me, this rapid backstage swapping of costumes that Henry seemed to delight in.

We found a group of dead boys lolling on a sandy beach watching the breakers. At least Henry described them so, I couldn't tell. Their uniforms were dirty and torn, but they seemed more playful than exhausted to me. A couple had their pants off and were paddling about aimlessly. Three or four more were leaning on their elbows smoking and chatting. They looked for all the world like factory workers on lunch break in summer, stretched out on the lawn in front of the plant. Henry said he was sure one of them had gone off, so while he went off to check I was left `in charge'. Of course I hadn't a clue what to do, so I just stood there, a few feet away, observing. The two paddlers began horsing around and were soon soaked to the skin. They returned to the group and shook themselves off like a couple of family dogs at a picnic, eliciting the usual howls and threats.

I stood entranced , not quite able to believe my... luck? All these dead soldiers and none of them had a clue. My own `death' seemed hardly worth bothering about. Much easier to fret over others than to face oneself. I see that now, but I certainly didn't then. It's all to do with projecting one's inner turmoil upon the world and taking up causes and issues rather than confronting one's own inner demons. And that I was certainly doing as I watched over those dead boys basking on the beach.

In his little pep talk earlier, Henry had warned me that some people's thoughts might appear in my own head, and if I took it calmly, the information could be useful in figuring out just what way would be best in approaching them. Well, of course, it started to happen. I was looking at one of the soldiers, a skinny, frail looking black boy when I felt I could hear him praying to his `mamma'. I could feel a great bond of love between the two of them, a bond that I instantly felt was unbreakable, no matter what. Just as I was wondering where this newfound sensitivity came from, Henry reappeared, as he often did, out of nowhere.

"Just as I thought, he announced, expecting me to know exactly what he was talking about, a habit I could see I was going to have to get used to, "A couple of them were drawn back to the Saigon brothels and opium dens. How are you with hard drugs?"

I had to disappoint him. Hard drugs were a no-no for my crowd. We considered them a tool of political repression, fashioned and sustained by the ruling oligarchy to control the indentured serfs of the miltiary-industrial complex, and we avoided them as a matter of course. Now don't forget, this was long before political radicals of my stripe turned to drug deals to support their more idealistic ventures. That was what the other guys did. The ones with the suits and late model cars. Now smoking a little home grown grass, that was different. Mostly because the chain of criminal command was not fed in any way. It was a gesture of goodwill amongst like-minded friends, a sacrament of some folk religion we were building as went along. So no, I had no experience with addiction to heroin or opium. I mentioned the boy praying to his mother. Henry seemed pleased with his new pupil. He asked if I'd approached the boy. No, it never occurred to me. Well, why didn't I try it now?

As I thought it over, Henry changed himself into a chaplain's outfit. A small black book lodged in his left hand. He smiled and said "There's always a couple of religious ones. What are you going dressed as?" Naturally I laughed, not then realizing the importance of dress in soul retrieval. I can tell you now, with many years of experience under my belt, the right costume counts for more than either attitude or skill in this line of work.

"How about an MP, that might get their attention." Henry seemed pleased again. He asked me if I was up to visualizing it. He'd hinted at this process before, so I sort of knew what was expected. I thought about an MP in any picture or movie and saw myself dressed that way, right down to boots and armbands. Although it's second nature now, back then it seemed quite magical.

We approached the group together, me imagining the role I had to play and Henry just strolling through his. Two things happened almost simultaneously: the guy who'd been quietly praying to his mother jumped up at Henry, and calling him padre, embraced him like some long lost brother, and another white guy, who I hadn't taken much notice of, pulled himself up and explained that they'd become separated from their unit, and were, basically, lost. They'd been expecting the choppers any minute for hours now. He was obviously feeling guilty about something but I couldn't tell what. While Henry was dealing with the freaked out black kid, I spoke in a commanding manner to the others. No choppers were available right then, but we'd been sent to bring them back. At the edge of the jungle by the ocean in the middle of what seemed like nowhere this must've sounded fairly bizarre, but it met with an immediate response. All the men were on their feet, dusting themselves off, in seconds, quite obviously ready to follow me anywhere. And to think only a day or so before me and my cell had been on the FBI's most wanted list. I consulted with Henry for a moment. Before turning to me he looked the boy in the eye and told him everything would be fine and we'd be out of here in a few minutes. I asked him quietly, "What next?"

He said, "Introduce me as Father Henry and say I'm going to make a blessing on our journey."

This I duly did. An MP handing over the mike to a chaplain seemed a bit strange, but the men accepted it as quickly as my first pronouncement. I stood back to let Henry speak. In less than a minute he compressed an introduction, a blessing, and some instructions for the trip, not to mention a brief gaze into every man's eyes. He projected calmness, sincerity, and a deep sense of purpose, convincing even me who knew it was all a con, albeit in a good cause.

We were to link arms and close our eyes. Needless to say this was greeted with murmurs of disapproval amongst the men, but Henry insisted. As they organized themselves Henry leant over to me and whispered that I was to imagine us back at the line of trees just outside town as soon as he gave the order to close the eyes. He placed me on one end of the line and himself on the other. The men looked puzzled, the black boy afraid. Henry made a point of standing next to him and holding his hand. He reminded the men that they must close their eyes until told to open them again, or the experiment would fail.

I realized right away his judicious use of the word experiment. It made them feel special, as though the army had selected them for an unusual mission. The order was given: I imagined the line of trees and the long swaying grass I remembered beside them and suddenly we were there. The `eyes open' order was given.

The men uttered a collective gasp.

I enjoyed their shock; it was a bit like taking ghetto kids to a circus, although I'll have to admit I didn't think of that comparison until much later. At the time I just smiled and welcomed them all home. They looked around and then amongst themselves and then cheered. Two of them fell to the ground and kissed the grass. Henry seemed to have seen it all before. I don't know, for a self-confessed old codger he seemed pretty hip. He told the men there was a new base nearby and all we had to do was walk there. The men asked if we had to march in formation. I said, "Nah, forget it." It seemed a popular decision. Henry, thank god, lead the way, talking to the scared young black man, reassuring him I imagined. A couple of the others dared to approach me with questions. I thought it best to lie through my teeth. It was the first time I'd been to this base. Yes it was a top-secret project. Sure it had a religious aspect to it, and that's why the chaplain was there. No, I didn't know him, I'd just been assigned to the project myself. Actually I was just as curious as they were. That at least was true.

I later learned that lying in a good cause was part of the

curriculum in this school for astral helpers, but at that point I felt kinda guilty about it. When the state lies to the citizens, as mine did, the citizens owed it to themselves to be truthful to each other. As radicals we certainly had a radical vision, but we never veered from telling the truth as we saw it. So all this pretending and lying took a bit of getting used to. When Henry suggested, sometime after we'd got the new arrivals settled, with a wry grin, that not only was lying in a good cause good for business as far as we were concerned, it was what motivated the politicians I battled against, I was not inclined to agree with him. He was pushing too many buttons at once; I was not nearly ready to take that leap. He was probably just playing with me, for as soon as he registered resistance the matter was quickly dropped.

Now perhaps you're wondering if I was starting to enjoy my eternal life yet, and my answer would be yes, very much. The endless charm and beauty of my surroundings and companions, and the insistent `newness' of every experience as the minutes rolled by, had quite submerged all the tension and drama of my other life. I've dwelt on the details because I think it's important for you to see my gradual unfolding into the new reality, and my various ways of rationalizing the ignorance behind my perceptions. By the time we'd unloaded the soldiers into the very capable hands who met us at the `base', my paranoid fantasies of CIA drug experiments seemed just that: paranoid fantasies. Even the agency couldn't organize something of this depth and complexity with this number of bit part players all executing their roles like Oscar winners.

We walked back to town discussing our venture. Henry said he was quite pleased with my performance and assured me I'd have plenty more opportunities to exercise my new found talents. That is, he peered at me, if I felt up to it. Of course I did, I wanted to help out, didn't he see that? Yes, he thought he did. But if I wanted to play around with Angela and Susan I was more than free to do so. There would be no coercion on his part. Or anyone's for that matter. I was to do as I pleased. I told him I surely would. How long had we been gone, I wondered out loud. Not nearly long enough for those gals to practice up their tennis apparently. Henry said he had to pop home on some business. Would I mind if he just disappeared for a while? I asked about accommodations. Should I just go back to the hotel? Yes, he was sure they could fix me up. And if I needed him for anything I was to just send a quick message. And how was I to do that? I was to summon him by thought. It was that simple was it? Yes it was. And with that he disappeared. One moment there, the next gone.

DOING AS I PLEASED

I was alone for the first time in I don't know how long. I could return to the hotel and settle in. I could seek out my playmates. I could just wander around and get to know the place. The last option seemed like the most fun. I was walking along a tree lined street towards what I thought was the center of town when I decided this, so I slowed my pace and began looking about in earnest. The street itself was a grassy thoroughfare completely devoid of traffic. But I knew that from my stroll around the day before. I noticed a woman gardening and called out an hello. She seemed about thirty and very intent on her work, which seemed to be a mixture of pruning and replanting.

She strode up to meet me with a big grin on her face and her hand her out.

"How do you do, Heather Bishop. Slipped on some ice while skating with my sister. New here are you?"

"That's right. Gene Norman. Shot in a shoot-out. Been here about two days I guess. Lovely garden you've got here."

"Actually I inherited it. Previous owners have moved up a level. Lovely couple from Rhode Island. Out sailing when a storm came up."

"Lucky you."

"Yes really, don't I know it. I was just walking by one day, finally got rid of my grandmother for two minutes, and they called to me. Just like you did actually. Looking for a home?'

She was tall and thin and schoolteacherish. Pointy nose and her hair held back with a scarf.

"No not really. I'm headed back to the hotel to get a room. I've just finished a mini tour of duty over Vietnam. My guide was showing me the rescue routine."

"Took some dead soldiers to the base did you? That's wonderful. Those poor boys are so mixed up even after they've been here awhile. Half of them still think it's some top-secret project . I help out at the little library there. There's a fine one in town here, but they don't feel welcome enough yet, so we started a little one there. Maybe we'll catch a couple of the more intelligent ones. Mostly they're high school drop outs though, and when they find out that they're really out of the war all they can think about is sports and chasing girls."

"Well I suppose they've had a hard time of it and just need to let go."

"Of course. Now can I offer you some orange juice?"

I'd no sooner accepted her offer than we were sitting in trellis lined porch overflowing with yellow roses and bougainvillea. I found out a lot about a childhood in Kansas and a summer trip to Maine, a holiday romance gone sour with pregnancy, a beautiful baby given up for adoption, and the shame of it all, and only one sister who cared enough to visit, and only one skating trip and only one fall.

"That's all it takes," she said staring into her juice.

She heard some stuff about political radicalism and how one is pushed by the tide of events from civil disobedience into active resistance. I could feel she was a bit uncomfortable with it, and I asked why. She said working at the base had brought it home to her more than anything when she lived in the states. Those boys were so messed up with guilt and anxiety and fear. Most of them had killed enemy soldiers and they were bad enough, but some had killed defenseless peasants and some children and they were just ruined. She'd been too wrapped up in her own little dramas to think about it much when alive, and dismissed folk like me as degenerate anarchists out to destroy. Now she could see we had a point.

I chuckled and told her that I would have been glad to hear of such a change in views when I was still alive, but now I wondered if we were ever more than a thorn in the side of a giant. The war would end someday, but not because of our activities, but because it was doomed from the start. As far as I could see it was all about helicopters and heroin. Building one and smuggling the other. And likely the other way around as far as financing went.

Heather seemed more mystified than ever, but before she could put together some kind of reply, neighbours appeared and made themselves at home. Martha and Ron were from Cape Cod. Actually Ron had strayed over from Vermont looking for work in the thirties and Martha had grabbed him and put him to work in the family store, which she'd just inherited, and they never looked back. Sold out in sixty-five and just relaxed and traveled. Driving through Nova Scotia when a sudden storm surprised them. Spun off the road and into a tree and that was that. Still they couldn't complain, they'd had a great life together and they were having a great life here. Martha's only regret was leaving their adopted daughter behind. Judy had always been a bit on the simple side, easy to take advantage of if you know what I mean, and kinda on the plain side so she hadn't snagged a husband yet, but at least she had a good job working at the power company.

Ron said perhaps they shouldn't be bustin' in like this, but they hadn't known Heather had a visitor. I said that was fine, that I was just passing by and noticed Heather gardening., and as I was new to town I was trying to get to know folks. Martha looked at Ron and smiled. Well, wasn't that just lovely, a fine young man like me, and how long had I been dead? Well, only a couple of days but I was feeling just fine thanks. Martha advised me to get ready for a funeral, she said it would draw me like a magnet and my folks' sadness would really shake me up. As Heather returned with some juice and cookies for them just then I did not have to explain the sticky business about my family. Politics had completely poisoned our relationship. We hadn't spoken in years, and my itinerant lifestyle didn't help matters. Anyway, knowing where I was at any one time would've been dangerous for them.

Luckily for me the gentleman visitor theme was pursued. That role I could live up to. Heather mentioned I'd been doing retrievals over Vietnam. Ron was immediately interested. Their son Rick had been lost in action a year or so before they died. Did I think I could find him? I told them my guide Henry would be the one to ask. I was so new at the game I didn't know what was possible. But I would definitely get back to them. I looked over at Heather; she beamed with pride. I could see Angela and Susan drifting away on the breeze like hot air balloons. Suddenly I just had to get to the hotel and find a room. Oh I was staying at the hotel was I, Martha offered, now that was a lovely spot. Heather said not to worry, there was always spare rooms, even after disasters. Her friend Lynn worked there sometimes when they were short. I should ask for her by name. She was the only Lynn that worked there. I made my farewells bright but brief, and promised once again to check out their son's situation with Henry. Heather walked with me to the garden gate, wished me luck, and offered an open invitation to return anytime. I thanked her for the hospitality and waved goodbye through the apple trees. Boy did I hightail it outta there in a hurry. Just a shade too comfortable for an outlaw like me. I focused on Angela and Susan and the fun we were going to have.

The hotel seemed to be the tallest building around; I could see it from blocks away, although I was beginning to notice that measuring out blocks was a whole different story here. There were so many little parks with fountains and play areas and band shells that I began to wonder if the whole town wasn't somehow inside a park. I thought I saw some of the kids from the hotel playing frisbee, but couldn't spy the teacher that had spoken to me at the elevator so I just walked on. Besides there were kids bouncing about everywhere, just like it was some kinda school holiday. I couldn't believe they were all dead. Where did they all come from? How many fires and accidents and whatnot could occur anyway. Well, way more than you think. Henry got me thinking about this later. He said you had to remember all the illnesses too, the crib deaths, the cancers and all that, the sort of thing that never got in the papers.

The hotel was just as busy as when I left, but there was no problem getting a room. I signed my name and went on up to the fifth floor. Showered and rested and wondered about it all. Fell asleep in about five minutes. A deep, dreamless sleep. Woke up hungry I don't know how much later. No bedside clock. No calendar. And somehow it didn't seem to bother me. It fit for some reason.

Well shit, I said to myself in the bathroom mirror, if this was some kinda agency drug experiment, it would definitely be wearing off by now. And there'd be guys with little ferret faces with clipboards asking you insane questions about relatives in Russia. I laughed at my own joke and headed downstairs for a bite.

A MEMORIAL SERVICE

I found Susan picking at some fruit salad. I asked her why she looked so glum. Angela had disappeared in the middle of tennis practice. Well that must've put a damper on things, I grinned to no response. She'd sat down with a headache, and seemed very distracted and then just sort of disappeared. I thought about Henry disappearing and tried to make a connection. Susan said that another tennis player had asked how long her friend had been dead, and then shrugged and said it was probably the funeral or some kind of wake that had drawn her. Susan told me she knew about that happening, but still found it very unsettling. She looked so sad I put my arms around her and hugged. I blurted out, for some light relief, that my own family was so distant that nothing could bring us together now. But that just made her worse, she said her own family was just the same. Angela had sorta become her family.

There seemed to be no consoling her, even though she had to admit that Angela couldn't stay away forever, so, remembering Henry's advice, I put out a call for him. I imagined his face and asked him to come. In no time at all he was walking up to us and sitting down. He resolved the situation almost immediately by suggesting that we join Angela wherever she was. And how were we going to do that, she wanted to know. We were going to close our eyes and think about her. Henry picked up a couple of my shrimps in a coconut batter and suggested we move to the garden at the back of the hotel for our little experiment.

We sat together under a giant willow tree, hand in hand, and focused our minds on Angela. The next thing I knew we were in some kind of church with a lot of strangers. Someone other than a minister was upfront speaking.. An elaborate closed coffin lay underneath the podium, with, I was guessing, the mortal remains of Angela. She herself stood right beside it, looking up dejectedly. Susan ran up to her and threw her arms around her. I looked over at Henry. He shrugged and walked over to a rather pompous looking old guy in the back row and began to blow in his ear. The guy scratched at his ear once, then twice, and then again, looking very irritated, as if maybe a mosquito had crawled in for comfort. Henry grinned over at me, looking very pleased with himself. I wanted to take him a Republican convention and see what he would make of that.

It was exactly the sort of nonchalance he displayed at my shoot out, only this time I saw the funny side of it. For the first of many times I thought I had Henry pegged, - a comedian at heart. I watched as he irritated several mourners about the neck and ears, creating a series of small disturbances that was passed off as an annoying insect. And I was to see such antics again and again as my `training' progressed. Henry always seemed to find human drama and pain a great source of amusement. After this particular display I confronted him on it. All tragedy is really comedy, he replied, and after some more experiences here, I would agree with him. Eternal life turns everything into a joke, a great cosmic joke. There was really nothing worth getting yourself upset over, every-thing worked out in the end, even if it did take several lives to iron out the wrinkles.

But I'm getting ahead of myself. Susan brought Angela back to where we were standing. They were both crying. I put my arms round the two of them. It seemed like the only thing to do. Henry came up to us and smiled. `Just tough it out', he whispered to Angela, `it'll be over soon'. And it was. But while it lasted I was quite fascinated. I'd never been to a memorial service before, and after Henry suggested that I try to tune into people's thoughts with empathy, it became even more interesting. Angela seemed to be going through the crowd with Susan, explaining who everyone was and what their relationship was like, so that left me with some time on my hands.

One old guy seemed to be bored and kept thinking of his favorite racetrack. I think his wife was a friend of Angela's mother, as she seemed much more in touch with the overall mood of the place. A couple of younger men seemed to be hometown boys still in love with Angela. Both their thoughts revolved around dates after football games. But their wives sitting next to them, that was a different story. One was quite relieved and glad. Secure I think, knowing that her husband's old flame was never going to show up and rain on her parade. The other was reeking with guilt, recalling all the times she'd been jealous of Angela's looks and popularity. The funny thing was, it all made perfect sense. It was just like high school always was, probably always will be.

Anyway, Angela seemed to be handling it a little better with Susan by her side, so Henry and I left them to take a stroll outside. If we'd been alive we would probably have been sneaking out for a cigarette. Henry of course, picked up on my thought, producing one between his fingers and offering it. I had mastered my nicotine habit a couple of years before and was still proud of my achievement, so I laughed and said thanks, no thanks. It was gone. We moved over well-kept lawns and under large spreading trees. I glanced at the neighborhood just beyond: it looked a lot like the one I grew up in and grew to despise as a symbol of the affluence created and sustained by Yankee imperialism. I should have known better than to have any thought at all, as Henry immediately commented.

"Imperialist expansion is endemic to the cause of civilization, surely you realize that. One piggybacks on the other, always has. What do you think pays for all those fine institutions of learning and arts? Men compete and the winner takes all. And for those who are willing to stand in line there's the inevitable redistribution of wealth."

I came up with my usual line on the importance of civil disobedience, embellishing it with passionate denunciations of genocide and economic slavery. All of which had gone on throughout history with barely a pause for breath, Henry reassured me. "Yes it's an honorable cause, Gene, but the problem with causes is that all their adherents think them honorable and are willing to have their lives subsumed by them." And what the hell did he mean by subsumed? Taken over. And what was wrong with that? It put limits on the individual's growth apparently. Made you think your cause was your life and let you lose yourself in it.

He had me: I couldn't see what was wrong with my cause or my commitment to it. Henry turned from his stroll and looked into my eyes. Fighting the good fight was no longer good enough. It was a phase of my growth and that phase should be over. Needless to say I was indignant and wanted to argue the toss with him. But Angela and Susan appeared and Henry immediately responded by slowly floating up into a tree and settling himself on a branch. Grinning down at us he patted the spot beside him and Angela floated up to join him. That left me with Susan, who seemed to have cheered up since I met her in the restaurant. I took her hand and we strolled on.

Seeing this memorial service had gotten her thinking about her own hometown. This of course tempted me to think about mine, but I narrowly avoided any confrontation with my past by asking her about hers. There'd been a scandal, and she'd left under a cloud, changed her name and moved to the big city. A bit like Heather, I thought. As we spoke she said she could feel the urge for going. Go with it was my thought, and I wondered if I should go with her. She said she felt herself fading fast; I grabbed her hand and in a second we were standing in a schoolyard smack in the middle of recess. Squealing children spun around us. Susan seemed lost in thought as she gazed at a group of trees by the fence. I lost myself in the exuberant energies of the kids: their frantic fun was infectious.

Susan squeezed my hand and whispered at me. A boy called Norman had kissed her under those trees one Saturday morning when she was seven. The strange thing was, as she focused on the memory the sensation of the kiss became stronger and stronger, drawing her back into the original excitement as if nothing else existed. I motioned to the swirl of screaming children all about us. She nodded, as if to say, `Oh yes that'.

This, of course, was her old neighborhood. Norman was killed while riding his bike a few blocks from here. He must have been about nine then. He was supposed to be coming to Susan's birthday party, and the next week they all went to his funeral. Suddenly we were standing at a leafy intersection, silent but for the distant drone of a lawnmower. The only thing that had changed was the trees had gotten larger. I saw a small boy standing under one of them. He looked a bit like one of my own boyhood buddies, Chuck I think . He looked lost as if he'd wandered out of his own neighborhood and couldn't find his way back. I did the same thing myself once, and it was scary. I moved toward him automatically, forgetting that I had Susan by the hand. Noticing the strain I turned around: her mouth was open in shock. "My god, she said, "It's Norman!"

We stood I the middle of the road, Susan unable to move, and me too puzzled to pursue my original intention of helping out a lost boy, which, when I thought about it later, was a pretty crazy thing to do. I looked at Susan and she looked at me. Frozen there so we were. An old caddy purred towards us. I was so busy figuring its vintage it drove right through us before we had a chance to move. I've been able, more or less, to describe all my post mortem experiences for you, but this one surpasses my abilities. It was just too weirdly indescribable. Henry had moved me through walls and doors before this, but so quickly that I barely noticed. This happened in a surreal slow motion. Gordon asks me (now, in real time, as he writes this out), was it like thickness moving through thinness? Well, I suppose... textures, very definitely textures... sand on glass maybe, I don't know.

I can tell you though, Susan was even more freaked out than I was. I had to put my arm around her shoulder to keep her from collapsing. I shuffled us to the sidewalk. The boy ignored us. Which was funny because he seemed to be looking right through us. Susan started to sob. "Oh it's little Norman, she said, "He's still here after all these years. How could it be?" I sure as hell didn't know. I turned from the lost boy to weeping Susan. "This looks like something for Henry. Let's go ask." She nodded. Keeping my hand on her shoulder I imagined Henry and Angela up in that tree branch and *wanted* to go there.

It worked. There was Henry and Angela still up in the tree. They both waved. Where have you two been, Angela wanted to know. "That's our little secret," I replied, smiling. Henry sensed something was up. He patted the branch beside him. Susan dutifully floated up and settled herself. I joined Angela and explained what we had seen. Susan was obviously discussing it with Henry. Below us people streamed out of the church, forming little groups and chatting. Angela pointed out her parents to me and wondered out loud if they remembered meeting up with her two nights ago. Henry had shown her how to do it. They still looked sad so she flew down to give them a hug. I watched the tender scene, enthralled, not knowing it was but one of the first of many for me, and that eventually I would become accustomed, if never completely hardened, to the emotional outpouring. After her parents she went about the crowd, kissing and hugging. No one seemed to notice, at least not that I could see.

I realized I was filled to capacity with fascination. I wondered if I'd remember it all later. I didn't know it then, but memory works very well in the spirit world. It's as if there's nothing to get in the way of what you desire, and if what you desire is memories, then presto, there they are.

Henry announced that he had a plan. I presumed it concerned the little boy. Did I wish to come along? Of course, but what about Angela? Henry suggested I try throwing a thought at her. I did exactly that: I thought about what we were about to do and projected it down to her. She turned and looked up. I gestured, smiling. Yes, she wanted to go too. She'd had enough of all this sadness.

En masse we shifted to the schoolyard. It was eerily empty and quiet. Susan led the way, explaining the birthday/accident story as we walked. Angela moved from my side to hold her hand. I wondered if we'd gone back in time somehow. Henry projected a thought to me; no, the boy had become stuck in time. I was formulating the thought `how?' when we arrived at the intersection. Two young women passed by pushing strollers, completely wrapped up in conversation. Of course they couldn't see us: we were dead, don't you know. Both Angela and Susan had a very tender look in their eyes, a look I would puzzle over , on and off, until they started helping out at the orphanage. That's not what we call them here, but it gives you the gist. But I'm getting ahead of myself again.

We watched the boy staring into space. He looked frozen, as if he started to wait for his father to come, and never stopped. I carefully avoided thinking about my own father. I'd given up waiting for him years ago. Henry asked Susan if she could see herself as a little girl again. She thought about it for a minute and said yeah, sure. They must've discussed the idea before, because her manner betrayed a confidence I couldn't share. Then I remembered the MP uniform. She'd do the same thing except she'd change her whole body. Henry told her to focus on a favorite girlhood image, a day, a dress, whatever, and see it not as *then* but *now*. She nodded and closed her eyes.

I mentioned earlier about how I was filled with fascination. Well, this is a perfect example. I'd been in this strange and wonderful new world. for maybe three days, but the magic of the place seemed to know no bounds. I watched as Susan seemed to dissolve. Yes, dissolve. She grew thinner and fainter and in a matter of seconds was no longer there. In her place appeared a little blonde sweetheart in a party dress, tied at the back with a blue ribbon. I couldn't believe it; she even had two blue ribbons in her hair.

I glanced at Henry: I got one of his *told you so* smiles. He looked just like a proud parent at, say, the school concert. Little Susan walked up to little Norman. From where I was standing he looked as though he was talking to her. Then he seemed to be thinking something over. The little Susan took his hand and they walked over to us.

She said, "This is my friend Norman and he wants to come with us. Norman, this is Henry, Angela and Gene." We all said hello. Norman kept his eyes down. Henry suggested we walk back to the schoolyard, which we did at a leisurely pace. Little Susan and little Norman were chatting away quite happily, so I fell in with Angela. We quietly shared our amazement. Henry sauntered along, unaffected by it all. He looked just like some retired farmer who'd gotten up off the porch to go to the mailbox at the end of the driveway and was maybe going to forget what he was doing before he got there.

Once in the schoolyard little Susan led little Norman over to the trees. The three of us big people held back and watched as they disappeared behind the largest trunk. We waited. I expressed my amazement to Angela. She shook her head and raised her eyebrows. Henry smiled his wry, smug smile.

I now knew better than to criticize it, even silently. The children reappeared and walked towards us.

Little Norman seemed a bit more *with us*.

Little Susan looked up at us, completely the precocious assertive child, and said "We're ready to go now Henry". Henry had us all hold hands and shut our eyes. I think you know what happened next: we reappeared under the willow tree in the hotel garden. A group of people sitting by a fountain I hadn't noticed before waved to us. One of them was, I was almost certain, the teacher I'd met at the elevator door, how long ago was it, a day, two days, I wasn't sure, but I remembered the little twitch of her nose that'd convinced me I wasn't in a giant CIA drug experiment after all. I waved back and I think everyone else did too. An older woman approached us. She looked and dressed about sixty. Norman suddenly ran towards her, shouting "Grandma, grandma!" and jumping at her outstretched arms. I had a feeling that Henry had something to do with this, but I said nothing at the time.

GREAT PLEASURE

It is with great pleasure that I return to the consciousness of you readers. Though many months have passed since Gordon last let himself be used as a conduit for my energy and intelligence, that interval means nothing to me, and I take up the reins as if I had never let them go. My existence, like all other higher selves/ monads, is not limited by the definitions of time and space. I am, always and everywhere. And, as energetic extensions of me and those like me you are, always and everywhere.

There is, as you may have guessed, nowhere where we are not. And if it could be said that we have an agenda, it would be something along the lines of creative play. We explore the confines of various levels of density and gravity, planning and executing experiments whose outcome we can only guess. If the ascended masters, some of whom you will be meeting later in this narrative can be said to be cheerleaders for evolution on this planet, we, the monads could be described as both the game and the players.

Though the demise and death of your bodies may seem to threaten your sovereign being, be assured that your individual consciousness will survive the change. Each of your bodies, when they fall away as simply as a snake sheds a skin, will leave you poised to explore another plane of existence. Each of those planes is populated by a myriad of sentient beings, all of whom are evolving, like yourself, back to the blessedness of omniscience and omnipresence, where all is revealed and nothing is hidden.

Well, what is the nature of that all, I hear Gordon saying, souls need to know. While I can reveal a slice of that particular cake, I shall not unveil the entire construction, for that would spoil your crowning achievement. Suffice to say, as the highest truths of the world's religions insist, you are all sparks of god consciousness out exploring the nether regions of his (her) creative manifestation, undergoing every possible experience in a variety of lives and forms. All challenge, all suffering, all joy. Despite all exhaustion and limitation, the divine spark lies deep within you, ever ready to light up a new path through adversity. If monads (or higher selves) are fingers on the hands of god, as is sometimes said, then individuals, like yourselves, are the fingernails. You grow out from us but you always reach farther. And the clipping that is death only appears to stunt your growth. You are always expanding, through every death and change of form.

Gordon says, be more specific. Well. (1) All human individuals, no matter how distanced from spiritual understanding, are sparks of divine energy, who live many lives in perfecting their being; (2) All belong to the group soul configuration known as the monad or higher self, and most return to that highly conscious state between incarnations to "recharge their batteries". (3) Those who don't, who become ensnared by the glamour of the many paradises, purgatories and hells, can return to earth without that recharging, but the dimming of the divine memories makes their path even harder then before. (3) You share your evolutionary journey with souls in the mineral, animal, plant and angelic kingdoms, and you have the opportunity to cross over, should you so wish. i.e. a fairy spirit can become a human spirit, and humans can merge into devas. (4) All sentient entities in the manifested universes are of equal value and no course of action is condemned; (5) All energetic interactions have causes and effects which manifest multidimensionally through eternity in the worlds of form; (6) Nothing is static, finished or finite. (7) All planetary bodies are ensouled, sometimes by humans who have graduated from earthschool.

How's that, I say to Gordon. Good enough for now, he smiles.

SECTION TWO:

A COUPLE OF HENRY'S PROTEGES

SERENE

The next guide up is Serene. This is not her earth name, but a representation of how she feels now, in spirit. Henry found her in a hippie commune, right after she passed during what appeared to be a difficult childbirth. She was not the first to feel that delivery under the influence of the psychedelic LSD would be a transcendent experience, but we think she was the first to feel, while out of body in an profound depersonalized ecstasy, to decide that her husband's new but barren lover was the rightful mother to the child, and that she was merely the vehicle bring these souls together, and that her selfless gift was actually the return of a two hundred year old favor.

Having had some experience with the expanded state of psychedelics, Henry had no problem fitting himself into Serene's sparkly universe. Or at least that's what he's telling me now. Don't take my word for it, let Serene tell the story. Which I shall do.

Yeah, Henry made a great clown alright. Juggling those little blue teddy bears just got me right off. I'd long past the stage of caring whether he, or anything else, was a hallucination. I'd settled into that all-knowing hyper-reality phase, where the thoughts and emotions of others were just waves of energy passing through me. And that includes a number of commune women who were totally freaked that I'd taken the acid without their approval. But the stuff we had was the purest Owsley and I knew it wouldn't do me or the baby no harm. I'd taken some the year before and had the most ego blowing trip imaginable.

Couldn't even talk about it when it was over. Out in the hills, almost a full moon, I seemed to merge first with the earth and then with the sky. And then I just kinda disappeared. I'd heard about the void from some zen buddhist types, but to be there, no-where, feeling nothing about to become everything, well that was just the best. So where else to be but there, no-where, when the child was about to become? Seemed obvious to me, and that was when I got all the past life stuff, the favours the debts and all, and just knew I had to go on. Jim, Ellen and the baby would be fine, I knew it. So I withdrew the spirit from the body.

How? I just didn't go back. And with Henry the clown juggling those blue teddy bears, I lost my chance to reconsider. Would I have used it? Hard to say now. Henry knew my guide who knew the karmic details and the pre-birth plan. (you all know about pre-birth plans doncha?). As it turned out my drug fueled enlightenment was an attachment free passport into what Henry called the upper reaches of spirit but what looked to me a lot like northern California minus all the eyesores. And it was there that I fulfilled one of my lifelong ambitions: living in a giant redwood. That's right, way up there. I'd dreamt of it since I was a little girl in Sacramento. Used to drive my parents crazy with tree talk. *Honey you can't live in a tree and that's that*, was my mother's final word when I was eight or so, and after that I just talked to myself about it. But I'm getting off my story, which is show you the kind of guide work I do here. Yeah, my transition was way outta line with what most folk experience, but let's not get hung up on that. As Henry will no doubt let you know sometime during this project, my passing was kinda like someone deep in meditation or prayer being slaughtered by a surprize invader.

So let me tell how I enjoy eternal life. I work a lot with sudden death, heart attacks, crib deaths, aneurysms and the like. Since I'd made that snap decision without regret, Henry reasoned that I could help others do the same. Turned out he was right, ...most of the time.

I am standing with Adrian, a dead young Jamaican-American athlete of some promise, in a typical den somewhere in middle class North America. We were watching his parents watching videos of their darling boy breaking county track and field records at eleven and twelve years old. We'd already seen the wedding and baby shows and joined in the teary celebration of his tiny angelic beauty. I'm still a sucker for that. No matter how long I work with the recent and suddenly departed, genuine family emotions still get me going. Hey, it's the astral plane we're on now, and that's the plane of emotions: crying comes with the territory.

But fortunately so does laughter.

Adrian suffered a heart attack during a very important sprint last week, and he and everyone else were completely baffled. No medical explanation was found.. It was just one of those things. God always takes the ones he loves, they said. Adrian was pissed: in almost perfect physical shape, with absolutely no steroids or other stimulants in his system, he stood there, hands on hips, staring at his crumpled body on the track while people freaked and fussed about him. I stood there with him, vainly trying to get his attention. Not an unusual experience for us, I might add. The dead do tend to be somewhat preoccupied with their own corpses. Much effort can be expended before they realize eternity is much more interesting than the breeding ground for maggots their former residence has become.

The earthly drama unfolded, as earthly dramas do, with much consternation and carrying on, all of which sucked poor Adrian into its stewpot of steamy energies. He followed himself on a stretcher to a first aid station, and then, via ambulance, to a hospital. Needless to say I went along for the ride, on the slim chance that he might take a second to turn around and look at me, instead of through me, as his panic vibration dictated. As with most cases I was left to calmly observe as he tried, ever more frantically, to get someone, anyone, to take some notice of him. Ironically, of course, the only one who would was the one he was oblivious to.

By the time we'd made it to the morgue and stood facing that dark cold drawer, I knew I'd never be able to grab his attention without some earthly help, so I left him there while I took a turn through my physical plane meditators and retrievers. The continuing surge of the new age movement has provided us guides with a pretty reliable and ever expanding stable of eager service providers, who somehow understand that their physical level of vibration can be directed by us to those earthbound spirits, `like Adrian, who cannot tune into our frequency, no matter how far we lower it for their benefit.

Two of my contacts were busy at work and were much too

preoccupied to even notice me, never mind take time out for a retrieval. A third was working in her garden, with a determination so fierce it shut out my prompt that she could use a nap after such a long morning's effort. Those short naps can be so useful to us here. An experienced retriever can often work magic in those eight or ten minutes, handing over a difficult client and returning to their couch refreshed by the physical rest and yet energized by the astral adventure. They all know that little psychic tingle means something, even if they're not quite sure what. A fourth I found at her dentist, shivering in anticipation. The fifth was Gordon, who, fortunately, was between shifts and just finishing his lunch. I knew that in a few moments he'd be lying down in the dark to listen to a meditation tape whose sound content would maneuver his brain waves into a frequency that could propel him in my direction. I waited patiently while he answered the phone and brushed his teeth.

Gordon's fairly new at retrievals done in the daytime meditative state, and finds it all frustratingly vague and unverifiable. Like many newbies he feels like he's talking to himself, making it all up to satisfy his expectations and ambitions. Of course, it's the old faith vs. doubt debate incarnate humans have been indulging in since time began, and maybe even before. Eventually his abilities will stretch far beyond his need for verification, but for now he will have to go on trust, which is a trip in itself. Funny thing is, at night when he's asleep he becomes this amazing spirit being, whose efforts in the emancipation of ignorance are almost endless. It's interesting for me to see these two halves of him, so different and yet so distantly related.

Guiding his relaxed mind to Adrian in the morgue, I let him do his stuff unaided. He knows, as do the others, that if a human, however vague, appears to him, that human is more than likely to be deceased, confused, and in need of their retrieval skills. I can see him interacting almost immediately. He doesn't yet have enough depth of vision to know they're in a morgue, but he intuits Adrian's basic medical state, anxiety and confusion, and knows, more or less, how to deal with it.

After a polite exchange he asks what the problem is. Adrian tells him about the sprint and the guy collapsing and nobody talking to him. Gordon assures him he's the guy collapsing and no one will talk to him because they can't see him as he is now. And how, exactly, is he now? In a word, dead. This at least gets Adrian to laugh, always a good sign. And how come then Gordon's talking to him? Well, he understands how it is for dead people and makes a point of seeking them out. And how is it for dead people, Adrian asks, not believing a word of it. Pretty frustrating and confusing most of the time, is the reply.

"And you're gonna fix all that up for me are ya?"

"Sure, especially if you let that attitude down for a minute."

Fortunately by the time Gordon had maneuvered him into the afterlife 'proper', as he calls it, Adrian, no doubt dazed by the thrill of flight, had let down his defenses long enough for me to be of some use to him. And having taken the heat for me, Gordon quickly bowed out and went back to his nap with only the sketchiest notion of what he'd just accomplished. But true to form, he did take a second to turn to me and wink, whispering , "I guess I'll get my reward in heaven, huh?"

So by the time Adrian and I were standing in his parents' place drying our tears I was just about his best buddy. The athlete's village I'd introduced him to would no doubt capture his affections in the days to come, but in this immediate post-mortem period I was still his staff and compass. It is often like that when a young person has no parents or grandparents in the astral that a guide can become more like family. He did have a couple of gangster wannabe cousins caught up in the usual criminal illusions of a lower astral neighborhood, but he was in no way keen to make their acquaintance. A service in a nearby Baptist church was more to his taste.

And so it was, after a week or so earth time, he was able to fly from the sadness of his parents den to the charismatic succor of his pastor, where I left him off, knowing I was no longer needed just then, and that months might pass before he realized that "training" here was less a matter of moving the limbs in the required manner, and more a matter of letting thought take you away. He would continue to believe in gravity and the necessity of effort in overcoming its pull until I, or someone like me, would arrive by flying.

Of course there was always the possibility that his pastor might convince him that such a delightful transport was but a demonically inspired bewitchment drawing him away from the true path.

Pastors here are like pastors there: they tend to their flocks tenaciously, especially when they see a loose cannon like me around. But we'll face that one when we come to it.

For now I'd like to move on to another part of my life here, something I hope you'll all find intriguing. I know from my cruising through your world as some kind of intelligent ghost on a mission from god to round up the lost and confused that the concept of a "shapeshifter" is very current in your culture, so perhaps you'll not be too shocked to hear that I spend some of my time looking like a soap bubble blowing about on the breeze. It's another childhood fantasy come true, and you can probably guess how often I drove my mother crazy with it. The bottom line for her was that little girls just can't be soap bubbles no matter how much they may want to. My dear old ma, and she is dear and old now, ninety two and in a nursing home, waiting out her time, she still thinks over the nutty stuff I used to come up with.

Pretty soon she'll find out it's not so nutty.

Of course it was Henry who taught me to shapeshift, but he says to remind you that it was Jack who taught him, and it's not as if he started the trend. It's just something you can learn when you get here. Some folk take to it like ducks to water and others, well, it just never seems to sit right with them. They'd rather be just who they are. As you can probably guess, Henry taught me the art so that I'd be a better retriever. Molding your body and dress to suit the unconscious expectations of your "retrievee" is one of our basic skills. Once you've got the basic "repertoire of characters", as he likes to call it, he leaves you to explore on your own. It was on one of these explorations that I wondered what it would be like to be a soap bubble. The sudden curious intensity seemed to have an instant effect, and quite dizzying it was too. You are light enough on the astral to begin with, but in a second I was no more than a balloon being blown about. Have you ever watched a leaf in the fall, swinging down from a high branch and looking so goofy and carefree? Well something like that.

That first time was just magical and my childish glee in finally living my dream had me enthralled for I don't know how long. That's something else that happens a lot here: losing track of time. Not that we pay it much attention in the first place, but if you're doing our version of daydreaming, you're just gone, bobbing-cork-in-the-ocean type thing. And sure, it's as blissful as you can imagine: not a care in the world. Not that I have many cares to begin with. But some people here do. They worry about their families that they left behind, they feel remorseful about stupid things they did, they wish they could do it all over again, they feel they've done nothing to deserve the heavenly life they've gotten. But I suppose that's another story. For now you should just remember how blissful that bubble thing is for me.

Another time, a few weeks ago as you would figure it, I was alerted by one of the personal spirit guides I work with that a certain soul was heading for a pre-arranged heart attack, and that I might want to be there to assist. I say pre-arranged meaning that the soul had set up the circumstances before birth. He had wished to become much more spiritually oriented in this incarnation, and in case this desire was offset by other karmically determined circumstances, i.e. family pressures and the lure of the dollar, the crisis would be triggered for full effect.

After the guide's tip I found myself in the large car of an obese attorney in a mid-sized southern town. He was hot and bothered by a whole pile of angers and anxieties as he drove across town to yet another appointment. The crappy diet and excessive tobacco intake was all he needed to overstress that most vital organ., so when he parked the car in a panic and then passed out I was there to smile and say "Hi, howya doin?"

His first response was along the lines of, "Who the hell are you and how did you get in my car?" And as he was driving through one of the tougher neighborhoods in town he thought I was one clever hooker who figured by dressing down in jeans and sweatshirt I could avoid arrest. I flipped him an angelic smile and told he I was only here to help him decide.

"Decide what exactly?"

"Whether you want to live or die."

"I ain't goin' to no church lady and I ain't givin' you any dough either."

"I don't want your money. You spent way too much on lunch as it is." That got him: I could feel his credit card anxiety and see an image of an attractive black woman. He was doubly trapped; having an affair was risky enough, but with his family's intolerance a black woman would be out of the question.

"How'd you know about that? You a witch or something?"

"Nope, I'm a spirit guide and I can read some of your thoughts."

"Great! You're gonna give me some advice are ya? How about fixin' up the air in this beast, can you manage that?"

"I'll do better'n that. I'll take you somewhere's really special."

Baffled between the angelic smile and the hooker invitation he just sighed and agreed. I whipped him up to a mid-astral reception complex. A couple of colonial style transition rest homes situated in beautiful park like settings. You know, ponds, fountains, swans, weeping willows, tennis and golf. Just the sort of thing Al would go for. I moved him there instantaneously, arriving right by one of the pretty fountains and seating him on a stone bench by the rock garden. I can do a bit of flying or I can do the instant transfer; a quick mental scan of the client shows what will sit best with them. Kids, of course, love the flying. But Al seemed like the sort of totally straight guy who'd be freaked by that kinda thrill. Poor guy, he looked so dazed and confused I gave him a little peck on the forehead. But to counteract any misunderstanding, I sat down very demurely next to him and gave out one of my church lady smiles. He asked me if this was heaven, but something about the way he squinted nervously and slumped his shoulders told me he wasn't too happy with this quick change of scenery. He was waiting for something, I don't know what, to catch up with him. A guilty anxious guy to be sure. I'd been told his much loved grandmother would be around to help. I couldn't see her anywhere, so while I made small talk with him I put out an urgent call. Sure enough a grandmotherly sort was soon sauntering our way. It's not maybe the nicest thing to see a fat, balding, bad tempered lawyer clutching his granma and weeping, but it's all part of my work here, so I kind of nod and smile with the best of them. Julia had obviously been briefed about the pre-birth arrangements and was soon dropping hints about it. When she said "You know Alan, you're just passin' through here, you're not stayin' " I knew it was time to step back in.

Having barely accustomed himself to the thought of being dead, Al was now being told he'd have to go back. Back and face the music I could feel him thinking. Back to that shopaholic bitch of a wife and that posse of drug addled psychos he'd called sons. Back to the ripoff ratrace they'd called law. Back to the boozing shark subbing in for his mother-in-law. I could see all the pictures he was shuffling through his mind and knew I had to somehow inspire him towards one of the possible futures only his will could spotlight. Julia kindly let me get a word in edgewise.

"Things don't have to be the same when you return Al, you can choose another life, one more suited to your original aspirations," I told him, using the tone of calm assurance I thought I'd perfected.

"You make it sound so easy girl. You got some methods of persuasion I ain't used myself?"

"I sure do Al. I got someone comin' along that was there when you put together your life plan in the first place."

"My life plan? What in the heck is that? Don't tell me babies sign contracts, 'cause that means they got lawyers in heaven too."

I laughed. "No lawyers Al, just advisers."

"You mean like those fellas we sent to Vietnam before the suckers like me were rounded up?"

I chuckled some more. Julia didn't seem too pleased, though she kept her opinions to herself. One of Al's senior guides finally showed up. I'd met Eons before, but I'd never seen him dressed as a very aged and respectable church elder. The costume had an immediate effect though: Al lost his sardonic edge, became respectful and compliant, and was soon walking off with Eons to a quiet spot somewhere where he would no doubt move him back in time.

Though I remained with Julia by the fountain, sharing the small talk of astral strangers, I sent part of my mind on with Eons and Al, to record what transpired. By most folk's standards this is an invasion of privacy, and I know exactly what they mean. But the circumstances, I think you'll agree, extenuate. Henry suggested I do this for the readers' benefit, and way later Al gave his consent, although in a situation I'm sure he would only recall as a dream.

In a nearby rose garden, the one with the "meditation garden" sign at its entrance that we often use here, Eons sat Al down, held his hand to Al's forehead and transferred the memory of his pre-birth planning session into his consciousness. Notice I say consciousness and not brain. On this level, memories, even reactivated ones, are not confined to the brain, as you suppose on earth. Everything is contained in the energy body of the being and can be read by any who have the ability. Some stuff is obvious and can be seen by almost anyone, but the deeper motivations are, how shall I say, encoded, and require a bit of training, the kind that guides and helpers like myself get. The gist of his aura read-out was this: after several lives nearly wasted by rash decisions sparked by passion and hot tempers, Al finally wanted some kind of progress. The riches and spoils of late-century America, falling like rain on the his desiccated and poverty weary soul would likely cast him adrift from spirit, so a mid-life medical crisis of the sort unheard of in previous centuries, which could be precipitated and resolved in an hour or two, might be extremely useful. To the pre-birth Al, nurtured by some seasons of astral r and r after a few very grim depression era years of hunger and despair, the idea was intriguing, but not nearly as glamorous as being a lawyer with a big car and a house in the suburbs. But up here we're used to that sort of thing, and we work with what we get.

Al looked a bit brighter after his "infusion", but maybe not as inspired as we would have liked. He'd been here long enough to get a feel for the glorious beauty and relaxed comfort of the place, and even if he wasn't entirely sure it was real, it was at least as good as that private golf course his one rich client had impressed him with. Eons brought him back to the fountain area just as Julia was excitedly telling me about her house renovations. Al took her hand and held it as he explained his remorse. Considering he was a full grown man I thought she did a great job of acting grand-motherly. Her turn of the century gentility may have been down at heels when she passed, but by now it had been refined to perfection.

Eons suggested that Al return to life with me as his guide. I could see that he was torn between asking for a stay of execution, being sarcastic about my youth and gender, and immediately complying with Eons wishes. Eons has this way of making folks want to please him. It's a trick I wish I could learn. Al finally went for obedience and we walked off leaving Eons and Julia smiling and waving. A discreet distance away, I grasped his hand and told him to close his eyes if he didn't want to get dizzy. Executing an immediate transfer we showed up as a paramedic, having laid his body on a stretcher, was pounding on his chest. We joined the small crowd watching the drama unfold. Al was entranced looking at himself. Sudden death types often are. He turned to me and grinned, "Sure beats reality tv don't it?" and then disappeared into his suddenly thrashing body.

For the purposes of this project, I checked in on him a few times after. In hospital he and his wife all tears and forgiveness and the sons all immaculately dressed. Some weeks later, post surgery and recuperation, the spouses had shared their secrets. Sherry was not shocked to hear about the existence of Gloria or the pigmentation of her skin, but Al was sure surprised to know that his wife had been seeing their accountant Don and wanted to move in with him. One son wanted to go to college out of state, another was going to Aspen as soon as he graduated grade ten, and the third wanted his legal savvy in beating a possession rap. Dad had been raving about his near death experience for weeks and they all thought to get what they could while he was still flipped.

Some time after that I found him in church, Gloria by his side, testifying about his encounter with Jesus and how it had turned his life around. A genuine fervor flowed about his aura, and I felt it would keep him on track even as it dimmed through the years. He was dedicating his life to the Lord's work and I was pleased to feel that I'd played a small part in his emergence. Eons had been mistaken for many a prophet in his work, and was not surprised when I told him. Senior guides like him often are. They get used to it, it's part of the job. They're way beyond having anything like that go to their heads. Tell you the truth, I think they're on a first name basis with all the big name prophets anyway. They're all on the same team if you know what I mean.

Just after that last Al stopover, I thought to visit my dear old ma. I often do, but this time was worth telling you about. She's having spells of senility now, and that often means she just goes with the flow of her imagination instead of trying to act nice and normal for the staff and other residents. She had been daydreaming for ages that morning and all I had to do was appear looking just like I did around the time I ran away from home, which means the uniform of the private school in which I'd been incarcerated. She'd been reliving our final argument when I stepped up in front of her and announced all was forgiven. Using a sort of imaginative willpower I'd overwhelmed the image she'd been seeing and the shock of the new had stumped her. Anyone passing by would've thought she was jabbering incoherently, but at least I'd gotten her to see me. Finally, after all my efforts!

I entered her dream, as it were, and we talked. I said I was in heaven and that dad was there too. I didn't mention he still wasn't speaking to me, but we could get to that later. Brother Tom was still trapped in his suicide's hell, despite the efforts of his sister and others, but that would just depress her. So basically I sinned by omission, but at least she could talk to me and hear how I was, which was fine. I also told her how much fun heaven was and how her sister Marlena was asking for her often. She told me she'd always missed me after I'd gone, wherever I'd gone. To a commune in California was the answer, but that's another story.

I wouldn't want you to think that guys like Al were all I dealt with, so let me whisper a few more secrets in your ear. Sometimes it seems to me that teenagers form a category of their own and then other times they seem just as varied as any other group. Maybe I should just stop making up theories. Sudden deaths in the teen years fall into two main camps: the unplanned, careless types, and the carefully constructed family drama. The tools are likely known to you all: cars and alcohol, cancer and meningitis. But the fact that they are used by souls as carefully as stock reports or computer manuals in constructing a purposeful journey of learning from creative possibilities of conflict and suffering may not be as widely recognized. Well, that's one of the things I'm here to talk about.

Teenagers are exploding with energy, that we all know. You call it madness, you call it hormonal, you call it peer pressure, but it's all that most adults can do to barely cope with it, the sudden highs, the depressions, the mood swings. Lost in this carnival of stress and excitement these young people seek the self-expression so necessary to the soul and its development. To adults it seems that they want the world and they want it now. They forget how it feels to be young and confined. I don't, but that's another story.

The first thing you have to remember is teens, like the rest of you down there in earthworld, are ageless beings bucking eternity for a bit of time. A bit of time to bite down on their karma. They may look younger and stupider, but they're only pretending. The soul inside is like all souls, ageless. But the body they're in and the emotions they feel can easily distract them from their pre-birth plans. But again, in that they're just like the rest of you, getting caught up in what society and personality tells you is important and forgetting what your soul wants. This is the sort of thing guides like me sit around and debate in our spare time when we're not getting the job done. Kinda like I'm doing now.

A while back I was working with Lena, let's call her that anyway, whose pre-birth plan included a short life for the sake of a short life plus a deep shock for her all-too-ambitious parents who had driven her to the brink more than once before. I say "included" as all incarnational designs attempt to fulfil a small army of purposes, but to list them all would be, as Gordon suggests, counterproductive. She chose to be a child whose every moment was a wonder, whose joy in life infected all those around her and whose love of the moment embraced everyone in it. She'd had that joy cruelly crushed out of her in three other lives and was keen to relive it without the punishment that rigid fearful societies usually demand. Not that she hadn't done her fair share of repressing individual expression, the stern matriarch and the obsequious bureaucrat were not unknown to her. She could see the theme and recognized its cause and purposes. As her guide said when she was filling me in on the details, "She knows that the past creates the future".

Lena was everyone's little angel from the word go, so when the seed of the brain tumour sprung to life right on schedule, the dizzy spells and headaches clouded everyone's horizon. When it was declared inoperable everyone grieved, including Lena, whose love of self, fanned by her proud and ambitious parents, had grown to obscure her original mission. As her decline kicked into operation I began almost nightly visits. Just little chats between dreams really, but I thought they'd be enough to start a reaction. What they started would be hard to define, but a growing acceptance of her departure triggered a sudden upswell of worry for her devastated parents. A knowing gaze settled into her sky blue eyes as she searched her mother's sad, self-pitying smile for any trace of the understanding she felt growing inside.

A word, a look, a nod, any little sign might have done it. But her mother's grief was clouded with anger, resentment at a god who would so poison her life. She wanted to get pregnant, fertility as revenge against cruel nature, and Lena could sense the calm plotting in her heart. It made her feel disposable, degraded and sad, and when we next conversed, that night by her bed, freed from the burden of a broken body, she seemed angry herself, mad at a mom who'd reduced her to a battle strategy. Yet as we talked, and I gently reminded her of the earlier arrangements, tinges of forgiveness seemed to surface in her talk, and the dread of departure seemed to be rearranging itself into the thrill of new adventure.

Often these nightly visits would be followed by yet another attempt at rescuing my brother from the lower astral Saigon he'd sunk into after od-ing on weekend leave back in, well I'm not really sure, `69 or `70, but way after I'd slipped the noose. Always rejecting my father's live-free-or-die pose, he'd somehow wound up going to `Nam instead of Canada, like at least three of his friends. I'd already run off to Frisco, my halfway house to full hippiedom at the commune, so the news remained a secret until I started roaming the ethers under Henry's directions, and seeing that you could discover just about anything about anyone anywhere, but how little good would come of it even if you had a mind to fix things. And Jacky was definitely one of the things I couldn't fix. Still can't. But back then I still had bags of enthusiasm. The sight of my darling big brother, who took me to the park when I was five and the carnival when I was eight and looked out for me at school when my mouth made me a target, sprawled on a dirty mattress in a gloomy cave of a room in some fleabag hotel was almost more than I could take.

Like all family members doubling as helpers, I wanted to share the joys of paradise with the terminally joyless, but I couldn't even get him to see me, such was his guilt and self-punishment. Not to mention no belief in an afterlife, or at least not in any afterlife that would take in scum like him. A sergeant had blamed him for the death of his buddies, and bummed out as he was he bought the whole trip without thinking it through. This was a dead sergeant by the way. Rank and retribution carries through.

I'd tried everything I could think of, the angel, the slut, the kindly grandmother, the Disney character (Mickey Mouse *and* Olive Oyl) but nothing seemed to work. If he'd been religious for more than five minutes in his entire life I might have had half a chance as a demon, but no, I was just some kinda weird dreamy hallucination, his useless brain dragging up butchered bits of his little sister in drag.

The hell realms, the lower astral, purgatories, call them what you will, are a real testing ground for us guides and helpers. The negative thoughts, destructive emotions and general overall hopelessness that hangs over the place can really drag you out and down. People are angry, frightened, anxious, confused and really really depressed. It's no fun hanging out there, believe me. Best you can say is it's a challenge.

My brother's building, a dump if you ever saw one, was typical of the worst Saigon neighborhoods, Saigon's lower astral Bowery if you like. Dead junkies gravitate to such places for the same reason other dead types move to their favorite spots, because they feel comfortable there, they feel they belong. That can be a hard thing for a paradise lover to admit, that others actually want to be miserable, but it's true. Maybe it's because that's all they know, but still, at some point in their cloudy past they made a choice. I guess I just wanted to help them make other choices. And if that makes me a goddamn do-gooder then so be it.

The best thing about my brother's life is the fifteen year old girl that brings him his fix. She was with him a couple of times back in the land of the living and his basic kindness kept her on some kind of leash until they met again. Henry says if we ever get them outta there they'll be a good team, such is her devotion. I find that hard to believe but you never know: I've seen strange and wonderful transformations here.

So for a while I had this rhythm of making progress with Lena and getting nowhere with Jacky. There's a way it's just like earth, here in astral illusion land, you win some you lose some. Lena, bless her, did a lovely job of leaving her house of grief with as much joy and light as she could manage. The angels she saw at the end of her bed were, of course, me and her guide Shelley, welcoming her with open arms. She'd seen us a few times already, but only her schoolfriend Ellie seemed ready to be convinced. Neither parents nor grandparents were ready to release their stoic materialism. (That's actually Henry's assessment, which I'll use as mine sounds more insulting) We flew her to a children's reception center and laid her on a bed in a room with a lovely view. She slept a morphine sleep the whole way; the drugged ones often do. With

Shelley to drop in regularly, I was free to check in once in a while on the family. Mother Alice, pregnant and knowing it by the time of the funeral, barged through the rituals of loss like a trooper, shouldering husband and parents the whole way. Those most affected were her classmates from Mrs. Piper's grade four, who built a rock garden shrine on the school's lawn to her memory, and Mrs. Piper herself, a woman who, unknown to her colleagues, had already suffered three miscarriages in her short marriage. I tried to communicate with her during dreamtime and was at least partially successful. An unconscious acceptance seemed to at least neutralize her grief. Observing her thoughts patterns and the network of interactions with parents I could feel the anger-at-god syndrome claiming a few victims. And though I tried, no one seemed to feel the love and understanding I sent their way. Even the couple of church goers didn't seem to get it. Saying that it must be part of god's plan, either to themselves or each other, barely covered the open sores of their rage. And don't forget, for us that's a very real experience. Angry clouds would sort of smoke out of tears in their aura as they sat in each other's kitchens and smoldered. *Such a beautiful loving child, such an angel, how could god take her soon,* I would hear. *Because she wanted to go, it was part of her plan,* I would try to feed them, to little, if any, effect.

It made me sad, but not despondent. People make their own way in life and can only be helped if they really want it. Struggling mightily with their burden is a big thing for a lot of folks. Giving it up is just too easy. Jesus doubted and suffered, they think, why shouldn't I? So who am I to disagree? That's kind of a big thing for souls in this line of work: realizing that you can't always help, despite all your mobility and knowledge and driving urge to help. Some folk love their misery and some wanna manage it under their own steam: that you gotta accept. And mostly I have. After all, I renamed myself Serene didn't I?

BRIAN ALBERT

Before I get started we gotta get one thing straight: there's angels and there's angels. Some are really angels, always have been, right from the beginning of what you wanna think of as time, at least on this planet where we take that kinda thing seriously. And some are just dead people with angelic leanings. I'm one of the second group. We'd like to be angels but we know we got a long ways to go. We've seen the real thing and were dazzled, like kids at a carnival. So we've been shown the ropes and set free to see what we can do. Apprentices, that's what we are, apprentice angels.

I got my start right after I died. Henry caught me hanging around a major league baseball stadium, in a city he asked me not to mention, napping between games. Had some kinda seizure on the way to the game and just kept going. Didn't even see the fuss I'd left behind on the sidewalk. Went through the whole game without realisin' a thing. Till a guy sat on me that is. Sittin' on me was bad enough, but havin' it not hurt was even stranger. Yellin' at him was no good either. My hand kept goin' right through him. I got so pissed I kinda lunged at him and lost my balance, fell down ass over teakettle about ten rows. Stood up, no bruises, and thought I musta bin' loaded. You know a drunk's made o' rubber, right? So just went right down to the pitch and stood right behind first base. And then the pitcher. What a blast, I could even hear what they were thinkin'. And not a soul could see me.

Except Henry, but that was later. A whole season passed I think, but to tell you the truth I kinda lost track. And how he sized me up I'll never know. Maybe he read my aura and saw me helpin' old ladies across the road, 'cause I do that sometimes. He's a sharp one that Henry, knows more about you than you do yourself. Sees what you really wanna do if you weren't so shy about puttin' your best foot forward.

Once he'd convinced me I was really dead and not just dreamin' or some weird thing, he asked if maybe I'd wanna try bein' an apprentice angel. I don't know why but I said "Sure!" Sounded as though I could check it out and maybe move on if I didn't like it, and really I'd more or less had my fill of great games and free food and booze. Not to mention those goddamn snotty managers and their wives.

Henry said he'd seen I liked movin' about town as if I owned the place. Well I didn't deny it. Ball games had been my passion, but I liked the fancy hotels too. His whole thing about me bein' a ghost didn't seem right, but instead of arguing the toss he got me goin' with the idea that I could be some kind do-gooder ghost. I kept thinkin' about all those rich guys doin' stuff for charity and how it ticked me off because it was never any skin off their nose. Maybe I just wanted to go them one better, show them that a guy like me could do it if he just got the chance.

Henry walked me to the nearest subway station. He wanted me to see something. I wondered what. We stood with our backs to the wall, just kinda lookin'. I noticed a few pretty ladies, comin' home from work by the looks of things. Henry said "See that guy there? The one in the ratty jean jacket and three day beard. I saw a guy scowlin' kinda, like he had a headache somethin' fierce. I wanted to give him a Tylenol and sure enough there was one in my hand. Back then I was still amazed that stuff happened. Henry had a glass of water suddenly. With that smile of his he said "Go on give it to him." Guy was so shocked that he just took the pill and water as if I was his mum.

He did seem kinda gruff, like some guys are, like things are buggin' them but they won't say what. He handed me back the glass, kind of forceful, like take it or else, so I took it and asked him how he was. He grunted as if to say could be better. I knew a few guys like that at work. Too lazy to speak most of the time. Henry came up beside us. Guy looked him over and snarled, sorta. Then he grabbed him by the shoulders as if he was gonna shake him about for stealin' his lunch. I've seen guys do that you know, steal somebody's roast beef cause they only had peanut butter. Hell of an argy-bargy. But before he could really get a grip Henry quickly snapped his arms back in place. It wasn't even a show of force.

More like a karate guy in double time. All over in a second. The guy looked amazed and just stood there. Henry leant close and whispered. The guy's face softened for a second, like an alley cat bein' offered some milk, and Henry lead him to the back of the platform and had him sit against the wall. Now he looked kinda dazed. Henry came to me and told me the guy had had some mental problems but got sick of the drugs that were supposed to calm him and jumped out a window. He didn't know he was dead and he was still pretty sure he was crazy. Henry wanted me to sit with him and keep him company. I said sure. Henry also said to call on him if I needed help. "Just think of me and ask and I'll be here". Okay, I thought, I'll give it a whirl.

Well we sat there quietly as all the people came and went, trains every few minutes. Guy said nothing, didn't look at me, didn't move really. I wondered what I'd do if he jumped into action, cause he kinda looked coiled, you know? But he just sat there, docile like. Maybe that Tylenol was really something else.

Things were so quiet, at least with my guy, I was starting to get a little fidgety for something to do. The station was as busy as ever, folk comin' and goin'. Nobody stood on us. It doesn't hurt when they do, but it still feels right strange. I thought on my days at the stadium and figured they were over. Still, it was a dream come true, so I oughta be thankful for that.

Henry sat down beside me and asked how I was doing. Holee, was I surprised. Didn't see him comin' up at all. Turned out his other business was done for the time being. For about a second I wondered what that other business could be. He said, "Our friend here seems pretty relaxed." "Yeah, I said, "He's barely moved a muscle since you been gone. What did ya do to him?" Well turns out he turned that Tylenol, which of course I just thought into existence, into a double dose of anti-psychotic and anti-depressant, and since the guy was missing his pills he was susceptible to just a little thought from Henry and the whole thing just kinda cooled him right off. Henry said he woulda tried to commit suicide again if we hadn't stepped in. Not that it would've done him any good as he was already dead, but he woulda kept trying anyway. He been jumpin' out his window for god knows how long before that. Henry said he'd tried to intervene several times but it did no good, guy was so rattled.

Why'd he see me then, I wondered. But instead of asking that, I asked Henry where he'd been. He stared at me. Did I really want to know? Well sure. Well he'd been checking out some fancy night clubs in New York. Oh, says I, thinkin' he's not exactly a party guy type. You're right, says he, I'm not. He was lookin' at the back doors, fire escapes and all. Turns out drug overdoses get dumped there to kinda cool off and if they die, someone gets paid to squeeze 'em in a barrel and dump 'em in the river. Henry tries to kinda jiggle the soul outta the body before it finds itself at the bottom of the river. Course this is all done so that the night club can keep their good name. Now I'm not exactly innocent you know, I've seen a few things in my day, but this I just couldn't believe. Believe it, Henry said. Happens in all big cities. People are expendable. But souls are eternal, he grinned, and if I can get them back on track I'm happy.

I wanted to know how he knew a certain person needed help hundreds of miles away. He didn't really he just checked all the clubs and at his flyin' speed that didn't take long. He'd found a dead girl slumped like a sack on a fire escape, her soul sitting' on its body dazed and clueless. He got her attention easy and took her to heaven, or at least the part of it she'd be happy in. And then he came back here. I don't know if Henry was tryin' to impress, but I had my socks knocked off. How could he do all that? Well, I was about to find out.

We got the other guy standing up, quite the docile patient now, and Henry put his arms round the two of us, told me to shut my eyes and when I opened them again we were standing at the entrance of what looked like a swanky hotel in the country. It was a really bright place, like the one time I was in Mexico and got pretty Mexican lookin' by the time I got back. Before I had a chance to squint a second time, Henry handed me a pair of pretty cool lookin' sunglasses. I thanked him and put them on. He's fast, that Henry. If you ever meet him, watch out. The gardens outside this hotel place were really nice. So nice you just wanted to lie down and have a nap. I could hear birds twittering, water splashing and way off in the distance music, as though there were some kinda concert about a mile away.

Our friend seemed even more stunned than me: he just stood there, kinda stiff, as if maybe he was too scared to turn his neck even. Henry took him by the arm and walked him forward. Very doctor patient you know? I followed along, glancing here and there, amazed at my luck. To think of all the dumps I coulda ended up in and here I was lookin' for the luxury cars. Which, by the way, I never did see. There were a few people strolling about, enjoying the weather and chattin' away. All well dressed too. Not a plaid shirt in sight. We wound about a few paths, in and outta bushes and little flower gardens, gradually coming closer to the front of the building.

Maybe the most amazing thing was that the steps up to the door were made of grass. Just exactly like about five steps maybe fifteen feet wide, but made completely of grass. Grass at the peak of perfection I might add. Grass that had gardeners fussin' over it all week I'll bet. Not that we saw any. The lobby was grand kinda but, you know, comfortable? You felt like you belonged there. Very quiet and calm, like those hotels often are. A woman came to meet us from a side door, like she'd seen us from her desk or something. She seemed to know Henry very well. Henry introduced me and Lila said she was very pleased to meet me and hoped I'd come by again soon. Our friend seemed mesmerised still, but maybe now by Lila's beauty, for she was a very pretty woman. She lead him away and Henry and I turned to leave.

Outside Henry asked me what I wanted to do. Walk around a bit was my answer. Henry seemed sorta proud of me: his eyes lit up and he smiled. Fine, he said, I'll come back for you in a bit then. And off he went. This was the first time I actually noticed him disappear. Before he sorta come in at me from the side and I figured he'd been walkin' quietly like. But this time, it was just poof, gone. I chuckled and shook my head.

The gardens about this place were wonderful. I'd never been

that thrilled with parks and the like before, only the odd time when I was hungover and needed someplace quiet for my poor head. I had a friend that usta love walkin' through Mount Pleasant cemetery from one end to the other, and once in a while he'd talk me into comin' with him. I have to admit it was very relaxing, just like he said. But morbid, you know? Anyway, other than that gardens were just places you walked past goin' someplace else. The bushes and flowers here seemed different somehow. More beautiful I guess, more...sparkly and shiny. I sat down on a bench at the edge of the path.

For a while I didn't think about anything. I got so relaxed all I could think of was taking a nap. So I stretched out on the bench. It was so warm here, just so right, that there was no way I needed a cover. For a second I worried about what people would think. Or maybe I'd get hustled off by security. But then I thought, nah, not here. Even though it did look kinda posh.

I musta fallen asleep in no time. I dreamt about my mother. She was pacing up and down in front of her tv, lookin' very worried. Sweatin' about my eternal soul no doubt. She was always worried about that. I got so sick and tired of it I'd told her to mind her own business. It was that little store front church she went to. They'd highjacked her brain and taken it to dopeyland. Not that she was too terribly smart to begin with, but that place didn't help any. They overloaded her with junk and it kept fallin' out of her mouth like so many corn flakes. And dad was no help, all the way up in Thunder Bay. He did his worshippin' at the legion hall.

So I'm standing near my mum in this dream and she's pacing up and down, not seein' me. I say "Mom look at me I'm here!" She says "You can't be here you're dead!" Now I'm standing in front of her, blockin' her way. "I'm here all right!" She glares at me. "So they wouldn't even let ya into hell and ya had to come back here to hide? That's a fine show!" That was enough for me: I told her to take a hike and left. Next thing I know I'm wakin' up on this bench in this lovely garden, feelin' all lovely.

Eventually I sat up and looked about. There seemed to be no reason to do so, and really not much of a reason to do anything. I couldn't have been more relaxed if I'd been lyin' in my own bed staring out at the street below on a Sunday morning. Brian Albert staring contentedly at bushes and flowers: I can think of a few folk who'd double over in laughter at hearing that. I was pretty surprised myself. Then I heard that way off music again. I had this feeling that I could walk and walk and never find where it was comin' from.

Henry came back, calling my name as he walked down the path toward me. Boy it was nice to see him. His grin just made me feel things would be okay. There's lots of other spotting and saving ghosts type stories I could be telling you, as Henry got me to go back to my city and kinda be his eyes and ears on the street, but he tells me that's about enough for now. Gordon's got lots of other folk to hear from and I guess maybe my time is up.

Right now we're standing near him in this huge library where he's happily typing away, which is so funny for me 'cause I never set foot in a library since I was about nine, and I think then I was just tryin' to steal something. I can't read his thoughts as well as Henry does, but Henry's tellin' me he only half believes we're here with him. Henry says he can communicate with Gordon from just about anywhere, their link is so strong, but that once in a while he comes by just to see how the old boy is doing. Gordon looks like a serious and dedicated guy to me, but if he's a friend of Henry's he must be a bit of a joker too. And before I go I want to say thanks for listening to my little story. Nobody paid much attention to me when I was alive on earth, so it's nice to see that somebody cares now. And that guy we took up to the hotel? Well, it was really a nursing home and he's still there now, but comin' around, you know? Even goes for walks by himself.

HIGHER SELF AND SIMPLICITY

Hello friends and readers, here I am merging my consciousness with Gordon's so that he can type out some of the eternal ideas I wish to donate to your day. Many thinkers and philosophers have touched on these notions before, some at great detail and length, but the sophistication of their language sometimes obscured their reception by any but the most gifted and intellectual among you. Simple but not simplistic is our aim here.

Simply put, Eternal life is forever. There is no end, only change. Every incarnation, every family and nation, every religion and type of government, every phase of hunting, gathering and agriculture, every planet, star and galaxy, is but another step in our continuing experiment with form, energy and modes of organization. We are children playing and spirits creating. We are the divine, neatly divided. I, and those like me, are divided from god; and you, as human individuals, are divided from me. There are fifty-two cards in the pack, but they are all cards.

The energy is repeatedly stepped down so that the power of god will not destroy the forms of density on the so-called lower planes. Each level has its requirements so that the "game" can be played with maximum challenge and ingenuity. Some of those requirements are willpower, courage, adaptability, compassion and mercy. Of course there are others: cunning, deceit and competitiveness are among the qualities we are trying to phase out and redirect, now that they are no longer needed. Many of you have evolved beyond them, but planet-wide the habit is still strong, and will take much karmic stamping out.

You have guessed that various qualities are required for the various stages of spiritual evolution, and you are right. Part of the learning process is determining which are truly needed and which are no longer useful. As all individuals, families and countries are at different stages there is no overall answer. You must all turn to your higher natures, as the religions say. And remember, there really are no wrong choices, just mistakes that can always be rectified. And who gets to define the nature of a mistake? You do. You and you alone. Judges and courts, like crime, retribution and redemption, are all created by you. With a little help from your friends. Like me and all the other monads out here in the divine light, twinkling.

SECTION THREE:

GORDON'S GREAT EXPANSION

HENRY: OVER TO YOU GORDON

Henry has just said, "It's your turn Gordon, tell them how you're enjoying eternal life." Well, let me tell you, that's not quite what I was expecting, but I should have learned by now not to expect at all. The spirits always surprise me. Their goal always seems to be growth, the kind of growth that has me constantly revising my estimate of who 'I' am and what I can 'do'. And every revised estimate quickly becomes just another rest stop on the way. On the way to where? On the way to an ever more all-encompassing embrace of who I am. Who is? Well, I'm not sure because it keeps getting bigger and bigger, in size, scope and ability. Okay, call me evasive. It's not that I couldn't care less, it's just that there's not much I can do about it as I charge about, gamely lassoing new self-definitions, only to find how quickly inadequate they become. Try it yourself sometime, you'll see. Eternal life sure is fun, but trying to put a lid on it for storage and safe keeping is well nigh impossible.

When I began to write out the material which became *A First Hand Account*, in the winter of 1998, I was well aware that many adventures were transpiring while I was out of body at night. Even though I could only seem to remember disconnected snippets upon waking, the jigsaw puzzle could usually be completed with some channeling later in the day. Some of them seemed to be Gordon's experiences, some of them Henry's, and some such a curious blend of the two that I quickly felt unable to determine whether Henry was taking me along for the ride, as an apprentice in spiritwork, much like Brian Albert in the previous chapter, allowing me to blend with his consciousness so that I lived for a while in his heart and mind, or giving me an energy boost so that the activities 'beyond the veil' would be available for transcription the next day. And other times it seemed that he unveiled a monitor on which was playing a movie of his experiences, which I would watch, quite enthralled, until I fell into the movie itself and lost myself in becoming part of it. This last, of course, I couldn't help but compare to the process of incarnation itself, when the personality merges with its movie so completely it forgets its origins and falls into a dreamlife full of oppressive forces and fates. That I was able to fashion some sort of persuasive narrative out of these almost nightly adventures, so wild and crazy I feared everyone would assume I was fantasizing, I attribute to the years of practice as a poet and novelist. Those years taught me to write through not only one's mood swings but also the ups and downs of life and to never judge the day's output relative to one's mood of the moment. I'd learned to *go with my inspiration* and *trust the process* long before those nostrums became the clichés they are today. It's a shame they've become so commonplace because they're far from trite. All that *journey and not the destination* stuff is true.

As I was working away on *First Hand Account* the giddiness of just touching the skirts of eternal life was having its effect. I made my way through the earthly day like an interloper from some divine elsewhere. From years of reading spiritualism, theosophy and the like, I understood intellectually that we do not belong here, that we're only passing through, but now I could feel the actual *experience of elsewhere* vibrating at my core, creating a quite palpable disconnect from the amusements and distractions of the physical plane. I could look at people embroiled in dispute or consumerist desires and see their self-willed entrapment as clearly as the grieving and fretting ghosts I was working with at night. The leg traps of fear and desire work just as well in the astral as the physical. Sometimes even better. I was quite able to see how belief systems simultaneously support and shackle the souls who embrace them, myself included. Find a belief system that suits your current requirements, I would joke with friends, for ultimately belief systems are all we've got. Like shoes, you may as well find one you're comfortable in as be hobbled by a bad fit.

HEMI-SYNC AND RETRIEVALS

My gradual but insistent sense of expansion was further fueled by my discovery of hemi-sync tapes. Developed at Robert Monroe's Institute in Virginia, I first saw them mentioned in the books of Bruce Moen. I'd discovered his first while I was finishing up *First Hand Account*. Some of his early retrieval experiences so paralleled my own patchy nighttime recalls that I felt compelled to try out the tapes for myself. A course at Monroe seemed prohibitive in Canadian dollars, but the Going Home set of tapes fit my budget perfectly. My Toronto friends Jim and Deb certainly recommended them, and it was only a few weeks till I had my own set.

I see from my journal that on Wednesday April 14, 1999 at two in the afternoon, I seemed to retrieve a local farmer who'd been wandering around his property in a kind of blissful daze for a couple of months since passing during some farm machinery mishap. As Robert Monroe had described in his books, bundles, or rotes, of compacted information would come to you while encountering another spirit, in the retrieval process or otherwise. Suddenly while chatting with this old man, I knew he'd been negatively affected by his parents' troubles in the depression and had shied away from religion and fell into the rhythms of nature, nurtured as much by her unpredictability as the rewards hard won from her bosom. Like any tough old farmer he'd seen his share of struggle and disappointment, but was shocked, I think, at how the removal of his physical body also removed a layer of reticence from his heart, allowing him to experience his love of the land and its moods more directly, and ultimately, more ecstatically. In this state even stormy rain and wind seemed a blessing.

Unlike someone from my sixties' generation, he was not accustomed to feeling 'blissed out'. Looking back on it now, I think that made him more malleable, for although he initially resisted my suggestion that he come with me to see heaven, it did not take long to have him take the plunge. He was reluctant, as many men have been since, to take my hand and close his eyes, but when he did and we changed levels to my request for the most appropriate reception center, we were flying over a golden valley of trees and rolling grassland with people on the ground gazing up and waving. Since I'd given myself over to the first of many invisible guides at the opening of my meditation I assumed these souls had been previously alerted to our imminent arrival. Or maybe they were strangers happy to welcome flying arrivals with cheerful waving. At the time it didn't seem to matter, and years later with an almost endless number of retrievals under my belt, I can't honestly say it matters much now. I seem to be the type of character who likes to get the job done and move on, a no-muss no-fuss kinda guy.

Within days I was doing more retrievals, some of them significantly more complex than the one above. I seemed to have no problem quickly adapting to unforeseen circumstances. Nothing was too much of a problem, no situation too challenging. While part of me was grateful to Bruce Moen for the retrieval examples given in his first book, another part of me soon realized that it knew just what to do, not just sometimes but always, and that that part had been doing retrievals, if not for years then possibly for centuries, in various guises in various cultures. For the usual delusions-of-grandeur type reasons, it was something I tried not to dwell on.

This attitude was only partly successful, for I quickly got to be such a smart aleck know-it-all, I again fell into the trap of being embarrassed to tell anyone except my Toronto area friends Deb Aaron and Jim Flynn, who'd had enough out-there experiences of their own that mine fit right in. Jim, for example, could see quite clearly at focus 27, telling you just what colour of shirt and type of buttons someone was wearing, whereas I, while telepathic to the max, often sensing the answer to a question not yet asked, couldn't see very much of anything too clearly. On one memorable occasion Jim was able to do a bit of matchmaking on focus 27: he merely introduced one recently dead person to another and let sparks fly.

And although I later met and repeatedly interacted with this couple and their adopted child, it was certainly years before I got up the nerve to post my experiences on Bruce's online conversation board. A quite intense humility settled on me, something I thought was quite appropriate for the work, but something my various guides sought repeatedly to depose. They seemed to want me to embrace my power to its fullest extent, rather than give it to them or anyone else. It got to be such a tussle I began to feel that it must go back to some other incarnation where power was deeply abused. Of course, the past life regression archives are filled with such tales. Coming to terms with the right use of power, that is the one without all the nasty karmic kickbacks, is one of the major incarnational themes on this planet of ours.

A CHAKRA READING WITH

DEB AARON

Whilst my seeming ease at retrievals expanded my sense of self and joy in eternal life, another experience around this time shook me to the core. While trying to uncover some of her obe and psychic experiences for possible inclusion in my book, Deb Aaron convinced me to come over and undergo what she called a chakra reading. It was a type of psychic reading she'd developed since attending a couple of courses at Monroe Institute. She'd always been psychic, she said, but being at Monroe had blossomed her abilities tenfold. This was the type of story I was to often hear repeated over the years.

We sat together quietly in a darkened room, breathing together. Deb opened her psychic vision. After a few moments she said "Gordon you've got more brilliant white light streaming through your heart chakra than I've ever seen before." I was astonished. Deb was not the type of psychic to butter you up for financial reasons, so I believed she was being true to her own lights. I said something lame like "Well, I guess I've always been a kind of loving type of person" and hoped like hell she'd soon skip on to something else. She did, but much of the rest was equally astonishing. At one point in the shared meditation, I found myself floating above the planet, looking down amusedly, sometime during the dinosaur era. This was "before I became human", when "I was a free spirit". I quickly expressed disdain for the incarnational experiment of the dinosaurs. "Tiny brains in huge bodies, it'll never work", I announced authoritatively. I may even have said "It'll never bloody work". Deb and I exploded into giggles. By that I mean a full tilt bozo eruption of hysteria, the sort of thing which lands folk on the floor or running to the washroom. Howling uncontrollably at ten am on a Saturday morning. Never before or since have I experienced such a disruption of serenity during a regression/meditation/exploration. Calm eventually reappeared and we moved on.

Somehow we arrived at the 'god level', as I called it, and slipped into its all-enveloping lack of activity, its endless comforting nothingness. The beautifully upholstered void, as I now sometimes call it. And as I now know, just a touch of omniscience is enough. A little too long there and you don't want to come back. Astral plane paradises are all very well, especially for the wounded on the road to recovery, but nothingness has got all those heavens beat hands down. Just wait till everyone else finds out ! Anyway, we slipped out of that one and I began chattering on about the next level down, what I then called the Jesus / prophet level. I expounded at length about the necessity of Jesus' sacrifice, how we needed divinity in a human body as an example to inspire and imitate as incarnate souls basically just could not relate to God. God was too remote to be of much use to the average schlep 2000 years ago in the Mediterranean.

Where was all this coming from, I wondered as I walked back to my vehicle afterwards. My expanded sense of self was the obvious answer. And that expansion haunted me for months, if not years after, until I learned to incorporate it into my daily life. The initial bout of haunting lasted a few weeks until plateauing out, the new level of being somehow incorporated.

A MORE DETAILED RETRIEVAL

About five weeks after my first hemi-sync retrieval, on the Sunday afternoon of May 23rd, I lay back to attempt contact with a local criminal legend. For about a week our newspapers had run stories on an escaped bank robber. He was one of those kind but cunning fellows who gain the public's admiration by repeatedly outwitting the authorities without ever harming anyone in his path. A born outlaw, he'd been in and out of jail all his adult life. In an age where violence and vengeance are all too common, there was a taste of refreshing old-fashioned adventure to the tale. While on the lam throughout our huge and largely unpopulated province he left taunting messages for police and sent a scathing letter to the warden of his institution. Finally he was trapped in a house in Toronto. Whilst police tried to negotiate his surrender, the unexpected occurred: he accidentally shot himself while talking on a cell phone.

A full schedule kept me from the nagging inner voice that wanted him retrieved for about three days. When I finally focused, I found him in what Monroe calls focus 23 that is just the other side of death, the gray area of mists and anxious confusion. He was sitting, slumped over, head in hands, glum and morose. I introduced myself and said why I'd come. My notes say that this was the 'beginning of a long conversation', but I'm afraid I cannot fill in the dialogue for you, as such details tend to be the first thing to disappear when one comes out of meditation. It is all one can do to sketch out the basic outline of what went on.

He tells me the afterlife is not for him. Criminals and suicides? Someone who didn't go to church? Hardly. I tell him that he's a bit of a hero and that people look up to him for not harming anyone. This seems to get him going a bit. Suddenly he cares passionately. This is good; passion is energy and can be easily retooled. "Like those bastards in Brampton? (referring to a recent local bank robbery where a teller was needlessly shot) No need for that. Just showing off. They should kill them." I could see that codes of honour had been broken, but use the moment to tell him that I knew he wasn't cruel and could fit into the afterlife. We talk some more, about his hero, a bank robber from the 1930's. Ask again: no, he still doesn't want to go. He asks if I will apologize to his warden for that 'smart aleck' letter. He's sorry now; it was just that he couldn't stand being locked up and could never go back. I tell him I'll try. I tell him that the afterlife's the best vacation ever. He tells me he's never had a vacation. I say, "Well you got one now, and it's more fun than you'd ever believe".

I somehow manage to get his agreement to at least look at the afterlife, and if he doesn't like it he can come back. This is a line I later used on a lot of souls, as the 'back door out' option seemed help with their sense of really not belonging in heaven. Centuries of various religious rules and regulations have left us with a populace that feels quite undeserving. It is as if you're inviting them to some A list party where they're convinced they'll only be found out and shown the door. He's still wondering why he should trust me, and I tell him he'll just have to go with the program and see. No jails in the afterlife? No cops? No and no. Not where we're going anyway. And no banks either.

Finally we float up over the Toronto skyline and out over Lake Ontario. This move had worked so well with a little boy I'd moved on a few days before I couldn't resist trying it again. My bank robber says the lake looks so calm. I say that one day he will too. After a moment I make the switch to the astral plane and we float down into some lovely gardens. Two men approach right away. Jerry and Sam. Handshakes all round. I suspect he knows them from jails or foster homes. They say they're gonna show him the ropes and he seems fine with that. It's time for me to be off and I make my goodbyes. He's surprised. Most retrievees are. I don't think any of them believe you're actually living on earth. If you can get them to take you seriously at all, then they assume you're some kinda guardian angel, even if they've never believed in guardian angels. I got this so often from folk over the years I started saying "No, I'm not dead, I'm meditating in Mississauga". As I'm disappearing I hear the words, "He's quite a guy".

THE LIGHT MEDITATION AND HIGHER
SELF CONTACT

Also in this time period, I began going regularly to my local recreation center to use the pool and hot tub. I had started the habit in the usual middle-aged attempt to keep the joints flexible. Creeping arthritis had given me quite a scare a few years before and I'd been told swimming was as good a way as any to keep from turning into a piece of plywood. But as is often the case, one's surface motivations are but the tip of an iceberg. Other, more profound purposes were being set in motion.

Quite spontaneously one day, while relaxing in the hot water of the whirlpool, I followed an urge to enter a specific meditation. Right from the beginning it was a 'white light of love and understanding' which I was drawing down 'from the highest level that this body can safely sustain', opening my crown chakra to receive it, moving though my etheric body and then out through the heart chakra to 'bless all the sentient beings in my vicinity'. It was a fun little fantasy at first, a cool game to amuse my newly awakened self. But it soon became a habit, something I would do on every visit to the pool, which would usually be at least three times a week.

Reacting to warnings in various metaphysical books over the years, I thought it wise to consciously shut down the energy flow before I left the pool. After all, I was about to drive a school bus full of children. One couldn't seriously expect to meditate and drive at the same time, now could one? Well, one day I hear this voice, saying, "Don't shut it down, let it continue". I give my sensible bus driver reaction. The voice says "That's okay we'll take care of it. You concentrate on your job." Which I did. There followed many months of channeling this 'light of love and understanding' while I was driving around the west end suburbs of Toronto. I got so I could start it up in a ten-minute morning break between schools. This would usually be sitting in the bus on a side street about eight-fifteen am.

My conception of what was 'actually' going on evolved. I soon felt that this golden white light was part of a higher vibratory energy washing through the planetary atmosphere, whose primary purpose was to raise the vibration of the physical plane closer to that of the astral plane. It was an energy which needed conscious grounding by willing human partners spotted about the globe, physical plane anchors for a process initiated elsewhere. Is it the energetic component of the ascension process? Quite possibly.

What I do know for sure is that sometime that July (1999) I felt my Higher Self contact me while I was swimming. The contact was so casual, so normal I could hardly believe it was happening. The feeling was very similar to a spirit guide contact, and it took me quite some time to distinguish the two. Guides almost always have a more specific, human agenda, whereas Higher Self just wants to shine on you like the sun, and shoot its light though every one of your cells so that they become a trillion tiny suns themselves. My initial disbelief was countered by Higher Self saying that it was not so hard for it to 'come down' to my level as I thought, mainly because I'd raised myself to the astral level by the daily meditation. To say that this went against all the traditional teachings I'd absorbed would be an understatement. Charles Leadbeater would certainly have considered this a gross miscalculation one hundred years ago when he was pumping out what would become the basic elements of the theosophical canon. Wild claims from a know-it-all neophyte it would have seemed. I wonder what he thinks now. Certainly crazy and unsubstantiated claims to any skeptic. But as you've no doubt guessed, I'm writing this book for those who wish their belief systems expanded, not contracted.

I know all this because on Wednesday August 11th, my notes remind me that while listening to a hemi-sync tape and not being offered any retrievals, I thought to try contacting Higher Self, only to quickly image a globe of glowing light, a sphere with lovely rainbow colors rippling across it, a sphere which soon announces that "There's lots of people doing retrievals, there's no need for you to get stuck just doing that".

Oh, I see. And was this the same Higher Self who communicated during swimming a month or so back? "Yes." And yes, it is pleased with my progress. Hmmn. Should I continue with Afterlife series? "Yes." And other, more personal questions.

Toward the end of the exchange, the sphere spits off a handful of little spheres, as if to show how souls are started out. My notes say, 'I still have some intellectual resistance to this, as if I can't see my individuality engulfed by this greater being'. Fascinating, as in the months to come I would dialogue and merge quite merrily with this oversoul entity. And as I bid a fond and grateful farewell the sphere shoots 'up and away'.

A word about the background to my conceptual understanding of Higher Self. Primarily influenced by theosophical teachings, specifically the writings of Charles Leadbeater in works like *The Inner Life*, where it is seen as an aspect of the Monad, a kind of eternal group home for souls, and later by the channelings (the Seth books) and thoughts of Jane Roberts, particularly *Adventures In Consciousness*, where she calls it the "source self", and then later by Robert Monroe and Bruce Moen, who call it the "Disc". Other new age writers and teachers, like, say, Chris Griscom, called it the Higher Self, and usually thought of it as that spark of divinity which never dies and which lights up all souls on their journeys through the valleys of the shadow of death. So, as you can see, I arrived at my own encounter armed with enough understanding to intelligently participate in the enlightenment, but with sufficient dogmatically derived insecurities to deem myself inadequate for the interview and subsequent job posting.

INTERLUDE IN AMSTERDAM:
THE PAST LIFE SHUFFLE

But despite all this high level fuss, a quiet inner voice reminded me that trusting in the process and proceeding was still the recommended mode. Which I did, arriving in Amsterdam for a vacation later that month, only to discover an ignominious past life as a moderately successful trader travelling by small boat to and from the capital with the desirable goodies from the far east which others had risked their lives and investments to procure. An interesting mix of business acumen, family and civic duty, moral flexibility and religious fear, this man, whose name I never did get, started an affair with an Amsterdam woman whose soldier husband had died and left her penniless. His motivations seemed to be an equal mix of compassion and vanity. Yet some deep well of guilt, specifically that of the Christian variety I suspect, would not allow him to continue. There was contemplation of suicide from an Amsterdam canal bridge, on which astonished me stood one sunny afternoon, dizzying myself in the sparkling reflections, feeling his despair and ultimate lack of courage. And later there was a drunken nighttime stumble, a head first fall into his boat, a merciful blow to the skull and a welcome drowning.

All this came in a series of flashes as I toured the city in typical fashion, and dipped into a book on contacting the Akashic Records. Having long since felt that we visit the countries in which we once lived, this came as no real surprise. My past life count, stemming initially from some professional regression sessions in the early eighties, was up to about ten at this point, and this Dutch fellow was just one more. If he had been my first, the discovery might have spun out more shame and despair, but by this point in my journey many exits had been effected by many souls and each seemed to voice its own validity. Doing retrievals one learns that judging the retrievee is useless; you're there to expedite a transition not harass them with your precious ethics. Absorbing the discovery of other lives is much the same: you're there to embrace the drama, enjoy the performance, be it tragedy or comedy, and let the actors finish the script and take off their costumes before you offer them a ride home.

That both wife and mistress were both present in my current incarnation presented perhaps a greater challenge. Which is, do you tell them or not? The ethical potential of such action is indeed complex. Is your revelation necessarily theirs? Will the information be more of a burden than a gift? Aren't present life challenges enough? And who are you to think that you are the rightful awakener? Not to mention the fact that they might think you crackers. I wound up splitting the difference, telling the one I thought would be receptive while respecting the other's need to remain unruffled.

CHATTING UP A STORM: PUBLIC
SPEAKING AND SOUL SEARCHES

And so the strange and mystifying expansion continued. Around this time, my manuscript completed and doing the rounds, I made contact with a local group, the Explorers Network, who put on talks and seminars in my area. I was soon chatting up a storm on the afterlife, reincarnation, and what you might call related topics. Decades before I'd been a shy young poet, nervously reading my work in front of small groups. In the interim I'd acquired this cool confidence I knew nothing about, and suddenly I was a teacher who seemed to be able to answer any question put to him. Was I channeling a higher intelligence? It sure felt like it. Was that intelligence a part of me or something quite distinct, an entity visiting for the purposes of performance? Was I in some kind of light trance? No, I felt quite rational, spoke with my normal voice, and yet seemed to easily access a source of almost unlimited intelligence that was greater than the sum of its parts, but, you know, still a part. I was not to do any serious dialoging or merging with Higher Self for several months, but sometimes I wonder if a connection was not somehow established even then.

Of course, the minute you appear in public with the mantle of teacher about your shoulders, people come to you with problems and questions. Someone asked if I did soul searches. I had to ask what that was. Oh yes, tracking down the recently dead to see what they were up to, I could do that. And so it was that I found myself in a fair resemblance of a dingy dark basement, by a grumpy old woman taking what amounted to a prolonged hissy fit. She knew she was dead, dammit, she didn't needed no young fool to tell her that. And she sure didn't need no talk about heaven. That was for church folk. She said the words 'church folk' as if she were spitting out some old smelly tobacco juice.

Was I religious then, is that why I was there?

"Naw, I tell her, "I just know my way around."

She thinks religious people are "pathetic liars".

I chat a bit longer and then tell her I'll be back later.

"Oh well, if you must".

A week later I appear to her again. She wants to know if I'm a missionary.

"No, I'm here to tell you about the afterlife."

"See I knew you were a missionary".

Then I ask how I look to her.

"Like a scrawny little fellow at the end of a tunnel with a light in it."

I ask if maybe she wouldn't like to see her family that passed on before her.

"One or two maybe, but most of them no."

"I could take you there, it would be no problem."

"No thanks, I don't believe you anyway. Maybe you'll take me to hell."

"So you believe in hell?"

"No, but you never know. There's no afterlife there's just this cold darkness."

"That's created by you Hilda."

"No it's not, I didn't create anything. I just died and here I am."

"Look you're saying here you are, you must be somewhere. Aren't you interested in who asked me to come?"

"No!"

"It was Lynda, your friend from Streetsville."

"What's she doin' stickin' her nose in? None of her business."

"She's concerned about you. Are you sure you won't come and have a look at the afterlife?

"No. There's that voice talking again." (Robert Monroe on hemi-sync tape: can't tell you the number of retrievees who heard his voice and asked what it was)

Two days later I try again. Unfortunately I'm sleepy and can't focus well. Notes say 'Still glum faced, still determined not to budge or believe me'.

A week later and she's just the same. Thinks I've been sent to bug her. When I suggest that this thought proves the afterlife's existence, she says no, I've been sent from earth. She can't see the fallacy in her thought. She asks why I'm so interested in her. Because I feel love and concern for her. We chat a bit more. Tell her I'll be back. A week later again I go looking for her. Was told, by 'disembodied voice' she'd been moved on. By whom? By mother, I'm told. Well there you go. This was my first taste of doing the legwork, of opening a closed door so someone from spirit could walk through. A taste of sacrifice rather than glory perhaps.

It happened again, not too much later. Only this time the experience contained my first, and possibly best, piece of verification. As Bruce Moen's guide 'Rebecca' says, *trust is always the first issue.* The neophyte meditates and moves around in spirit, projecting consciousness through space and time in a way that seems to deny the commonly held actualities of those dimensions, and interacts at a distance with entities embroiled in ignorance. And this tender and dedicated newbie, despite all advice, can hardly believe it's happening. How can something so profound be so easy? Don't you have to sweat years of effort to achieve anything? Not with hemi-sync you don't. Hemi-sync helps rearrange the connections in the brain so that a portion of the energy it organizes is released to roam as it pleases.

There you are, lying on your bed in the darkened bedroom, listening to the musical sounds and the voice of Robert Monroe telling you you're *free, free.* And eventually you believe him. Sure, it's the hypnosis of advertising at work, but you're not buying anything but a new belief, the belief that part of you can be anywhere, anytime, at will. Doubts, of course, try to hog the wheel and steer you back to the known. And even though they fail they keep jabbering away, hooting and jeering from the peanut gallery.

Is that you on the bed, *mind awake, body asleep,* or is that you in the astral plane bar, drinking the Guinness that was offered you by the man whose still living cousin asked you to check on? Eventually you have to admit it's both, and drink up. The man, middle-aged at best, has passed after cracking his not too sober head on the sidewalk near home. Upon waking in the other side of death, his thirst was the first thing on his mind and he found his local had been transferred to the astral almost intact with all the fine old fellows who'd passed before him, one of whom now says, "Isn't it grand that this young chap came all the way from Canada?" It had to be his local because here he was standing in it, saving yet another pint from oblivion. And there I was standing next to him as the hemi-sync entrained my brain, dimensions and distance away.

The week before I'd found him near the accident site, on his way home to check on his children. His routine seemed to consist of shuttling between pub and home, convinced his children still need him around. He hovers about their sleeping forms, the custodial ghost. It's an easy continuation of his house-husband life. He knows he's dead but doesn't want to go on, as I suggest. Doesn't believe in it. And besides, no hired help is gonna care for his kids like he did. This time he's still decidedly against even a peek at the afterlife. Naw, that's just for 'priests and do-gooders'. He spits this out as someone else might say 'hookers and junkies'. I say no, it's for everyone, not anyone special, but no, he's happy where he is thanks. A thought appears in my consciousness: it says he's been abused by a priest as a boy, feels unworthy and full of hate. About two months later, the cousin who requested the search called to say the man's wife had been told by his sister something she'd never known about her husband: as a boy, he'd been abused by a priest. It's not much of a verification, but so rare are these pearls we grab at them with glee, despite their often sad and sombre payload. Three weeks later I returned, only to be told he'd been moved on by a relative to a shabby purgatory where he could combine a modicum of growth with the drinking schedule he so treasured. A later visit by his cousin suggested he'd moved even a bit beyond this.

PLOUGHED UNDER WITH
ASTONISHMENT

This verification came about a year into using hemi-sync, a year in which many other experiences ploughed me under with astonishment. One of them was a request to remove the ghost of a suicide teenager. It came through a friend of a friend and involved distances of over 2000 miles. I contacted the stranger easily and working my way though his defense mechanisms, moved him on. His fuck-you attitude did not fizz on me: I work with teenagers in my day job and know bluster when I see it. Those in the haunted house reported no further activity. Hey, I was a ghostbuster too! Cool!

I started joking that it must be some kind of an accelerated learning program. Not a week would pass without some other jab to startle me out of my three dimensional snooze. Such intense psychic stimulation can feel exhausting: I would sometimes wish my life reduced to mere coping with work and weather. There is something reassuring about the daily bitch. But eternity beckoned from every glint of light or rustle of leaf. At any point in almost any day I could spin out of the dreary procession of seconds into an eternity peopled with lost souls, spirit guides, past lives and higher selves and feel myself bobbing like some super-conscious cork in an ocean of light, easily in contact with anything I chose, and easily contacted by any who chose me.

For example, my old friend Gerald Byerley, dead at least three years, appears during a hemi-sync tape exercise, wearing the black beret of the pretentious artist he never was and doing a funny imitation of a friend from crop circle days in England, where we spent many happy times together, John Haddington. He's having a blast living in some artists' colony in the astral, and has defeated the rancors and anxieties that defeated him in life. Happy as a lark he is, and he wants me to let our mutual friend in Tennessee, Oliver, in on the news. Also my sister Irene and her son Charles, who seemed to share an abode and are having a wonderful time 'here', saying how could you not, and asking why I don't come to visit more often. This makes me laugh, as she would often say that back here on earth. My father, with whom I've had 'dream' contact for decades, almost since he passed thirty years before, often drops in while I'm listening to a tape, telling me what he's up to, like helping other family members 'get settled', fretting about the ups and downs of my (still physical) mother's daily trials, and giving me the odd message to pass on. His appearances are so regular he might as well be living down the street.

The previous year, flush from the shock of actually having the nerve to write *A First Hand Account* and circulate it in public, I was able to retain some measure of normalcy by believing I was being allowed a glimpse into Henry's amazing life and adventures. The *It's not me it's my guide* prevarication in bold living color. This year it was me, majoring in revelation for a degree in divinity. Was there anything I could *not* do? The guides said no, the only limits were my courage and imagination. And sense of civility and dignity, I was often tempted to add. I mean, was all this stuff appropriate behavior for a respectable, well behaved citizen of the state? Laughable perhaps, but it bugged me. Maybe some leftovers from lives of magic more black than white or respectability at the expense of honor and decency.

In this period I lectured to audiences, gave private instruction, facilitated past life regressions, performed hands-on healings, expelled entities from suspecting and unsuspecting humans, both in person and at a distance, consulted with other psychics and healers, studied like a man possessed, and generally expanded in all directions at once. Exhilarating? You bet. Enervating? Sometimes, especially when I forgot to seal myself energetically after a particularly intense session with say, a nasty earthbound entity not particularly inclined to leave the host in whom he'd nested for decades. Exhausting? Only when I insisted on my small and stunted personality and denied my eternal limitlessness, which, believe me, is easy enough to do trudging through four feet of compacted snow or sagging under the weight of an invasive flu.

HEALING AND ENTITY REMOVAL

When synchronicities become so common they're passé, you know you're riding the crest of something. Each week would bring fresh examples of old blinders falling off and new vistas opening up. People would come for healings and not tell me they were clairvoyant until later, when, with surges of emotion, I'd be told that I had the clearest aura they'd ever seen, or that I had the most amazing team of discarnate doctors and healers working through me. My friend Deb nicknamed them the 'mobile mash unit', and by mobile she meant they moved about the planet with a rotating crew of members and worked through as many incarnate energy workers as would have them.

Others would phone in a frenzy of need, having heard what I'd done for their friends. From a restful oasis of twenty years, my apartment was transformed into a vortex of tremendous energetics. Strangers would phone for appointments just as clients were walking in the door. *Excuse me, I have to go now.* Other healers would forward me their toughest nuts. *Well, I guess I can give it a try.* Eventually I learned to say no, but it took a while. During the hands-on work, I would oscillate from cool cynicism to sweaty commitment, from watching myself pretend to be a healer to groaning and gyrating like a man possessed, my palms like mini-furnaces and my legs all weak and wobbly.

Entities I had no trouble with: no threat, curse or trickery seemed to stymie my intent to remove. The more snarly, proud and powerful the entity, the more I liked it. The challenge seemed to amuse me, for immediately and instinctively I seemed to know that I'd done this type of work many times before, and that I was the last physical plane link in a chain of light beings who could blow the cobwebs out of any basement anywhere. I'll never forget the one who snarled. "Don't give me any of that mealy-mouthed do-gooder Christian shit, you think I give a damn about any of that?" He'd mistaken my initial politeness for woosiness. Well, I soon cleared up any misapprehension on that front: he was outta there and he was outta there *now*. *Game over dude*. (Yes I actually said that). Then he upped the ante to some serious cursing, assuming that there were words that I would shrink from using. Not so. And thus the battle escalated. Notching up the pressure from beyond seemed to act like a wind tunnel, with us finally just blowing him out and away from his longtime power spot in the host's solar plexus.

Of course, most entities are harmless enough, - confused children, lost grandparents and the like, souls who merely need some gentle urging and redirection. Dead alcoholics and drug addicts need a little more persuading, but as long as the host is truly willing to let go, they can be moved. Now some hosts have issues of guilt, responsibility and inappropriate compassion to work through. If they feel that they "owe" the entity something, whether it be a favor, some nurture or protection, or perhaps they see themselves as "deserving" the treatment meted out, then the removal can be difficult or well nigh impossible. Such hosts usually have a variation of the martyr complex to work through, and until they have the entity will be able to extend its lease indefinitely.

Such situations are dealt with in greater length in books by Louise Ireland-Frey and William Baldwin, so I shall restrict myself to adding that this work of spirit releasement certainly contributed to my growing sense of self and my further establishment of a home in eternity. Which brings me to the cottage and how I rediscovered it.

THE COTTAGE IN F27

Establishing your place in focus 27 seems to be an integral part of the Monroe system of consciousness expansion. I encountered it through Bruce Moen's books, and his approach is largely based on what he absorbed during his several Monroe courses. I see that by November 7, 2000, I was attempting to "establish my base in f27" but that I seemed to get sidetracked by expressing an intent to contact two recently dead teenagers that I was concerned about. In this I was successful. Already in focus 27 they did not need retrieved, but I did manage to disseminate some 'useful tips for new arrivals'. Sidetracked by this small achievement, I let my previous purpose slip for about five weeks.

On the afternoon of December 17th, five days after awakening to one of those disembodied voices which reserve five am as exclusively theirs, telling me that my "life as a medium was now ready to begin", I had another go. Arriving under the drooping caress of a marvelous willow, I enter a 'long encounter with being who lives there', and who is 'a permanent resident of the upper astral' and whose 'life has stretched through many physical incarnations', starting with the druid incarnation, whose 'astral consciousness was quite strongly activated' and including many others, some of which are already known to me. 'Is this character Henry? Yes and no. Henry is part of him, as I am, but he is much more. And the more I tried to focus on him, the more different aspects seemed to manifest, including gender changes. 'He said he has the ability to change appearance at will, and often does. And he pointed out that female forms that 'I' desire he can actually *be*, since 'I' am 'him' in a sense, I am, in a way, reaching out for myself. He is like a half-way resting point between the physical and Higher Self level.'

While pondering the enormity of all this I was shown about the cottage, 'traditional thatch type at front, heavy oak door with arch style front, large terra cotta tiles with Persian carpets and exposed beams, with large and long rectangular music room at rear with many French doors onto garden...much elaborate 18th century furniture about the place, the kind of furnishings that a period reproduction of the Brandenburg Concertos would need. Lovely grand piano in library which Henry tinkled on and invited me to join in. I gave him a spontaneous big hug and said how happy I was to be there. Of course I've been there while asleep at night, apparently many times. Henry also spoke about his many educational and artistic activities geared to helping people there grow and explore'.

(Readers of A First Hand Account will note the strong similarity to the cottage Henry describes for his musical get-togethers. And although Henry and I shared, in the most intimate of manners, many explorations, some of which resulted in the narratives of that book, I'd assumed the cottage was 'his'. On speaking engagements I would joke about how Henry and I had some 'serious boundary issues' and that I couldn't tell where he ended and I started. And although this identity confusion ran fairly deep, I could not see the sense in torturing myself over it. Seemed to me that the illumination offered by the details of his astral navigations far outweighed the lack of analysis of their anomalous source. Since then I have opened up several of the many more locked doors in the mansions of mystery, and my personal collusion in the construction of my father's house seems all the more obvious. Was Henry fibbing in the first book? I think he was telling me what he thought I could then handle. The 'me' here can only take so much, while the 'me' there can dish out plenty. I now suspect the cottage has been 'there' for a couple of hundred years earthtime, which of course, is next to nothing in the astral, and has been modified from time to time, as 'my' talents and inclinations evolve. If this is just too weird then just skip it; can't say as I blame you, as it was too weird for me for quite some time.)

Further explorations, some partnered with my friends Robert and Elizabeth, revealed more details about the building and my part in its life. Once while several of us were marveling at the hand tooled leather bindings of library books, and I suggested that Elizabeth direct her congratulations to Henry, he appeared and pointed to me as the perpetrator of that particular luxury.

Indications were, if other hints of his were to be believed, that 'I' created much of what we were seeing before I was born as 'Gordon'.

Henry had a habit of appearing as soon as his name was mentioned. Perhaps he had a cueing device manufactured by god. He certainly had a divine sense of humor. During another spontaneous hug from me, he warned me not to 'get too intense else I'll disappear into him and merge for good'. And lest you suspect, as I did from time to time, that he worked well as a Freudian style father substitute, let me mention that my birth father, with whom I'd been in regular psychic contact for some time, once appeared at the cottage door to join Robert and Elizabeth and myself in sociable chat and what my notes refer to as 'piping hot and tasty cups of tea'.

SPARKLY NEW PARADIGMS

I had about one month to accustom myself to this sparkly new paradigm, and several weeks of winking at myself in the bathroom mirror and singing "Who's loony now?" to the tune of "Who's sorry now?", when on another tape exploration, this time of the Monroe Institute 'there', specifically its earth core crystal as described by Bruce Moen and others, when I made a discovery that rather put the cottage and its glamour in the shade.

But first the crystal. After arriving by a crystalline structure at least ten feet tall, hugging its 'loving feeling', I 'merge and go inside'. It has a 'lovely warm vibe' and, as it seems only right, I 'give thanks to those who thought it up and sustain its creation'. I can see why 'people get stuck at it and don't want to leave,....it's like spiritual opium.' Perhaps that realization shocked me, because the urge to continue exploring overcomes me, and I'm off over lovely rolling hills until I see a very 'modernist structure with long thin horizontal and vertical oblongs poking up and out'. Intrigued I move closer and 'sense music coming from building', actually hearing 'string quartet stuff', then 'bits of singers practicing and jazz'...'must be a music school'. Then a disembodied voice tells me 'you should know you helped create it'.

Oh god, not again, says I. Oh god, yes.

"Create it before I was born as Gordon?"

"Yes."

'It's called the Arboretum because living trees are part of its structure, trees rising through glass domes and slanting curving arcs. Visions of string players sitting between huge roots and performing. Am shocked at information - one more bit of the greater me I'm too humble to recognize. It's all too much. But given my strong attachment to Druid lives, with their deep devotion to trees, it's maybe not surprising in its detail. I don't see a body behind the voice that dialogues with me about all this. I ask if it's a guide, or Henry, or another part of 'me' left behind when I was born. Am told I will have to figure it out for myself.'

And figuring it out turned into a task with many twists and turns in its path as I paved a psychic highway between physical Gordon and Higher Self, a highway with many turn offs, rest stops and dimensional interfaces. Perhaps the notion that 'I paved' that highway is misleading. It existed long before I opened myself up to it. Only my dismissal of doubt and acceptance of possibility allowed it to appear. Much as a child might try to scramble through the thick undergrowth of a forest only to discover an easy path the next week.

The farther end of that highway, which was likely just as far as I could then currently imagine, was Higher Self, and it seemed by that point, (Feb.2000), comfortably established. A series of conscious dialogues, conducted at the laptop, and later printed up as *Being Watching Doing And Feeling Desirous*, had convinced me that our connection was as real and rewarding as any I might have with a sentient being anywhere.

Was it like talking to myself, as one old friend queried. Yes, but the Higher Self is your self, as in self to Self. The incarnate 'little me' is merely a portion of the discarnate 'big me', the group soul of HS, as I came to call him, projected onto Earth to play earth games, to win and lose, to learn all that needs to be learned.

'Merely a portion?' Well, a very carefully constructed portion, put down in a family/society/epoch, perfectly positioned to test its various characteristics, so maybe 'merely' is unfair, but when you consider the small hotel of souls residing in HS, and all they have lived and done during their tenure in the eternal tragicomedy of life, it does but seem a part, albeit a unique and unrepeatable part.

What about the soul? Well, the soul was the divine presence within the incarnate individual, the light which tried to shine through the haze of distractions and defense mechanisms which make up the personality. At that point in my journey I could easily distinguish these two, and I was rapidly clarifying my understanding of HS. It was the notion that there were other energetic projections, other aspects of self, residing on the various planes, I had trouble with.

Their potential existence seemed to upset the apple cart of my paradigm, which suggested that retrievals and explorations were conducted from the base camp of incarnate personality, during either meditation or sleep. Now it seemed as if an opposite were true: that the process of incarnation, beginning as a ripple of desire in HS and ending as a baby in a womb, not only picked up causal, mental and astral bodies on the way down, but deposited independent entities on various planes as it ploughed toward the physical.

Although I could not find anyone on Bruce Moen's conversation board who was as concerned as myself, this apparent paradigm shift seemed fundamental, and I agonized over it for quite some time. I was able to discover reassuring references to the soul dwelling on all planes in both the books of Charles Leadbeater and the post-mortem communications of Frederic Myers, but they were brief and far from definitive, leaving me still thirsty for either a paradigm reinforcement or a paradigm shift. Tantalizing hints just would not suffice.

A new contributor to Bruce's conversation board, Jeff, wrote of an entity he channeled from time to time called Bartholomew, and the material quoted seemed impressive, so I asked Jeff for a Bartholomew session. Having been inspired by some of my earlier posts, he was more than happy to oblige. The response I received some weeks later was likely just what I craved, although it took me some months to fully realize it. It would seem that HS, in response to Gordon's expanding sense of self and abilities, projects various energetic beams onto various planes, as they are needed, and these beams can manifest various aspects of Gordon's soul energy to accomplish various tasks. As Bartholomew pointed out, "This can be done without your awareness".

I began to tell various email correspondents to call for 'me' while in meditation/obe and see if I showed up. Well, needless to say, versions of 'me' did appear and respond to requests, including one where the very creation of this planetary body on which we plonk ourselves was visually displayed for an amazed friend, Marilyn. This sort of shameless showing off occurred often enough while I was busy at work that I began to accept that versions of 'me' were in full operational mode, guiding, healing, exploring, and just generally fooling around, without the slightest need for 'my' knowledge or approval. A slight, but for me, very significant, verification of this, came through in Bruce's third book, during some partnered exploring experiments he shared with his friend Denise. On their first trip, Denise appeared to Bruce and said "I don't even know I'm doing this, I'm slumped in front of the tv."

This admission more or less blew me away: it was just what I needed to hear. Denise, a relative neophyte, unlike Bruce's years of experience, could project without even trying while sitting bored in front of the television. If she could do it, anyone could do it. Which, when I come to think of it, is exactly what I said to people when I first began teaching them to do retrievals.

LINKING WITH JESUS, LIVING

IN CHRIST

I believe it was the Austrian mystic and educator Rudolf Steiner who first introduced me to the notion that Jesus was the man, albeit a prophet and initiate, and that Christ was the cosmic being who overshadowed him in the all important months leading up to his martyrdom. Later the theosophist Charles Leadbeater reiterated the concept. And I believe the British esoterist and composer Cyril Scott took much the same tack. And, of course, many observers thought Krishnamurti was overshadowed in much the same way. I devoured many esoteric writings in my spiritual seeking youth, and as I drift pleasantly through middle age, sunbathing on my raft of enlightened timbers, they have a tendency to blend together, all warm and fuzzy.

There are many versions extant of the Jesus myth, and I do not seek to harm others as I propagate my own. Each soul shapes its destiny from what it deems appropriate. Throughout my cycle of lives on this planet, many teachers have influenced the 'me' that wanted teaching. Gautama Buddha for one. And others. But for this section of my expansion in eternity, I need to focus on Jesus, he who lives in the Christ.

I'd been healing for some time when I finally convinced my friend Heidi to come by for some hands-on. She was a relative newcomer to all things new age, but mysterious flying dreams, and later, bowel cancer, had delivered her to my teacher door, requests in hand. Having already met up, fortuitously shall we say, with a healer specializing in cancer treatment, some months before, I was not entirely surprised, but the presence of an anxious, tearful young mother in my life left me spinning in something I would not describe as delight. No doubt about it, it was my turn to bat.

Given her initial resistance, distance healing seemed the best option at first, and I'd worked out an early morning meditation that catered to both tumor reduction and etheric body energy maintenance. A 24 hour psychic IV feed is not an inappropriate comparison. Still, I thought hands-on would go one step farther. I'd had great success in energy transfers with my friend Jim, over the long and tedious months as he waited for his heart transplant. Channeling the universal energy of life through my hands seemed somehow second nature.

When another friend had significantly reduced Heidi's pain level with a Reiki treatment, her attitude turned. One of the most powerful healings I'd experienced occurred that Friday morning, March 9th, 2001, as I bent over my prone client in something approaching supplication. Utterly breaking with decades, maybe lifetimes, of resistance to the church of the Christians, I appealed to Jesus to heal this poor child of god. In doing this I yanked open my heart in complete submission. The tidal wave of love which then engulfed me and brought me to tears was the classic Jesus connection as reported by many experiencers. I just couldn't believe that it was me experiencing it. But it was. During the contact we seemed to speak, and his simple "the church has not always appreciated your gifts my son" brought many a wall tumbling down, for after my last Druid incarnation, guides had convinced me to join in the Christian experiment, and I spent at least three lives trying, and failing, to balance the bureaucracy with the belief. Of course, to HS it's all happening now, with each drama's script leaking into all the other's, bringing about a multi-dimensional interface of staggering proportions that I somehow propose to encompass in part three of this trilogy.

Meanwhile Heidi emerged 'exhausted' from the session, but reporting an inner vision of many black spheres popping open and disappearing. In the weeks ahead I facilitated several regressions, both to 'this' childhood and several past lives, hoping to trace the source of the illness and eradicate it by confronting it, but although she was perhaps the best hypnotic subject I've ever dealt with, reliving scenarios in great and vibrant detail, we discovered no direct karmic cause, but a very interesting pattern. Out of six lives, two were male, with calm, untroubled deaths in old age, and four were female, with youngish women dying in childbirth or wasting away long before middle age. Strange as it may seem, Heidi seemed addicted to dying young and tragically. And although my Jesus connection helped dissolve one of two then current tumors, in a year they returned with a vengeance and she passed into the realms in which she'd long been traveling by night, and it was there that I found her, much later, living happily by the astral version of the Black Forest in whose magical shadow she'd shared a German childhood.

Since then there have been at least two other occasions in which this particular son of god came to visit. In both he appeared to the clients, both of whom called him Sananda, and not to me, enmeshed in the mechanics of healing and not feeling the need. One of them seemed like such a minor healing, helping someone overcome serious jet lag, I thought he needn't have bothered. But who am I to judge either the merits of each case, or the fantasy factory of each client's needs? I go where I am needed and act accordingly, serene in the knowledge that I have finally figured out how to separate Jesus from the bureaucracies which bear his name, and confident in the understanding that he comes in many colors, not all of which we have words for.

Does Jesus ship out when asked or just when he feels like it? And which aspect of his being arrives? Long could one wallow in questions like these. Archangels like Michael appear to many, often spontaneously. Guides and ghosts pop up everywhere. If Robert Monroe can divvy himself up into twelve aspects, as he said the last time I chatted with him, then I'm sure Jesus can project plenty. Heck, I can do three myself, and I'm just starting out. Linking with Jesus, in prayer or meditation, may be some folk's definition of a miracle, but perhaps no more so than the fact that we continue to draw breath every second. For me living in Christ is the real challenge. For that you must embrace everyone and everything with the energy of unconditional love, recognizing that they're all spirit evolving through various grades of matter, disregarding whatever you happen to dislike while devoting whatever energy you have to spare towards their education.

To live in Christ is to recognize the sacred brotherhood of all sentient beings as they paddle their way back through darkness to divinity. Easier to spout than to practice, of course.

TRAUMA ABROAD

During its long slow drift of allegiance from the British to the American imperial imperatives, Canada and its citizens have become accustomed to feeling safely distant from the mangled turmoil of world events. As a society slowly carved out from an unforgiving landscape and climate by successive waves of determined immigrants and with a long history of liberal tolerance of both political and religious diversity, our internal troubles often seem miniscule in comparison with the traumas glimpsed from abroad, and there's a marked tendency towards a rather smug gratefulness for our geographic remoteness. As we look out at the planet we know that just one January in our northlands would cure a lot of those hotheads out there. But that cool, calm assurance is repeatedly challenged out by the brutal winters we must endure every year.

One September morning in the middle of all this inner growth, I walked into a local coffee shop for a brew. The proprietress and a couple of regulars were glued to the tv set on the wall. I couldn't make out what exactly was grabbing their interest. Mostly blue sky and a skyscraper. Then smoke. And then it was the living legend of 9/11 unfolding before our eyes. The next couple of hours seem something of a blank to me now. Did I read that morning's paper? Did I go swimming at the local pool? It was a lovely day in September, I may have gone for a walk in the park. Around lunchtime, shortly after delivering my afternoon kindergarten children to their school, I sat in my school bus and attempted a meditation. As my spirit moved up and away from the body I felt layers of anxiety and fear blanketing the urban area around Toronto. I would describe these layers as pronounced. They seemed to say *Uhh, we could be next.* I struggled to move beyond the choking grip of these clouds. Eventually I seemed to feel a giant dome of light had been thrown over Toronto, no, no, that's too local, it was over all of north America, and it had been placed there by the planetary hierarchy of ascended masters, angels and their like-minded compatriots to absorb the arrows of fear, anger and vengeance arising form a jolted populace, to deflect and dissipate their toxins before they could drift together and form the dark roiling masses of demented first chakra energies which assist in propagating the blood lust of war. As one who had felt such dark energies and their cumulative effects over Israel/Palestine and the former Yugoslavia I thought it was a marvelously astute move. And I soon realized that this dome of love/light, though created by others for our benefit, was meant to be sustained by our meditations and prayers and that I was one of the ones who'd volunteered to disseminate this information through the medium of the internet. Though such self-selection can be as risky as it is inspired, I guessed that leashing my arrogance with as much humility and dedication as could be then mustered might just do the trick.

That afternoon I made a few phone calls and posted a call for partners to Bruce's conversation board. Though several email buddies responded quickly, I was never quite sure just how many joined up over the next few days, but my own meditations were as powerful as I'd ever encountered. That following Saturday, I announced on the board that I felt the next night would be pivotal and that as many of us as possible should dedicate our sleeping hours to contacting the priests and pastors of that very Christian country under attack, that their sermons might be the servants of tolerance and compassion rather than righteous retribution. As only complete, continuous out of body consciousness would reveal the results of my, and doubtless others, initiatives, I shall refrain from claiming any kind of victory for meditation and the internet. But I did notice that Monday's news saw the first words of kindness and understanding towards the Islamic community from U.S. political leaders.

I have learnt many things from dwelling in the Christ, but one of them is surely that there are many ways to turn the other cheek. Keeping alive the suppleness of that dome of lovelight, that it might continue to perform its intended function over the weeks, kept me quietly focused, and dare I say it, employed, for the next while, so that I didn't actually retrieve as many of the recently dead as I might have, although others on Bruce's board did a stellar job, and our efforts can be viewed to this day.

Certainly the experience expanded my sense of self and ability, causing me to leap out of my reserved Scottish self and shamelessly proclaim a vision and a duty, the sort of task I'd normally be loathe to embrace. Something else I'd rather deny than admit is this rather embarrassing notion that I'm some kind of useful underling of the planetary hierarchy. But the above experience seemed to cement me in the role.

As a long time student of the western esoteric tradition, such quiet discipleship to the adepts of spiritual evolution I knew was not unheard of. It was merely considered wise not to go about bragging about it, that is if you could even bring yourself to believe it. On an ego level I had absolutely no wish to follow in the footsteps of Madame Blavatsky or Alice Bailey, and for three years or so I shared the story with only a couple of trusted friends. It would seem that I was visited by a card-carrying member of the hierarchy the week before 9/11, ironically, just as I was diving into a solitary supper. He was not 'there' as the table was 'there', his words did not 'sound' as normal conversation does, but my developing clairsentience assured me someone was with me, and it was not some confused entity seeking succor or advice.

Visually a cross between the later Meher Baba and the various renderings of Count Racokski, he smiled and asked me how I was doing. In response to my gushings of gratefulness, he said 'I've always got time for people like you Gordon'. I gushed some more. In response to me 'Is there anything I should be doing that I'm not?' he joked that I might shift a little more energy from my second to my fourth chakra. As I was just then entering into the joys of a new relationship with S., I took this to be more friendly banter than esoteric seriosity. When it all boiled down beyond my initial surprise, it seemed he'd done no more than come by to say hello. Even at that I felt deeply honored. Okay, I thought, I'm an accepted pupil who needs encouragement from time to time. Fair enough.

But during the next weeks' intense psychic activity and subsequent fear of futility, I saw the beautiful simplicity of it all. He'd come by just to reassure my possible future insecurity. He did not give me a mission, I'd felt no closer to god, delusions of maturity were as distant as delusions of grandeur. He'd merely come by to say hello. The masters do indeed operate with subtlety and grace. I'm telling you: these guys are seriously cool.

ADVERTISING ETERNITY

For a few years I felt like I was advertising eternity to those trapped in time. I still do really, except I'm so used to it it's become second nature. Old friends find me funny, but then they always did, and I can't say I blame them. I'm as wingy and eccentric as they come. I do find it intriguing though, that the one thing which has liberated me from illusion - the understanding that we are eternal spirits struggling through time in many guises - is the one thing which makes me certifiable to many. What a classic paradox, the key to freedom is also the key to the box society will put you in. And that's why I follow the three c's, - civil, charming and companionable - for it helps to soften the blow. People will tolerate a great deal if you don't badger them. Mostly, of course, I'm preaching to the converted, those who acknowledge the presence and power of spirit outside of institutionalized dogma, and who want to feel more of its many unpredictable, and generally unacknowledged, manifestations.

Freelance spirituality is always an adventure. I could never say I was bored. Spirit brings many opportunities and challenges to my door. And as the years go by I'm beginning to see how each of those challenges was called forth by my increasing aptitude for the seemingly unannounced. Retrievals have become so commonplace I only take notes if they're out of the ordinary. I did at least four last week, for example; a couple of traffic accidents and two soldiers taken in action, and that's just what I can recall right now. Strangers email me for soul searches and distance healing, and unless I'm outrageously busy, I do them without a second thought. And at last I am comfortable with my fee schedule.

The abnormal becomes the commonplace, clients come by to be regressed, I make supper, I meditate and maybe merge with Higher Self, I make some cocoa, I go to bed. Sleep is a blessing. The body rests and recuperates, but the spirit soars. Since finishing *A First Hand Account* I seem to have come full circle. My obe contacts and retrievals were vivid but patchy. I wanted to do away with the channeling necessary to complete the picture. Hemi-sync then helped and extended the experience, but did not lead to the full visuals I'd hoped for, and as I went on I began to wonder: was I doing them in real time, or was I experiencing a rerun of the previous night's obe work? I puzzled over this for months. Guides were cagey when I asked, but eventually fessed up. Mostly my meditations were reruns, to further unveil the greater self 'there', and by posting help others on the board.

Some months after the 'take your own power' campaign had successfully subverted my humility stance they moved from carefree joshing and teasing to more open mockery. This turned into a 'do-it-yourself' campaign. Starting, as far as I can tell now, on January 6, 2003. I had been prompted by reports of a suicide bombing in Tel Aviv. Making contact, I asked was there a need for me in that city. The response "Wait a minute, let me check" looks a bit cheeky in retrospect. Then, "Yeah if you feel like it, most have already been moved but there's a couple of sticky ones" seems more purposeful. Then my "take me there" is cut off with "No, take yourself, you know how to get there." *Well, excuse me.*

In the dusty ruin I encounter a young woman who seems quite disappointed that I'm not a more Jewish angel. I assure her I'm a Scottish angel on a special mission. "Oh, she tells me, "I met some Scottish people and they were really nice". Course that helps and soon we're off to one of the several astral reception camps over Israel/Palestine. As with many long-term trouble spots, they are very well organized. "Come, come, says the rabbi who meets us, "There are many people waiting for you, come!"

That was quick, so I go back for seconds. On request the guide shows me a curled and quite dead body. Somehow I know there's a soul still in it who won't come out. Bad case of denial, I smirk to myself, and seem to know just what to do. Beam of light from my crown chakra to his. Woops, too much power: he shoots right up through the planes to his HS and right back down again. Another beam this time from throat chakra to throat chakra. He starts to moan and writhe about. The 'me here' is baffled. What am I doing? Then suddenly I know to shoot a beam from the second chakra to his second chakra, which results in a sort of sexual excitement infusing his writhing, bringing him back to life, although we know he is 'dead'. Like an old pro I leave the rest to the helper and buzz off. No wonder they've got attitude. Later I wonder, as I often do, or did then, where exactly I got the techniques. The answer I come up with is obe at night. This is all about remembering, about bringing the hidden out into the open, where we can see just what a clever little chap I am.

A week later, and the guides are still teasing. When I ask for a mission, a guide appears flipping though a clip board list, going "Hmmn, let me see now, you'll be wanting something backwards in time, huh?" Methinks, reading my mind is he? Then a chorus appears, "Yes Gordon, and we know all your little secrets too!". When I ask to be guided my request is granted. 'Impression of whipping through a time tunnel, suddenly a darkness, but a darkness with texture, oh it's soil, I'm under the earth'. Wow, it's a grave of some ancient warrior, not killed in action but tricked and held by witchcraft. The robotic spirit jailer has faded with time, and I apply a light energy to the whole body this time, vivifying it. A sleeping astral body, by the way, not a bag of bones. He seems to know he's dead, but not the passage of time, which feels like a thousand years or more to me. Takes me for a messenger figure from his pagan style world-view and wonders if he's been brave enough to merit a position in his heaven. No matter, I say, offering him the heaven of his choice. For some reason he trusts me, we move levels and arrive. Someone immediately strides out to greet us. The two of them hug and erupt into some ritualized sword play/dance thing and then howl with laughter.

Back to base and ready for more. Guide flips chart, "Not so far back this time maybe?" English industrial town, 1930's. Cobbled streets leading me to graveyard on hill. Impression of man sitting on gravestone, deep in thought. "Good day sir, my name is Gordon Phinn". Jumps to feet surprised; asks if I'm like him, a soul awaiting judgement day. "That is not the case sir, I am here to assist you." Then I must be some kind of angel sent to fetch him. "No sir, I am not an angel, nor am I fit to be one. I am but an apprentice in the ways of divinity. I am but a helper's helper, assigned a duty." So is this the day he's waited for? "Sir I am here to tell you of the Lord's infinite kindness and mercy. All are forgiven and welcomed to heaven." Surely not grave sinners like him? I have an impression of sexual problems in marriage, times secretly spent with a local prostitute, and a strict christian sect with very definite ideas of who gets to go where. "Surely sir, I am sent to bring you into the welcoming arms of the righteous." I think the language convinces him, for we change levels without a fuss and arrive outside a church where a woman appears out of the group to greet him. "John you are here!" she exclaims, ignorant of , or beyond caring about, his perceived transgression.

Three days later, when asking if "they've got anything for me" I'm told, in a slightly mocking tone, "Oh we've always got something for you Gordon." It's a young woman, victim of a highway collision in 1979, who will not believe that it's 2003 until I show her the new model cars in the parking lot of the building in which I am meditating. One month after that, when declaring availability I immediately found myself in the charred remains of the Chicago night club fire, quickly working on two ladies trapped in hysteria. One I calm verbally, the other with soothing hand gestures, and eventually mouth to mouth. After a few minutes of going back and forth between the two I realize 'I'm' actually doing both simultaneously. Another big *Oh wow* experience there.

About ten days later, asking for guides, one appears, irritated. I ask why. Told, "You can do them on your own. Don't need me." "Aw, what's ten minutes to you?" I josh. "Ten minutes where I could be helping someone who really needs help." I ask where he wants me. Told, "Where do you wanna go?" I say "where I'm needed". "You're always needed, pick something."

No mistaking that tone is there? I think of the Korean subway fire of some days before, express an intent to go backwards in time to just after the disaster and find myself flying through subway cars angel like, with remarkably large wing-like arms upon which I encourage people to cling. We go back and forth to an astral plane hospital courtyard. They slip off me almost as if they were jumping from a helicopter. Bizarre, but any more bizarre than anything else from the past three years? I ask guide if this was happening in 'real time', or was I rerunning it from obe at night work to recall and share it? I get an answer, "Yes." So why can't I recall this stuff when I wake in the morning? "I don't know. Why don't you tell me? Why are you blocking it, why won't you embrace your full being?"

Feeling somewhat chastened, I approach retrievals during the US/British invasion of Iraq, that spring of 2003, using a direct 'Iraq now!' expression of intent, which I think I picked up from William Buhlmann's *Adventures Beyond The Body*. It works quite well, and I begin to see I can go where I'm needed without guidance, as part of me already knows. Like any aid worker I make no distinctions, - Iraqis, Kurds, Americans, British: they're all dead and need a bit of direction. Civilians, combatants, journalists, they all have their priorities and agendas. Mine is to help them avoid becoming grieving ghosts in no man's land, or focus 23, as Monroe christened it. It's a giant, gloomy, misty-gray nowhere-land where anguish is the norm and ignorance the great leveler. In short, a great place to get away from.

Before one retrieval I pause for a Higher Self 'merge'. They're great little pick-me-ups, which I learned to do while sitting in the hot tub at the local pool. HS is always so calm, the original meditating Buddha, it's fun to stop by for a quickie. I ask if he knows there's a war going on. A 'Yes so I've heard' response emerges, accompanied by what I feel is a shrug. 'So what, there's always wars going on somewhere. It's an important part of the human experience. What are you learning?' I answer that I'm keeping a philosophical attitude I've had for years. "Which is?" "That there's sides with agendas and the agendas conflict. That each runs on fear and longs to gain or maintain power. And that aggression arises from the fear of losing power." As we share these ideas I lose track of where they came from or whose they are. That's what merging with HS is really, forgetting who's who. Finally HS shares her other, simultaneous war experiences. A collage of glimpses floods me. The comparison to downloading a deluge of relevant information from the mainframe computer is not too far from the mark.

That summer there were a couple of headline earthquakes, first Turkey and then Algeria. I 'worked' them both, but felt a bit muddled about the Algerian one. I woke up a couple of mornings feeling totally exhausted, but otherwise memoryless. In frustration I ask a guide. A guide who would not answer. Suddenly I found myself going to the cottage in f27, walking into a small room never previously entered, touching a screen mounted flat on a wall and watching the events of the previous night unfold. Images of imagining crumpled buildings whole again and dead folk walking out, and ambling around astral refugee camps, nodding and greeting residents like a, well, friendly official, soothed my troubled soul.

This lead to a summer of meditations expressly designed to capture those elusive hours of nightly freedom. I named the journal OBE@NIGHT.

OBE@NIGHT

The background to this would have to be a brief understanding of the five month decline in health of my girlfriend's father, J.A.W. An extraordinarily healthy man of eighty who I'd only recently met, he succumbed to esophageal cancer. The invasion initially stymied by some fast thinking Christmas Eve surgery, he lay in a variety hospital beds, enduring the usual depredations of various assaults to his weakened immune system and the isolation imposed by the then infamous sars epidemic.

I was not the only one, of course, to feel terribly sorry for his situation, or to wish for his full and complete recovery. Several in the family prayed daily for him. And actually, I was not the only one practicing distance healing on him. An early morning healing visualization, focusing on the etheric body's contribution to a depleted immune system, and carried over from my work with other cancer victims, was my principal contribution. This, I felt, was to enable him to have enough time to, firstly, decide on whether his reduced physical capacities were acceptable, and secondly, to facilitate the space for bringing as many personal relationships to mutually acceptable fruition before passing on. While the rest of the family engaged in the stresses of his day-to-day decline, I focused on this healing meditation. At no point did I feel I was curing him. During the initial surgery, the 'mobile mash unit' participated and seemed inordinately proud of their accomplishment, but said the rest was up to me. And as the chances of a man his age recovering from such serious surgery were so slim, their claims seemed not unrealistic. At this point for me, proof was no longer an issue: I was sailing along in trust, a trust which seemed remarkably similar to the faith espoused by others. Trust, faith, devotion, love; perhaps they're all aspects of the same phenomenon?

I played my role to the best of my then-current abilities, neither hogging the limelight nor clinging to the shadows, but sharing the stage with all the other actors and feeling the whiff of the transcendent in the tragic.

At the time of passing, which of course was traumatic for those physically present, I attempted several projections to J's hospital bedroom. Twice I saw assisting spirits waiting in the wings as I attempted to chat with J. about the actual mechanics of the physical to astral transfer. He was already outside the pain-wracked body that so disturbed his gathered family, but was quite vague on what to do next. He complained of feeling tethered to *their* pain. I, of course, urged him to dissolve that connection and pointed out both the friend and mother waiting nearby. His response, although not what I'd call strong, seemed sufficient for the journey, and I left him in the care of those from the other side.

Time, sometimes that most useful and comforting of illusions, passed. And as you will see, J's passing and my 'need to know' coalesced rather nicely for the *obe@night* experiment. On June 3/03, only about ten days after the Algerian earthquake experiences above, I lay down to listen to the 'free flow focus 27' hemi-sync tape, reenacted the cottage/screen scenario and watched the events of the previous night's obe unfold.

After a brief swirl through the trees outside my fifth floor balcony, with whom I've become inordinately affectionate over the last decade, and then down though the leafy structures of my town's main street, it's off down the delightfully winding river valley of the Credit, stopping off briefly in my girlfriend S's neighborhood about one mile south in a futile attempt to wake her out of an astral sleep, and then off again along the river valley, out to Lake Ontario, where I seem to know where to hover to be in the body of the, well, giant deva who broods over that aquatic structure, embracing rather than controlling the myriad forms of marine and aerial life. To this I would add air and water currents, whose endless intermingling is an ecstasy in itself. The human life around the lake's edge seems also to be included in the mix, as if the deva's embrace was a harmonizing influence, an attempt at blending nature and society.

From there I seem to shot up a plane or two to find myself checking in on S's father J. A somewhat typical astral rest home for those convinced recuperation is the first item on the agenda of their post-mortem schedule. A 'nurse/assistant' tells me he's resting, but awake from time to time. A question re. the relatives who appeared to me on his initial transition is answered with "I'm just a nurse and don't really know, but I have seen a lady who might be his mother", and makes me feel a 'bit daft'. I should've known better.

Then I'm suddenly in an Algerian 'astral refugee camp', walking around like a local and being accepted as such, chatting away like a cross between some long lost cousin and a reporter. Lots don't know they're dead, and think they're just homeless. Of course they'll be given as much 'time' to adjust as they need. Others have realized and moved 'on and up'. Also seem to know, without doubt, that the main retrieval work was done days ago and that I participated.

Then I move up to formless worlds of transcendent energies where Higher Selves dwell. Been here many times in meditation. Move into HS and interact with other 'personality projections', those souls who, gladly or otherwise, took part in history. The whole notion of their lives being complete and their being 'permanent residents of HS, while I'm still doing my thing here and only visiting, appears, and I juggle with it, as it seems to contradict the notion that all lives are simultaneous for HS.

Then I slide down the 'column of light' that connects me here to HS and slip into the astral levels where the dead live and love. I'm visiting my father in a house I recall from other astral visits, up in some hills overlooking a valley, a sort of bungalow with a slanted roof, low at back and high at front. He's very comfortable here and enjoys receiving guests. His brother B, dead fifty years and his wife, dead only five, are present already, 'happy as clams', and we chat away, just like families always do, bit of info from my side, bit of info from theirs. We've done this before, so the chat is relaxed and accepting of the astral/physical state of things.

Then I'm somehow amidst ethereal golden beings who live in the spiritual aspect of the sun, our sun, the one we can't live without. Been here before, but not sure what my purpose is here, but know that the purpose of the place as a whole is to continuously pour love, light and understanding onto this earth, the sort of deep continual embrace that god gives to those who are open and receiving. The beings here have lives, although I'm not sure what that consists of, other than the action above described. Don't know really where it is, but feel it's not where the Higher Selves/Monads dwell. Spend 'time' here and then reluctantly leave.

The very next night it seems I am on much the same journey: out through the trees, down the winding river valley, over to S's, where she is ready to awaken and we interact 'gladly and sensually', like lovers do. Later satisfaction parts us; she to more sleep, me to more adventure. Some of which involves 'splitting into three aspects who go their separate ways, like three old friends who have hatched a plan'. The first goes to a church, apparently Episcopalians with 'open minds, ready to hear other viewpoints', to give a talk about the many dimensions/planes between earth and god, where they as a group are situated on this evolutionary spiral, and how one has to give up one's personal identity to fully move into the 'god' level. The second goes to a lower astral level, a sort of 'bad-tempered, narrow minded rural community. Drafty damp cottages with drafty damp people in them, most likely dead, unemployed Welsh miners'. I appear to be in one cottage, speaking to a small assembly like some itinerant preacher, where I try to adapt what they expect into something more subtly spiritual, but without much success. My attempt to gladden hearts falls on stony ground in a miserable damp foggy forest atmosphere. Lines like *What's to be glad about*, and *If this is heaven it's bloody awful* and *Might as well stayed old and alive as this* and *Bloody religion always was a lie* reverberate in memory. It's the usual lower astral self-fulfilling negativity, but you work with what comes up. The third appears to be attending an 18th century style French harpsichord recital in full period clothing, at, where else, the music annex of the cottage. It's the essence of refinement and decorum here, souls who crave being cultured. As many earlier explorations and partial dream memories indicate, this is definitely one of my gigs, as part of me loves this culture stuff, and is always has an eye out for those ready to move on and experience more. A definite sense of all three sharing, in some simultaneous fashion too subtle to currently encode in words, the three streams of experience. The itinerant preacher seems to move on to some decayed urban ghetto scene, where he transforms into a version of the enthusiastic Black Baptist type, bringing the word to the brothers on the street.

Then numbers one and two seem to remerge while three is still at post recital reception. Other two, now merged, seem not to care and sped up to Higher Self and do a bunch of mingling there. Then all three seem to reunite in cottage garden, after the last of three guests depart. A return to 'here' with a distinct sense of reentering the body and its brainwave patterns, some of which continuously generate muddled dream scenarios.

These two nights of stupendous activity are followed by a relatively uneventful night, where an initial indecision is followed by a trip to J's rest home, where he is, in fact, still resting, and then a move up to a formless energy plane which might be the Void, where *being nothing, doing nothing*, is all the rage. I ask for the significance and am told 'doing nothing is as important as doing something', and am reminded not to get hung up in being useful. Then into one of the heaven worlds, one of the more refined ones where folk are just about ready to drop the body. I seem to be talking to one such candidate, trying to make them more at ease with the bodiless/formless scenario. Then a quick move down to S. who is 'completely ensnared in sleep'.

Five days later, a fly along the river valley to meet an awakened S., and we dance around, holding hands and twirling in a circle. My suggestion that she come and visit father J. is greeted with nervous apprehension. Eventually we go, and are in a bedroom with J. propped up in bed. A very emotional reunion between father and daughter, with other deceased family and friends in background. Then a return to S.'s own bedroom, where she retires, and I move on, to split again into three, this time for retrievals. One is a car accident mother, another a murdered prostitute, and a third a child of indeterminate trauma. All the details are fuzzy, but rather than be annoyed, I flow as another part of me moves up to Higher Self and merges there. And there's a definite sense of an entire night's activities compressed into 'headlines' for the duration of a meditation.

While typing up notes for this last, there's a surprise intervention from HS, who wishes to communicate the following: *Gordon it's wonderful to see you doing this kind of exploring. I know you're wondering how I'm aware of this right now, but it's still the same as before (as noted in earlier dialogues). The connection between us is now permanent and very strong, so when you're engaged in the type of work that resonates with my being I feel it right away. ...And what you're attempting now is a great leap forward, and I want to give you every encouragement to continue, despite any doubts that your imagination is making it all up. As you have been told before, in your 'next' incarnation you will be aware of what you're doing at other levels day and night, so this is your first baby step toward that level of layered consciousness. Don't be dismayed if at times the meditation you've adopted seems a pale version of what's really going on. It is a pale version, but it's the best you can do right now, but it will strengthen. Not with time, but with practice. Your physical level consciousness is, indeed, as you've joked, in the basement with the lights out, wondering what the heck is going on. For reasons related to other, more undeveloped character traits in your emotional life, you decided before birth, to expand in the planes without expanding in the physical. Now that you have matured the emotional wine, as it were, you see how bruises can make you beautiful if you display them unashamedly. This beauty born of suffering is the stuff that character is made of. And that stuff is now ready to consciously blend with the other stuff 'here.'*

The following night, I experience myself as a glowing sphere of light who radiates love to his two favorite trees, Walter and Wilhelmina. My ability to thus shift seems a matter of simple choice, and one that can easily be reversed. After a exemplary dawdle down the river valley to S.'s neighbourhood, where she seems quite ensnared in sleep, and I think of the deva over the lake, but feel an urge to hover over Toronto for a while. Close to the top of the CN tower, where amid the delightful breeze and counter breeze of the night, I expand to feel all the fears and desires bubbling up from below. All the anger, lust, ambition, anxiety, pride, honor, love and envy and vengeance. Also the long sigh of relief that is sleep. All the chatter, both expressed and held in.. Am I inside the deva here, to be aware of so much? Is it the same deva of the lake? Yes it is: it ensouls both, and they are a balance for each other. This is a realization, not an intellectualization. And I know folk will say, more please.

Then I move, vertically as it were, up through the planes, one by one, feeling out the various levels and the collective psyches of their inhabitants. Right up to the god consciousness level and then down a bit to the Higher Self level. In HS I feel a sudden urge to communicate with a future rather than a past self. HS says why not, she's always available to you. Quickly sense a being named Cassiopeia, a 'strong sensual and spiritual woman of indeterminate age living in about 2150. There's plenty of chitchat, much of which I forget before taking notes. But I do recall that she travels backwards in time to visit with many past lives and I am about the only one who does not take her for an angelic being. She seems to find this more funny than frustrating. She also seems to have easy access to all the planes, day and night, whilst remaining a physical being. She informs me that what I am trying now is an important step towards this state of affairs. She seems very happy and fulfilled with her life, and says she is a winning combination of elements from all past lives, of which I am one. It's as if HS finally got the right combination, but that may be my antiquated notions of linear progress butting in. We hug at my request and she's an interesting mix of strength, love and sensual 'beingness', almost a goddess figure by current standards. but perhaps not her own era. She doesn't feel like a future me, more her own person entirely, the kind of friend one is intrigued and pleased to have.

As more info melted away, I determined to meditate in the hot tub the following afternoon to reconnect. Course this lead to sitting on window ledge at the pool, scribbling away on a bit of paper. Cassiopeia: born about 2110, talking to her in 2150 approx. Life is very different then, as wonderful in its endless opportunities for growth and fun, as we seekers in our time imagine the astral world to be (which of course it is). C. very definitely lives in a physical earth reality where many of the predicted disasters from our day have not occurred. Maybe they've happened in other probable realities, she says, but not the one I'm in. A single woman, without children and without the desire for them, she does teach fine art and dance to young ones, and loves it. The kind of multi-dimensional astral travel through space and time that she freely indulges in, both while awake and sleeping, although practiced by many others, is still not for everyone. Many still live quite traditionally, family, career, religion etc. Visual and audio links with the dead are by then easily available, but not everyone indulges. Some still think it's the equivalent of sinful or black magic. Medical and scientific advances enable folk to live a lot longer if they wish, though not everyone does, and some are still quite self-destructive. Teleportation of human bodies is quite a reality in her epoch, almost, you could say, all the rage. People have to be taught how to do it properly, to avoid collisions and other accidents, eg. crashing through walls on arrival. To me it seems like the racing motorbike syndrome of the future. There are schools, accreditations, fines for carelessness etc.

She has lovers of both genders and is married to none. Lots of folk live like this, although to be fair, lots don't. (Whether there's no shame attached to this type of lifestyle or Cassiopeia is beyond the reach of such triviality, I'm not sure.) Jealously is almost extinct, she tells me, and illustrates the remark by saying that if your lover goes home with someone else, you can always go obe to Jupiter for amusement. This is obviously intended as humor, but I sense an important point is underscored by it. The backwards-in-time-to past-lives issue comes up again. C. feels such visits to connected souls are a bit like taking the time to go see your theatrical friends in all their plays, even if you're in a darkened theatre and they can't see you very clearly. There was also some stuff in here about C.'s psyche being partly a mixture of elements from myself and S., that S. and I decide, after this physical life to merge our beings, and that as we belong to the same HS, this is not as arduous as might at first seem. (Both S. and I feel quite strange about this)

That was what I received that afternoon. That same evening, connection was reestablished in front of laptop...

"Cassiopeia, what are your impressions of the epoch I live in? For some reason, I am suddenly fascinated by this."

"We have connected many times here while you're obe at night, long before your current explorations of this nature, so to some extent I see your world through your eyes, plus the various memories of 'mine' which were born from your life, those karmic seeds which connect me to you, not to mention all the others emanating from HS, but I think I can say a few things from what you would consider 'my point of view'. The world you live in now is an amazing mixture of violent destruction and highly energetic creativity. The earth has always seen those forces, but in your time the balance is definitely shifting to the creative. Fear and greed are being slowly swamped by love and fun. Computers and telecommunications, now within reach of almost everyone, are making the greatest contribution to the concept of one world, much more than any religion or empire ever did, although I'll bet there's thousands who would disagree. They are breaking down all barriers, mocking all pretense, and exposing what I know you call bullshit. Already, as you know, some adventurous spirits are communicating from the astral planes through friends' computers and tv screens. Let me tell you this will only increase in frequency, as the technology becomes more finely adjusted and people's belief systems opened up. This techie aspect will help as the spontaneous eruptions of astral plane consciousness enable the average person to glimpse the worlds of the dead and auras and all the rest. As you suspect from your meditative practice these sudden visions will upset the innocent citizen no end, but the technical side of it will help them cope, as many souls will still trust a machine over themselves. Many of these trends will have matured by my lifetime, and will be taken for granted by many, but when I look at your epoch I see the roots of such fundamental change and wonder why you're not more excited about it."

"Oh I'm excited all right, but I still have to live from day to day in a mundane world of moderated behavior and civilized restraint, and that's what I think you see. Can I assume your current facility in astral/time travel gives you windows onto many historical periods and cultures?"

"Yes you can. And what a fascinating education it is. Of course other activities claim my attention. In my time leisure and fun come close to obsessing people. Sometimes I think we make work to keep ourselves in line."

"How's the weather there?"

"About what you'd expect, but our adaptability has progressed greatly. Whether you live in a climate controlled city or in the mountains/rainforest desert extremes, your personal adaptability is what counts. Bodies are altogether more resilient in our time. In a word, they don't break down as easily as they used to, and when they do we have many clever ways of fixing them. Replacement organs and joints, artificial blood that blends perfectly with the real stuff, eyes, teeth, you name it we got it."

"What about politics and the environment?"

"Various purification machines, for air and water, offset any environmental degradations, and their invention is closer to your time than mine. And, as you probably suspect, fossil fuel dependence is long over, wind, solar and gravity, and let's not forget, thought, being much more useful. Certainly the changeover period is turbulent, but not nearly as turbulent as many of you fear. Several of the new technologies, once their covert suppression vanishes, are able to appear virtually overnight, and they race through the infrastructure as fast, if not faster, than computers and the internet. Politicians have to cope with the newer psychic atmosphere: many will intuit when they're lying and ways will be sought to blanket those perceptions. Democracies, and there are many more of them now, are still all about reasoned dispute, with gungho agendas grappling for dominance, so elected leaders are still stuck trying to appease various interest groups simultaneously, so the diplomatic arts are still very much in evidence."

"I feel quite confident now that I can contact you, so will you forgive me if I bow out now as tiredness is getting the better of me?"

"Yes of course. Wonderful to bring our ongoing contact to light finally. I wish you well."

"Thanks Cassiopeia."

Well, as you can imagine, these last two contacts threw me for a loop. As I said earlier about HS, talking to Cassiopeia was just as simple as talking to any guide or soul needing retrieval. Once you get over your reluctance, or insistence on inability, the communication just flows. Doubt is like a cloud which chokes everything. Also, my intellectual prejudices set up roadblocks to future selves. Do they not make a mockery of free will? Is everything then predestined? What if I decide not to reincarnate as Cassiopeia? Who am I then talking to? Is it just a probable future, as many have suggested? And if it is, how many other probables are there? Three? Five? Twenty? It's not a model I've ever been comfortable with, as it just doesn't seem workable.

HS is outside time; past and future are equally theatrical to him/her. A thousand plays with five thousand actors, almost all of who reappear in different roles. But the same caveat appears. If the outcome is set then what freedom do we have as actors? We know very well scripts are not set in stone, regardless of how programmed we are by our neurotic behavior patterns. I sense there's a resolution to all this, a resolution I have yet to uncover. I trust that it's discovery will be sometime during this trilogy. And until then I hope that the reader can relax in my uncertainty and still enjoy the ride.

About five days later, a meditation reveals that S. and I visited her father in his rest home room. J. is now sitting up in an easy chair, cool in his blue robe, looking relaxed and almost regal receiving his guests. After a joyous reunion between father and daughter, we depart for "my" cottage, where we spend the rest of our time, S. delightedly exploring, and me kind of amazed I hadn't taken her there before. Returning to her garden by her bedroom, we pause to absorb the pre-dawn chorus, and I have her watch her sleeping body before reentry, in the hopes that the transition will register on a deeper level of her psyche.

Three days later I meet up with a very awake S. and we travel to J's rest home to find that he has departed to watch some local tennis tournament, and no one knows when he will be back. We seem to move on to the cottage, where we relax in its homey atmosphere for the rest of the 'night'.

Four days later I again experience myself as a glowing ball of light which 'radiates' loving energy to my two favorite trees and then splits into two, only to chase itself about town, playing a sort of mad 'dodge and dash' game around the Bristol street bridge. Quite like how two birds will swoop and dive about each other: much giddy fun. Then a float down the river valley to S's neighborhood, where I turn back into a fair resemblance of Gordon and we dance about in a circle holding hands, all goofy and joyful like children. This leads to some horizontal intimacies about a floaty three feet off the floor. Marvelous stuff, and I wonder how many couples do it and then forget.

Then we decide to go see J. He's not in his room and we're told he's gone walking with friends. We find them easily. It's J., his mother, long deceased, and his friends N. and P., both of whom have passed in the last three years. J., of course, is stronger, but still thinks he's recuperating, a belief that everyone indulges him in. S. thrilled to see him and they sit together on a bench and chat excitedly. P. introduces me to her husband N., telling him I came to her while she was hovering near death, helping her through some issues, which I did at S's request. More group chitchat, which I can't recall, but I do remember John exclaiming "This place is just so invigorating!" I make some comment about him playing tennis and he replies that he hopes it will be soon. I sense his inner schedule of expectation and smile.

After this there's a scene of Lake Ontario, where S. seems quite thrilled with the sensations of merging with deva's aura.

The next night I am filled with a 'wild, crazy rock n' roll energy', and don't know why. Shoot out of window and into trees' aura, where I shoot a kind of 'starburst of little sparklies' at them.

Then I'm heading north on river valley, away from the lake for a change. I'm really zooming, like some astral speedboat, with a very giddy, couldn't-care-less energy. I hover over the highway, comparing its traffic flow to the river flow. Then off to countryside northwest of city lights, where I hover again, recalling the times twenty or more years back, when I lived here and first felt the contours of the landscape way below me. I gaze up, to feel the thrill of a million stars in the huge sky. Then I shoot east, passing over central Canada's landmass, cutting a path between Montreal and Quebec City, then out over Nova Scotia and on to the Atlantic. About half way over dawn shows in the east, that familiar golden glow. I realize it'll be about six am in England, and then it suddenly hits me: I'm going to look at a crop formation. Ireland and Wales are passed on my way to Wiltshire. I love them both but I've got things to do apparently. Then I start to think: which one did I really like that I saw on the web? Well, of course, this switches me from 'knowing' mode to 'gee I wonder' mode and slows me right down. Then I recall: it was *Ogbourne St. George*, the one with the little lights seen speeding about and caught on film. Then I am there, engaged with the overlighting deva, exchanging thoughts as one would in a human discussion. I express my love for the formation, and my congratulations. Deva is grateful after a fashion, but says many were involved in planning, and I know he means human spirits as well as nature beings. Including 'me' at another level? Possibly, but I'm not sure, and she's not giving away any secrets. Of course the energetic template for all this activity was laid down back in Druid times, this I already know, but the actual mechanics of the plan and its activation are still mysterious to the astral level of being I'm at now.

Of course, this formation is a slice of a 3-D shape, and fills many functions which my current level of being does not consciously know. Deva is happy to hear how inspiring the design is to me in my daily human consciousness. The speeding balls of light caught on film here are part of the deva's aura, which can be witnessed as any of several aspects, one of which is playful fairies involved in a project much grander than they can imagine, but spinning in delight at the energetic rush of it all. Much like me earlier tonight. I fly back to Canada, hitting the darkness mid-Atlantic. Visit S., who is still sleepy but responds to my whispered advice about her being in astral body now. Feeling that perhaps we've visited J. enough for now, I suggest she see some of the buildings where 'souls sleeping till judgment day' are stored. We arrive at rather functional looking barrack type residences, long and rectangular and maybe four floors high. Nurse type figures sit behind desks at ends of wards, reading mostly as there's not much to do. The wards have a long row of beds either side, all filled with sleeping figures, some in very old style clothing. All floors are the same and a gloomy silence prevails. One of the 'nurses' tells us he was like that before he awakened, and felt that he should be here for others, just as someone was here for him. After about the fourth ward S. gets a bit depressed and suggests we leave. We walk in a formal park like area while discussing the effects of strongly held belief systems. I suggest going to a level where believers are happy.

We arrive at something like a church picnic: all kinds of social and playful activity as we wander through a large garden setting with church visible nearby. We chat with various people we encounter, and at some point it becomes obvious we're just dreamers passing through. I think I actually say this to someone. Then I sense a whisper campaign behind our backs, and soon a pastor appears to engage me in conversation. Polite but very guy-to-guy, as if S. was not there. It would seem that they've been having a problem with 'dreamers' (i.e. not dead people) coming here and disrupting things. I assure him that is not our intention, that we're just exploring. I sense what's up, but keep my mouth shut till S. and I are on the periphery of the group, when I explain that in the various heaven worlds/belief systems, even vaguely dissatisfied souls can, and do, attract, 'outsiders', often those obe during sleep, to help them move on. The various pleas and responses are often enacted unconsciously, but the resolution, someone disappearing from the community, is always noticed by those who would have them stay and support the consensus reality. And in some of the lower astral hell-like states, the removal has to be executed with an almost military style precision, such is the fear and control exercised in those places.

We move into the forest we're at the edge of, well, the cleared area, and S. quickly becomes her happy pagan girl self again, thrilled with all the life of the woods. It's a joy for me to see her like this, after the last couple of experiences which have depressed her. I know I have shared such physical lives with her many times, and that this series of meditations is as much for her and her father as it is for me.

Five days later S. asks me to check out the experience three nights before, as she wants some dream memories checked. I oblige. We visit J., finding him walking alone on grounds, slowly, as if he can't imagine going any faster. S. joyously hugs him. I ask about his entourage and hear that he's asked to be left alone for a couple of days to 'find his feet'. There's a real assertion of independence here, tinged with a crustiness I find typical of J. as I knew him when 'alive'. We watch some tennis being played by fairly good players who have not been here long enough to know that their minds can control the ball with ease. J. seems happy.

He invites us back for lunch, and we accept in the time-honored fashion. The cafeteria is really quite good, he tells us. When there J. enjoys some eggs benedict, a high cholesterol feast he wouldn't have dared touch on earth, while S. and I nibble at fruit salads. When I tell him we're dreaming and not really hungry, it leads him to ask about my afterlife experiences. I launch into my little talk about my father dying when I was young and that giving me the impetus to explore. He asks where my father is and I explain a couple of levels beyond this. I mention some experiences I think he's ready to hear... the complexity of the various realms, how he's absolutely free to go anywhere he wants, but that he might want to use N. and P.'s spare room till he gets a place of his own. I tell him he's landed on his feet and how there's plenty of opportunity here for growth and exploration. He seems to be taking it all in, which reminds me of S's description of his information gathering abilities. He does make some remarks about "how marvelous it all is here". And just after saying something about asking his own mother to leave him be to find his feet, he asks S. to tell her mother N. that he is just fine. S. asks about a message for M., J. reluctant to give any as "she doesn't believe in an afterlife" and how it might only upset her.

After this S. says she wants to do something 'fun', so getting her to hold my hand, we float up vertically, gradually assuming that bird's eye view of buildings, people and nature. We notice the multi-cultural nature of this astral level, quite like the part of urban Ontario we come from. I briefly wonder if the various ethnics groups disperse, after a time at this entry level, but do not pursue the thought further. At about a height of one hundred feet we begin to float horizontally over the beautiful countryside. Standing and gliding gracefully: it's fun. I see a small lake up ahead and decide to glide, ever so slowly, down towards it. Like aerodynamically perfect little planes we land on the water with barely a ripple. Due to her unconscious expectations, S. sinks in. I yank her up and tell her how easy it is to walk on water here, that it's only a miracle in the earth world. We tread smoothly across the lake, S. a bit giddy from it all, saying "Oh this is so blasphemous". I, of course, beg to differ, and rattle on about the various conditions pertaining to each of the planes, all of it depending on rates of vibration. Some swans glide by, not giving a hoot either way. After a bit we return to earth and I suggest she try to recall some of the night's events.

S. asked for this as she'd had a couple of symbolic dreams that night, one, waiting for me in a darkened bedroom, and two, traveling in her own vehicle with some functions not quite responding as they should, but not seeming to impede her ability to travel and 'do things'.

Four days later I seem to merge with HS, only to feel myself at such a high rate of vibration I can neither cope with nor sustain the experience, and 'wink out'. Then, with S., visit J., who is now living in lakeside cottage with friends N. and P. Seated comfortably on a lovely wooden porch, we chat convivially and J. enthuses about all the birds he has seen since being here. Much discussion of M.'s difficulty in coping with J's "death". Some suggestions by me, on how he, together with N. and P. can project positive loving thoughts in her direction that might well lift her spirits.

Two days later, another startling set of experiences. One, a dream of a future me channeling the Maitreya 'live' in front of an orchestra. Two, a meditative recall of astral 'me' splitting into two, one going forward through time, the other backward. All to experience various incarnations, with a view to simultaneity. A third 'me; offers sardonic commentary on it all, mainly directed at *little gordon* who cannot yet accept his multidimensionality, never mind take it all in. Many details of 'past' incarnations I've already touched on, but with more focus and intensity. The future stuff is mainly about Cassiopeia and Gordon's Maitreya connection. Certainly more successful than the previous experience of 'winking out'.

A week later I feel impelled to research Maitreya. In David Anrias's *Through The Eyes Of The Masters*, channeled in 1932, I was heartened to find this: "Henceforth I come not solely through groups with recognized officials, through organizations rendering me what is often no more than lip service in their assumptions of Brotherhood; I come to each and all who love me, no matter of what race class or creed. The greatness of their need of me, the strength of their desire to see me, shall be the measure of their power to see me. The peasant in the Swiss Mountains, the scientist in his laboratory, the artist dreaming of his creations; the mystic and the psychologist; the spiritualist and the musician - to these and many others I come if their intuition, their inner vision be true enough to recognize me, if there be in their hearts that which responds to the Love which eternally flows forth to them from mine."

Of course there are websites, who appear to compete, and the channelings, though generally feeling genuine, at least to me, are tainted in various obvious ways with the personality assumptions/ restrictions of the medium. In one of my favorite outdoor meditation spots, on July 13, after a couple of unsuccessful attempts at contact in the previous days, I manage to touch base with the exalted being, who I sense would rather not be so exalted, at least for this phase of the program. A pleasant and polite chat, including a very gracious response to my offer of honor. And although obviously a great cosmic being he definitely has the ability to downsize at will. And yes my dream was an upcoming possibility which could easily manifest, should I decide to take it on. Yes, it was decided upon before birth, and some 'training' was undergone, but it is not the only project of this incarnation, and I should not allow it to outweigh the others. And yes, he can split himself up into dozens, if not hundreds of aspects to do the work. Also, I can bring to the project an individual touch, my own spin on the message, as it were, that will do much more than duplicate what is already being offered, both in print and on the web. It would seem that Maitreya wants many mouthpieces with no overriding authority. Whether this will lead to a chaos of dispute rivaling earlier religious squabbles remains to be seen. I certainly hope not.

Although more was experienced during these summer months of exploration, including some very intimate connections to the energetic creation of crop formations, the above catches the essence of it all, the core of my rapidly evolving consciousness shift, which I believe is what Henry was after all those pages back. I am now no more than a spark on a spiral of beings which connects the dots between the sleep of dense matter and the eternal delight of divine life, the recording secretary for a host of souls, acting and interacting on behalf of divine consciousness and its conspiracy to contaminate all of creation with the clear light of illumination.

SECTION FOUR:

HOW ABOUT FOUR HENRYS?

A RETURN TO RETRIEVALS

Some weeks back, that is in the real time composition of this narrative, Henry requested that I hold back on some retrieval stories, as they would fit in with his plan much better here. And so we return to the beginning of my daytime hemi-sync tape-assisted retrievals. As you will recall, I took interest in a variety of 'criminal' activities and their afterlife consequences. High school massacres and their perpetrators struck me as an interesting challenge. As with all other traumatic situations, one must have the practiced insouciance of a snobby maitre d'i with difficult customers. He must have seen it all and act accordingly, as if no suffering was worth the drama expended upon it, as if all such traffic required only direction. Compassion, of course, is a pre-requisite, but can be rather a burden when in action. Singleness of purpose is what's required.

According to my notes, I spent well over three weeks working on the case. With a first attempt spoilt by the sudden irruption of an upstairs vacuum cleaner, and a second with the overkill of imaging myself as a brilliant ball of light which unfortunately sent the perpetrators scurrying sway in fear of a being they called the *avenging angel* and shooting at 'me' with thought form automatic weapons while I sang out "Come out come out wherever you are! You are forgiven!" and a third where I was accused of being an emissary of the *dark lords* sent to drag them into underworld slavery, and then a forth where I actually managed to converse with one of the students. This boy was quite sure heaven was only for the kind of assholes who made life hell for them at school. I countered that heaven was for all, including those who felt shut out by class, crime or fear. After more debate I finally convinced the two of them to come and take a look at the afterlife and then return if it wasn't to their liking. The lakeshore holiday resort atmosphere, complete with squealing bikini clad girls playing beach volleyball certainly surprised them. Of course, I assured them, they're all dead too. I sense they're tempted but not ready, their old empire, the astral replica of their high school, an empty shell over which they now rule, being much too tempting.

Earlier I'd sensed the teen cult movie *The Crow* had been a major influence on these boys, and on my next visit I bring the matter up. A kind of *Yeah! Right on!* response let me nod in assurance. I then explained how its message of afterlife vengeance against those who oppressed you in life was completely wrong, and that they'd never be able to go after the tormentors they'd failed to shoot. One of them argued that he was able to meet his girlfriend almost every night. That was because she was out of her body and wanted to see him, I told him. His old enemies might never leave their sleeping bodies, and if they did he could do them no real harm as astral bodies can't ever be wounded. I avoided the haunting entity option, hoping that he hadn't read about it somewhere.

As we continue to debate I feel I am slowly getting through to them. Assurances that they'll never have to face their enemies if they don't want to, or atone for their crimes until choosing their next life seem to have a lulling effect: soon I'm convincing them to come back for another look, and we're quickly at the reception center being met by a friendly parental type couple named Maury and Esther, who seemed very glad to take the boys off my hands. They offer them a tour, and by observing the drag to their walk as they move away, I sense they still don't feel a real belonging, but I somehow know that will come.

A couple of weeks later I encounter one the boys on focus 27, and he is very effusive in his thanks to me. I told him no problem, it was an interesting challenge. Is that why I persisted, he asked. Yes. I ask if he's met any of his victims. Yes, a couple. How did he know I was coming? (this was still early days when I would ask such naive questions). Henry told him. His colleague in crime was around and okay, apparently. I told him I was available if he had any queries, but was also sure that others around focus 27 could also help if asked.

Now many months after this, with retrievals of all kinds safely under my belt and many more of the expanding-sense-of-self experiences mentioned above already encountered, and the school shootings almost completely out of my conscious mind, I was given some information on falling into a short afternoon nap. It was the images necessary to understand the past lives of those young 'shooters'. Poor blacks bundled into the army and then Vietnam, where they each died the most undignified of deaths, embittered by their country's callous disregard for their people. Once moved on and enjoying a brief respite from earthly pressures, they, like many young soldiers cut down in their prime, wanted back in the game, only this time with a better hand to play. Why not be the rich white kids who avoided the draft and got to party like pigs? Their guides arranged it and they were incarnated as babies headed for privilege and choice. How they came to their impasse of anger and vengeance is perhaps a matter for less esoteric psychologising, but the general picture has been imprinted.

And although I wonder why I was given such a snippet years before I could effectively use it, let's just say that god moves in mysterious ways and Henry is likely taking over the narrative from here.

HENRY AND FOUR OF 'ME'

You're right there, Gordon, I'll be doing most of the yakking for the next section. Readers have already witnessed a selection of soldier boy retrievals, and I think they have a fairly good idea of the various challenges we face in this aspect of the work. Some retrievers, like Gene, are on the Vietnam 'team' as it were, and some, like Serene, are more interested on a personal/family level. Those two examples comprise the vast majority of those currently involved in this work. Others are still working away at World War One and Two sites, and of course, all the wars, international and civil, since. If you're getting an inkling of the sheer vastness of these operations throughout the space and time zones of this planet I am pleased, but understand that it is but one of many activities which engage those of us here who feel they are graduates from, rather than residents of, paradise.

Many are those on the belief system levels, as Mr. Monroe called them, who act out the habits of heaven as they are envisioned by their sect or community. Just as many on the physical are happy to leave the guiding and retrieval work to the others they feel sure are better equipped and motivated than they so too are the vast majority on the astral content to contain themselves in definitions supplied by others. Although hierarchical authorities play much less of an enforcing role here, many individuals still prefer to live within the subtly expressed behavioral expectations of their communities rather than risk the exhilaration of outsider status. Reckless explorers like myself are graciously received almost anywhere, but the wary eyes of self appointed community guardians rarely rest when we're around.

Gordon is sensing that the narrative can go in any of several directions at this point, and realizing that if he were not working on a book, with its structure of linear narrative, several lines of enquiry could be followed simultaneously, and in this he is correct. Much teaching on this level is thusly conducted, and some of you have experienced this when obe at night. Could this be a prelude

to the multilayered effect of emulating the consciousness of Higher
Self, which is coming up in part three, he asks. The answer is, of
course, yes. And why not? Let's take a peek, shall we?

Those of you who are familiar with the literature of remote
viewing will know of various people's efforts, using that technique
to approach and communicate with various alien and otherwise
exalted beings. Well, we do that here too. Those who make the
attempt receive the experience they are expecting: if you suspect
that Jesus, say, cannot be approached except through an initial
'drowning' in unconditional love will receive such an experience;
if you expect to be blinded by intense white light you will; if you
feel that He is much too busy to be bothered with a little guy then
absence will be your experience; if you think an underling will be
dispatched then you will get that kind of visit. And if a selfless
devotion to prayer or good works is your prerequisite then so be it.
Of course many, assuming complete inaccessibility, will count
themselves out from the word go. I figured I could just go and chat
with him so that's just what I did. Very affable and charming he
was too, the most gracious of hosts. I seemed to be in a modest
dwelling, completely lacking in any ostentation but as comfortable
as an old shoe. I was told how kind it was of me to drop by; he
understood that this visit was for the benefit of Gordon's readers,
and would be pleased to lend himself to the project.

We spoke of matters I'd already been informed of, but which I
knew would be just right for the book. As others may have told
you, the kindness of his eyes and the love in his voice are so
wonderful one really wonders whether words are necessary. But
as words are the means of book encoded communication, words it
would be.

"No, I am not strictly speaking Maitreya, for he is an extension
of the being known as The Christ, and although I contribute to his
work and am intimate with its progress, I am more concerned with
the prophet of Christianity/son of god role I chose to inhabit two
thousand years ago. Many are the souls who still look to me for the
type of guidance and inspiration associated with those role
models. Even as I sit here in this appearance of a body, another

aspect of me dwells on a higher level, raining down love, compassion and mercy continuously upon not only those souls who crave such inspiration, but also those who barely acknowledge it, the so-called sinners who have separated through transgression and forget or deny the mercy and forgiveness pouring from my fingertips. And certainly I am not the only one doing such service. Many other beings, some recognized in the world's religions and some not, act as such continuous lighthouses of love and mercy. The guides who respond to requests along those lines are like motes of light on those powerful beams. Together we pour light onto the planet, enough to inspire but not so much as to deny the possibility of shadow. The rebel angels, god bless them, still need space to operate, as was decided at the opening of experience on earth; maximum density to offset the influence of divinity in the experiment of separation, and maximum free will to choose paths to cope with that separation. Dark and light are really simplified terms for these guides and angels; there is much that is a mixture of both. They are there to tempt you onto certain paths, should you feel the urge, and to aid you in dealing with the unforeseen complexities of those paths, for all ways are beset with challenge, both the light and the dark.

"There is much talk amongst those who follow me concerning striving. Striving to emulate my earthly life and deeds, striving to be a better human, striving to be a more devoted servant of god, always striving. as if to cease from striving were to fall irreversibly from the grace of effort. I am asking you to think of just being. Just be who you are and know that I am glad. That I am pleased with your ability to be fully human. I know: you ask what I mean to be 'fully human'. I mean to be complete in your identity, to be fully functioning to the current best of your ability, to radiate as much of god's life, that is divinity, as you feel you can handle. Thousands of years of striving have left you feeling wanting. Something, you think, is missing, but what? Nothing is missing: for despite the ever-evolving struggle for survival, you are surrounded by as much love and light as you will ever be. The only thing that will change is your ability to perceive and receive it. And those in the midst of destruction and agony can access it just as quickly as you in the lands of comfort and productivity. Opening to divinity is opening the heart to pour love, forgiveness and mercy to all who surround you, be they family, friends, rivals, enemies, or merely one of the millions of strangers. Victims of violence can accomplish this as easily as tv couch potatoes or angry fearful gang members. One who dies in a bomb blast can actually transcend the planes and return to god if they're willing to renounce not only the angry rush of vengeance, but also the very pleasures of paradise itself, which of course few are, as their religions have convinced them that the celestial picnic is not worth missing.

I am called the son of god by many who would crave such a father divine. It is also said that I pointed towards the divinity in all men, insisting that the things I did some day all men would do. Both these ideas still are true. May all humans who read these lines be inspired by such notions. Know that you can rise to this level without sacrificing what you think of as your humanity, and know that it is your very humanity which enables you to do so. You are all endowed with this spark of godliness; let it shine from your heart, speak from your mouth, and launch thoughts from your mind. Let no man make you ashamed of these talents, for as God lives in me, I live in you. And do not forget, I also live in your rivals and enemies, for the spark is given to all, regardless of race or creed or personal ambition. As stars in the dark sky we all shine, some brighter, some dimmer, but as light we remain, source and reflection.

Henry sits before me now, a welcome guest. Gordon receives and transmits the words, as is his desire. Any one of you could do the same, should you so wish. For I am many, as is Maitreya and Buddha, to name but two. We can be with all those who wish to be with us, in heart and mind if not in body. We exist to console and inspire, not to grant favors. We exist so you can see where it is possible for you to go. The ascent may seem arduous, but the arrival guaranteed.

Let your differences of opinion become as so many summer breezes on the beach of eternity. Let your arguments be waves, ever slapping on the sand. Let me be the water in which all of you swim."

Henry: I do not know exactly what that aspect of Jesus did when I left the humble dwelling in which I discovered him, but I suspect he remerged with what I might call the source entity, as that is what I do when I've finished some particular task on the planes. I'm good for about three or four aspects operating simultaneously, as is Gordon when he's obe. Jesus has so many aspects I would imagine they're beyond counting, partially determined by his evolutionary level and partially due to the number of souls who urgently require his presence.

Now as this interview was unfolding, another aspect of 'me' was working the astral jungles 'over' Vietnam and Cambodia, where many soldiers and peasants are yet stuck. Jeanie, a woman who felt suicide the only option when her own husband did not return from that very karmic catastrophe, was learning the ropes, much as you've already witnessed with Gene. We'd been working with some dead GI's who'd 'gone native', hooking up with some dead Vietnamese girls, whose prostitute life style had alienated them from the heaven of their culture, living almost happily in a replica of a Mekong Delta village, fishing and harvesting rice and vegetables and trying not to wonder overmuch as to why their couplings had not produced babies. We'd taken to regular social calls, not so much masquerading as missionary and wife, but allowing that impression to settle as the most useful.

As you already know, the first level post-death is so like the physical as to be almost indistinguishable, and the main hurdle is to convince them that they're actually deceased. They've got almost everything they need, are much happier than before, and cannot imagine any benefit in leaving with you. Since our previous visit they'd been joined by newcomers, long term loners, scavengers from the remotest parts, who looked to me like they'd tired of loneliness and were ready for a little community.

It was a fairly standard visit under the circumstances, some tea, some small talk, some laughter. They were warming up to their mysterious visitors, and suspicions were slowly melting, but it would be quite some time before any visit to heaven could be arranged.

Another 'me' was participating in what you might call a group meditation over the Holy Land. It's part of a fairly regular attempt to balance out the dark clouds of fear/anger/blood lust/vengeance with the divine light of love and understanding (as Gordon calls it). Teams of discarnates and earthside obe's continually blend, merge and move on as other activities beckon, and although the project is work, it's fun work, as that particular energy we're channeling is from a much higher level than we normally reside on, and the effect, if you surrender to it, is not that different from the excited dance of bubbles in a pan of boiling water. Visually it appears that we're poking searchlights into roiling mass of dark fog. I say 'balance out', as the idea is not to clear up a problem, but to offer avenues of escape for those who tire of the struggle, and who truly seek to transcend the iron grip of their culture and ethnicity, those who would forgive rather than inflict.

The dark clouds are the centuries accumulation of competing ideologies and the willful perversion of prophets' divine inspirations, which were all intended to draw a direct line between Judaism, Christianity and Islam, one that would link them in a giant historical design of godly knowledge and devotion, but seems to have had almost the opposite effect, if you read the headlines in your papers, as I do when I'm passing through your plane. And they are as self-perpetuating as any organic system on your plane, as the vibrations of the continued intolerance and ethnic strife feed them as surely as rain on soil.

Of course, this is not the only area of the planet with such energetic accumulations, but it's one of the worst, and left unchecked, would quickly feed others. Though all these nodes of conflict *need* to exist so that the tensions inherent in evolving personal identity through the various stages of growth through family/community/tribe/nation and preferences of a religious, social, economic and political nature can be accommodated with the amount of flexibility necessary for the almost infinite variety of individual characters completing their journeys, they have to be monitored so that the 'escaping steam' of tensions does not completely obscure the light of love which bathes them. Fortunately there are always dedicated discarnates available for such work and the balance of opportunity is always maintained.

Readers will perhaps not be surprised to hear that such work continues unabated, but I feel that the detailing of my personal experience will aid in their deeper understanding. Some of you, of course, have already participated in such service while either obe at night or during meditation. Those of you who wish to start need only express a strong desire upon going to bed, and that wish will be heard and aided.

Now another part of 'me' was in attendance at a temple of wisdom on the mid-astral, similar in purpose to the one described in Gordon's first book, but with a completely different style and attitude. Disguised to accommodate the more recent arrivals from the younger generation, this building was placed in an urban atmosphere and was designed to appeal to the youthful taste in dance clubs and rave drugs. A goodly number of the creators and appreciators of this subculture are here now, and we quickly realized the need for a cultural focus for them and their soon-to-be-arriving compatriots. The disused warehouse ambience was noted and employed, sound systems and light shows installed. Some of the attendees had been scooped up personally by me, as od-ing and dehydration related heart attacks were, and are, quite common as the subculture makes its way across the planet, and all one had to do was a quick nightly drive through to find a few lost partiers in the immediate vicinity of their last transit. A few would be in subway stations, waiting for trains, all giggly and silly, not knowing why they'd gotten separated from their friends. I got so I could do the European big cities one night and the North American ones the next without even breaking into a sweat. The kids liked the club and made suggestions as to its improvement.

As the drugs and dance of their culture emphasized an ecstatic togetherness and empathy for the other, their bonding here was almost effortless, and my role was limited to appearing in the quiet chill out rooms and dispensing advice to the pleasantly tired and lovelorn. My preferred look was that of the old and genial hippy, tie-dyed and pony-tailed, with belly pleasantly pillow-like. My language, a bit stiff at first, soon morphed into the required shapes. Some were no more than happily childlike and affectionate children, others were explorers, and an understanding of the psychedelic gurus like Leary and McKenna and Castaneda, was necessary, but I dutifully did my homework and soon warmed to the ancient plant based shamanism they espoused.

Aside from the usual hints on how to move around the astral and visit still living family without getting trapped, my basic aim was to show these arrivals that they could *think* themselves into the altered states they so loved, that their prized substances were like training wheels: superfluous when you knew how to ride. And so imagine yet another 'me', sprawled on a couch in a darkened room answering questions like 'When I'm so, like, gone, where do I go?' and 'Do you know where Jerry is man?' To the first I say 'You lose your vibrational focus and become a willing slave to sound and light. You are inside form looking out, rather than outside form looking in'. To the second I say 'No but I can guess'. Jerry is Jerry Garcia, former leader of the rock band Grateful Dead, whose passing, it seems, saddened many of several generations. I'm interrupted by a 'Hey man that was so cool' from my first questioner. She's referring to my sudden appearance on the couch across the room, and my sudden wink out when the question was answered. This projection of mirror images to questioners is one of my little tricks here. There's a touch of the shaman that's just right for the consciousnesses I'm dealing with.

Meanwhile Gordon's been wondering why I asked him to hold back on the retrieval stories of the school shooters and why the brief snippet of past life info was given to him months later. He was thinking it would lead to much more Vietnam stuff, I suppose, whereas I merely wanted a nice tie in to return the readers from their extended stay in Gordon's experiences. The past life info was passed on by two guides who wished closer ties to Gordon at the time, who basically wanted to be his astral secretaries, and whom he employed as such until his quest for HS contact quite overwhelmed him and he lost interest in guides of that sort. This was some time before other guides, as he has portrayed, lost interest in him! Still, all's fair in love and war, as they say. Old Henry just wanted to clear up that little discrepancy before moving on to Gautama Buddha, who has greeted Gordon on more than one occasion, as he might recall, if only the poor boy could reconstruct the fragments into something like the short movie I'm now going to show him.

"Souls tend to see only that part of me which they have realized within themselves, but I greet this partiality with as much gratefulness as I would offer any visitor. Gordon looks to the tiny smile in my traditional meditative pose and feels himself blending with its humorous acceptance of all the desperate and passionate illusions of form which animate his and every universe. When he thus merges, we breathe I AM and know who we are not. And like all true bodhisattvas, he wants to share this liberation beyond bliss with all those who suffer from its lack, and like all true bodhisattvas knows that he cannot, that he can but point a finger in the appropriate direction and wait while the wounded unwrap their own bandages.

Merge with me, thou born of light, and live for a time in this timeless plight, before moving back to the woe of thankless tasks! Join the design of noble desires, see dragons breathing fire and deities redeeming wreckage! The billion particles of becoming are ready to dance."

Some movie, Gordon's thinking, all I could see was blinding light.

I accuse him of being obtuse in the creative use of metaphor: he grins, hoping that no-one close by notices. It is his long established writerly habit to compose in the public library, and, as I focus on my end of the communication I can sense the human presences about him as dimmer shades darting about the flame.

Are you wondering what happens to my other activities when I'm thus engaged with Gordon? Well, the simple answer is I expand and contract as necessary. If a need is expressed, somewhere in the planes, for me, or someone like me, an aspect can be dispatched, almost without thought, to perform whatever function is necessary. And since I've been at this for some while there's no problem with losing focus or getting confused. Yes, it takes confidence and practice, not to mention a sincere desire to help others, but anyone really can master it, if they so desire. Some of course, assume such siddhis (psychic powers) to be akin to black magic, and will not come within a mile of it, and will assume deception should you try a demonstration, so for them we leave a wide berth, and leave all discussions of saintliness and multiple manifestations for later.

EONS OVER EASY

Readers will recall the senior guide Eons making a short appearance to assist Serene in her work with Al, some chapters back. Well, I am Eons, and I have presented myself to Gordon's consciousness so that he can record some of my experiences. I generally have very little contact with incarnate souls as my specialty is the grand overview. I assist souls in considering the completion of their evolutionary path on this planet, this very special planet of high density and low divinity. I do this assisting on a variety of the spirit planes, almost never on the physical. Gordon says 'You're one of those between life boffins, aren't you?' I am graced by his humor, for it will ease the transition into some fairly complex lifelines.

I dwell in that realm of spirit which has the body of the sun as its physical sheath, and as that location might imply, part of our existence is taken up with a continuous radiation of sustaining energies to the planetary bodies of the solar system. To explain in detail would be to launch into a wealth of technical detail of which my recording secretary has not a linguistic clue, so my assertions will have to suffice, fantastical as they may sound. Another part of my life involves high level guiding. I appear to souls at critical stages of their growth, usually at the request of their regular guides who sense that a deeper perspective is necessary.

Let me begin with a soul we will call Sabrina. She has, of course, had many other names in her long cycle of lives, but that is the most recent. An automobile collision brought her to spirit some time back and I have spent several sessions counseling her, sessions she has permitted me to quote. Although she has made great strides of progress over the centuries, a lack of forgiveness and love of ambition still hampers her prospects of graduation. We can plug into her journey almost anywhere along the line, as it were, a line that has no beginning and no end, but whose human component can be conveniently expressed.

Perhaps starting at the present and moving backwards would

be useful. Marriage to a long standing antagonist could be seen as cementing her fate, had it not been carefully set up beforehand. Habitual enemies are often encouraged to try that most intimate of relationships; some guides will go as far as to say that murder is the best prerequisite for marriage going. Sabrina and Harry could certainly make that claim. More than once they'd settled their differences with deceit and murderous cunning. With others they each achieved a measure of live-and-let-live, but with each other their desire to outwit and control became an almost unbreakable habit. Even as she was planning the extended poisoning of her husband during 1972, Sabrina felt a peculiar nagging urge to quit her low down ways, but the benefits of Harry's unfortunate demise quickly outweighed any other considerations. The prospect of freedom from debt and spousal oppression plus the chance to cruise with not one but two lovers while her two children sweated out their studies at distant universities seemed almost too good to be true.

The plan worked well: though suspicions were rife and accusations murmured, official investigations came to rest on the history of Harry's weak heart and high cholesterol. The autopsy which would have revealed the poisonous traces was never conducted. Sabrina buried him with a smile cloaked in tears. The children returned to classes with promises of new cars and increased financial assistance, and the widow wisely held back from the more immediate displays of merriment.

There followed twenty odd years of romance, party and travel, interrupted only briefly by a daughter's marriage and a son's surprise defection into seminary school. When Sabrina had had her fill of such pleasures and could clearly see age soon crippling any further access, her frustrated soul set the cancer process into motion, hoping to gain at least a few days of rigorous introspection before the transfer.

Despite the tears of her grandchildren and the petulant disapproval of her daughter, death was a relief for her glamour obsessed psyche. After a few days at a reception center, where the promise of returning youthfulness gladdened a slumbering heart she gravitated to a sub-astral where permanent vacation is the defining attitude. In these areas all the props and conveniences of hedonism are provided in abundance, as the underlying prerequisite of paradise is that all desires are gratified. Of course, some residents reach satiety sooner than others. Seeing that Sabrina, true to form, would be one of those others, I decided to approach her elegant townhouse, and enter her dream of heaven. I found her reclining on a chaise langue, admiring a recent gift of orchids.

A flicker of recognition momentarily lit up her suspicious doubts, themselves at war with the prospect of demurring to flattery. She didn't believe we were acquainted. Perhaps we'd met at the last governor's masked ball? I apologized for the sudden intrusion, but her guide had requested my attendance. Yes, that interfering fusspot Helene. And what good could I possibly do her? Well, I could take her back to before her first earth incarnation, and taking her through the last few thousand years, show her the highs and lows and help her rechart her course. Well Sabrina didn't know about that, the one previous life Helen had shown her was bad enough. Raped and left for dead indeed. Who needed to remember that? What possible good could it do? Frankly she'd rather I picked through a chicken's entrails and foretold her future. I chuckled and admitted that while that method may have been all the rage thousands of years ago, we now had much more reliable methods, especially here in spirit. Would she care to come and see them? Well, she'd have to think about it. And before I went, perhaps I'd be good enough to tell what other secrets Helen had revealed.

Poisoning one's spouse is perhaps a common enough miscalculation, I continued, but as she had already sought that solution on three other occasions, it was felt that shouldering her burdens rather than shaking them off would be not only an opportunity taken but a lesson well learned. She flinched and wished to dismiss me like a servant, but soul somehow asserted itself and in that moment of downed defenses, she agreed to come, even if only to get Helen off her back.

I advised her of the necessary arrangements, the vibrational shielding as we moved up through the planes. Although she still thought she saw the elegance of romance in my eyes, I managed to convince her that closing hers would be more than useful, and taking her hand in mine, we moved to a more refined state where the thought form of a small but ultra modern movie theatre presented itself. Sabrina admired its architectural delicacy. I explained that inside we would view the lives in question. Anticipating her enquiry, I suggested that the experience need not be as disquieting as she feared. All souls regretted certain choices made under seeming duress, and all souls needed a measure of darkness to complete their education. The point was to recognize when enough was enough and to know that relinquishing the old was to begin receiving the new.

And as that seemed to satisfy her need to be both soothed and impressed, we entered and seated ourselves before the screen in a suitable darkness. The structure, imagined by me and refined by an architect friend, had a direct energetic connection to the akashic records, that level of light impression upon which are recorded all physical level planetary activity, so while Sabrina considered the following a movie, I knew exactly what we were tapping into, and directed the 'editing' with that in mind. As with much that Henry has already revealed, it is a task that seems almost miraculous to the newcomer, but is actually quite straightforward to the regular practitioner.

A tall, proud princess, who has inherited her father's lands and peasants, she rides with a trusted servant to the forest. A witch of some repute carries on her existence there. Besides the usual psychic powers she is supposed to be a very knowledgeable herbalist, with a trunk full of remedies of which it is rumoured she will only unlock for those who strike her fancy. She has been careful to let it be heard about the castle that a potion is required to bring on a miscarriage. Her two sons are handsome and healthy and to risk the sickly daughter so prophesied in her youth is too much for her to bear. But on arrival an undetectable poison is sought, that the bully in her bedroom may be forever silenced. He is but a husband, and a bad one at that. The witch is persuaded on both counts: the princess stays over till her bedclothes are bloodied and leaves with a vial and two secrets.

A husband back from hunting, more wine than is wise, a supposed philtre which leads to deep sleep, and a pillow on the face: it is all over in a matter of days. She rules unchallenged till the eldest son marries, and then she rules from the shadows. The forest witch is often consulted and well rewarded, including the potion which will part the queen from the insults of age. Upon leaving her body she is met by the husband so long ago dispatched.

At my side Sabrina gasps and sobs. Passing her some tissues I encourage her to keep watching. Not only is it important for her to break through her denial but also the emotions it kept damned up. She recovers her composure and we watch as the two figures struggle for dominance. The husband has patiently watched and waited for his turn to inflict damage. As an angry ghost he'd tried to tear her limb from limb many times. All in vain of course. His obsession had kept him from gaining any insight into his current state other than a few tips gleaned from similarly deranged wandering spirits. The cuts and bruises of domestic carnage follow physical plane expectations; a no-win exhaustion settles in after that.

Someone appears between the sprawled bodies, ... a mother, a guide, a guide looking like a mother. Sabrina gasps again, it is her most recent life mother, Anna, and her loving concern for the erring daughter is apparent. But the warring couple are too exhausted to care, or even notice, and the spirit melts away. Further bouts of marital fisticuffs follow, with neither clearly emerging as winner. Sabrina hangs her head in shame. I quietly leave her to the freedom of her experience, freeze-framing the action until she's ready for more. When she looks up, I let it continue. The couple onscreen are reduced to a sort of wary snarling. Into the etheric version of her medieval boudoir comes an old friend, a neighboring aristocrat whose taste for self-indulgence suited theirs. Laughing at their depleted state he invites them to a kingdom of pleasures beyond. Both are intrigued and follow his bidding while keeping their distance.

One of the lower astrals hells for the rich and corrupt emerges. A decayed port with a semblance of a castle on a hill. Workers in shabby homes surround the docks where a handful of men o'war sit idle. Noise erupts from taverns. Emaciated rags slump in smelly alleys. They are lead up a winding cobbled street to the castle, where, they are assured, their kind await them. A kind of smorgasbord of cruelty and debauchery plays itself out. Lusts of every type are wantonly indulged. Sabrina howls in grief as her former self flounders in this gruesome swamp. There are rooms for endless banqueting, rooms for endless sex, and rooms for endless violence.

Do years pass by before the misery of such pleasure finally grinds her down? Ritualized cannibalism was what eventually did her in. Even depraved souls have their limits. She staggers down to the docks, where dead sailors loll about, waiting for a new pirate captain to emerge from their midst, and throws herself in. Nobody stirs.

Drowning is more difficult than she had at first supposed. Water fills her lungs but choking is quite absent. In the grimy oily harbour she floats, quite perplexed. An astute lower astral helper, long disguised as a tavern owner, suddenly floats beside her, grinning. The thought appears in her head: you cannot meet death here. She looks at her saviour and snarls. Gratitude is the farthest thing from her mind. He knows she feels humiliated, but senses her pride is so beaten down that the smallest effort will overcome it. He lets her feel the thought: you are far beyond death.

Sabrina seems absolutely transfixed beside me; wallowing in self-pity has been put aside. The incarnation finally has her in its clutches. Her good samaritan on the screen, knowing the density of such a lower astral, returns her to shore in the traditional manner, forearm under chin. An enforced rest in an upstairs back room follows. Her demonic nature is gradually subdued with the recurring milk of human kindness. The fevers of her feral nature finally subside; the provocations of lust and anger, constant rivals in this pocket of hell no longer have a purchase on her soul. She spends many an hour kneeling by her bed, praying.

A traveler arrives at the tavern and is made aware of her condition. Under cover of night she is removed from the clutches of her former life and taken to a somewhat fortified retreat in the mountains beyond, where a rigorous purgatorial regime of labour and prayer fits the penitential expectations of the ragged arrivals. Sabrina is still absorbed in the images, her pride and disdain quite forgotten. When she sees this former self praying in a small bare cell of a room, she turns and whispers "I used to dream of this often as a child". I smile.

The retreat is run by some astral helpers whose previous life experience of the redemptive and restorative power of silence, prayer and contemplation have lead them to reconstruct an amalgam of several earthplane retreats for those emptied and exhausted by the devouring energies of hell. After several months of this secluded and calming routine, the former Sabrina asks how she can make use of this newfound serenity. The dull glow of her aura has brightened considerably and it is felt that she could now handle an elevation. She is conveyed by foot to the next subplane of the purgatories, where small villages are clustered by the edge of a forest and narrow minded, superstitious peasants work the barely arable land. A few guides move through the area as itinerant peddlers, always on the lookout for hearts ready to open. The former Sabrina is guided to a run down cottage, introduced as a widow and left to pursue the mandate of her request.

We watch as she treks her uphill battle amongst the gossip and tempers of her neighbours, most of whom are as far from heaven as they were on earth and to whom anger and resentment are the common fuel for the daily grind. Their lives being so similar to the earth state, they cannot believe they are dead, and when pressed, will use these commonalities as undeniable evidence of the lies of religion.

Having only her hunches of the heavenly state to go on, the former Sabrina lives and toils alongside her neighbours, her steady cheerfulness slowly warming some hearts. The expected seasons come and pass with the monotonous regularity the locals assume is their unalterable fate. As perhaps you will know, each and every sub-plane of the astral has its own landscape and ecosystem tailored to the needs of its inhabitants. Although in the populous summerland there is neither day nor night, summer nor winter, in the lower planes these are needed and useful for the growth of the stunted spirits seemingly stuck there.

A helper, disguised as a traveling shoe mender, intuits her frustration and asks if she would like to move on. Despite the flutter of romance, she can sense this would be the smart thing to do and quickly readies for her leave taking. Her mysterious departure, when noted at all, matches the villagers' superstitions about their state and shifts through their hushed gossip to dust.

She accompanies the shoe mender through several valleys as he plies his apparent trade, being taken by some as an apprentice and by others as a wife. Over a rugged mountain pass they struggle; miles of beautiful meadowland stretch before them, dotted with lakes no bigger than ponds. She knows she has arrived somewhere. Her guide points out a small town in the distance and soothes her with comforting predictions. There will be a place where she can rest in peace and gather strength, there will be souls she will find congenial. The remainder of their walk is passed in relative silence.

The town is well laid out according to the fashions of her day; the dwellings are humble yet beaming with pride, and the industry of artisans is everywhere in evidence. Folk seem cheerful and greet her with a smile. The place hums with the immanence of greater things. The shoe mender takes her to a larger home and introduces her to the master of the house. An upstairs room is soon provided. A comfortable bed and lovely view are her new best friends. She settles into the rhythm of the household, making friends with the other boarders, allowing herself to relax after prayers. She knows she has escaped damnation, struggled in purgatory and is now waiting. Her wait is not long. The shoe mender returns, takes her aside and explains the plan of evolution. It is, simply enough, perfection through effort, mostly repeated effort. She has, he tells her, two choices: move onward to the heaven worlds, where devotion to God will eventually dissolve all that she now knows of herself, or return to earth and try to accomplish the goals of her last life left untouched by her greed and ambition. While her love of god has increased tenfold she cannot bear the thought of such dissolution, and so the challenge of triumphing over old adversaries is taken up.

Recognizing the ambition fueling the piety, the guide smiles and assures her it will all soon be arranged. After his departure she thrills to the possibility of a second chance, and renews her prayers with vigour. I glance at Sabrina to see an exhaustion shading her excitement, and sense a short walk outside would be in order. I mentally freeze frame the motion and lead her gently out. Arm in arm we stroll as the energy of her concentration slackens. In a few moments I lead her back inside without resistance.

Rebirth without remerging with the Monad is only advisable under certain conditions, namely the possibility of fulfilling the original birth contract by a remorseful astral personality. Often that remorse does not last much beyond the new birth, but that is the chance we are willing to take. A rebirth, of course, can always be repeated, should the original contract be once again aborted. Now, if the former Sabrina had decided, before birth, to consciously experience the powerful pull of lust, greed and ambition, to round out the dark side experiences of her Monad, things would've been quite different. Those who consciously aid the Plan in its unfolding, by volunteering to be tempters, tricksters and destroyers, will always be recognized for their invaluable contribution to the strategic set-up of this free will system, which, of course, requires opposing players and endless opportunities to practice. But the run of the mill egotism, overweening pride and ruthless ambition usually results in the kind of lengthy purgatorial remorse you have just seen unfold.

A birth is arranged to a pious and childless couple in a mid size town in what would later become Germany. Through certain processes, the former Sabrina is put to sleep, moved upwards to the first of the formless energy planes, where her astral and mental bodies are more easily dissolved, and the bright spark of the causal body can be brought back down into the womb of the baker's wife.

Sabrina watches this seemingly magical process unfold. A difficult birth is followed by a more than happy childhood. A collage of domestic scenes swiftly move by. Church going figures strongly in the family's life and the young girl's eyes seem to shine with devotion. The progress to the convent is palpable. Once ensconced she takes to her labours and devotions with a gusto that only the young can generate. The community is served and god is worshipped unstintingly. But as might be expected, ego gradually reasserts its force, blending with the energies of ambition circulating the institution, and another former Sabrina gets her way no matter what. The love of god becomes so identified with love of self that the two cannot be separated. Spiritual pride consumes her like a cancer, and she passes into the sleep of anger, going about the place as a ghostly caretaker convinced of her indispensability. Decades pass as she instructs her successors in the fine art of managing god's house. Many see her during their devotions and sense she should be gone. But the years of what seem like dedication have allowed her to devise an angelic status for herself, one so convincing that even a variety of guides cannot dissuade her. Finally I show up as a figure from the Bible and command her presence in heaven. A sudden meekness makes the ruse worthwhile, and off we go to Christian heaven, where a rest cure is ordered and dutifully accepted.

Watching another former self sleeping, Sabrina turns to me and chirps, "Well what's next?" Well, as it turns out, a life as a simple shepherd in Greece, whose wife dies in childbirth, leaving him with a son who's the poisoned husband from before. The father cares for the young son and the grown son cares for the aging father. Some equilibrium is reached and some debts settled: Sabrina seems gratified. She allows herself to pass through the levels, shucking off all that she knows of herself, leaving only the divine spark to merge with the blissful fire of the Monad. In the time of no-time, the Monad modulates her energetic makeup to make room for more of the creative masculine, and basically, see what happens there. And so her next two excursions are military males, one caught by a press gang, the other fired by empire and adventure. The first dies young and so full of life angers that he immediately returns to more or less replicate his dilemma. Just about orders his guides to find him a well set naval family from which a career can be launched, and soon he is serving under Nelson and helping to defeat Napoleon. The sisterhood of nuns becomes the comradeship of sailors, and although his life is cut short by a cannonball, honor and courage have constructed a character which can balance ambition with service to an ideal and pride can be tamed with respect. That respect from his men follows him through to the astral, where a heaven for Imperial Britain is in full bloom.

Sabrina is enthralled with herself as a man, a noble and respected officer of the Royal Navy, now retired to the country estate he'd dreamed of at sea. Life is indeed sweet and he reclines in its rewards for a century or so, until guides do their job of convincing, and she returns as Sabrina in 1938 to the German peasants of five hundred years before, whose skills and empathy with farm animals have set them perfectly to be horse breeders of distinction, providing their offspring with the first class education they hunger for themselves, and just enough money to tempt Sabrina into the spoilt princess act she's so familiar with. The pre-birth plan involved using the post war economic boom to set herself up as a millionaire horse breeder with a burning desire to set up charitable foundations, so that her propensity to egotism and love of power could fuel ventures of a more altruistic nature. But alas, the pleasures of the horsey set were not to her liking and an early impetuous marriage slid her into quite another world, where old temptations were easily enflamed and lead to the woman and the scene you see now: Sabrina and I strolling about arm in arm, discussing the various ramifications of what she has just witnessed. That she is a changed woman is undeniable; what she chooses to do with that new knowledge is what interests me. For now she wishes to be returned to her home, where a much anticipated ball is to be prepared for.

A settling of accounts with poor poisoned Harry is much to be desired, but as he has already chosen rebirth in Washington State to pursue a long repressed love of forestry, a meeting can be arranged in only two ways: a sleeptime visit to the astral form of his new personality, twelve year old Eric, who will likely be more confused than fulfilled by the experience, or a conscious ascent to the Monad where the completed essence of Harry now dwells. Now *that* Harry, having successfully unhitched from his incarnate attachments, would be more than pleased to blend with Sabrina in a forgiveness merge; the question is, could I keep Sabrina conscious at that level of vibrational intensity long enough for the experience to sink in and take hold, or would she phase out, the meeting becoming a vaguely recalled dream to be discussed with the ladies of her astral community? I shall ponder the various possibilities as I prepare some other cases for similar advancement.

Higher Self Merge (1)

Friends and followers of the word, can you feel this moment as the archetype of all moments, a space in which time is suspended, and the sphere of interaction is blown by divine breath into a bubble of breathtaking proportions? Can you see your selves as present in this moment, as purified of the past as you are prescient of the future?

If you can, then please join me here, in this effortless vibration, resting in this ancient endless activity of energy as it surges and pulses in the seeming stillness. Join me as I watch the action unfold on the many levels of manifestation, the multitudes of actors pursuing their passions, all the stages for fear and desire, all the infinite complexities of karma, all the candidates trying to catch or cling to power, all the forms of life feeding on life. Join me here as I exult in the bliss of this knowingness, seeing the action as blessed in its blindness, seeing the shadows as short interruptions of the light. Join me in exuding this beautiful understanding, join me as I broadcast this effortless blending to my distant personalities, that their struggles may be illumined from time to time with a temporary grace.

HENRY AND ED AT THE
HEALING CENTER

There are many types of healing centers scattered throughout the spirit realms. While some are what you might call all-purpose rest homes for those recent arrivals who just need a comfy spot to hang their hats while they learn about all the options available, many of them cater to very specific ailments. And the closer they are to Earth, the more attuned they are to the ever changing psychic needs of newcomers.

Henry is rather proud that he helped set up one of these and wants to show you around. I think I'm invited too. He's the tour guide, I'm the transcriber. The specialty of the house, as it were, is bringing together the "victims" of aids and those who denied or condemned them.

Henry has me meet Ed, who tells me that he chased away his own son he hated homosexuality so much. An abomination unto the Lord, he called it then. Randall then took off for San Francisco and put himself through law school, where civil rights issues are now his specialty. He and his 'man' share a Victorian mansion they renovated themselves.   Though his daughter married within the faith and produced grandchildren to be proud of, Ed suffered a sudden heart attack and died an angry man at fifty-five, unable to reconcile his faith with his son's life. His wife quickly remarried a friend from their congregation who had recently lost his own wife to cancer. In the midst of his betrayal he tried to bless them, a hollow effort to begin with but he's gradually filling it in with sincerity.

Alone with his anger in a rural astral community not unlike his old, Ed soon joined a church of his liking. Finding themselves in a shabby heaven more like the catholic purgatory they'd heard about than any eternal reward worth having, they were a congregation in prayer and self-examination. For him, it was as if the sin he'd seen all around on earth had somehow settled within him in death. When he tried to share this with the others he'd been rejected, shunned and eventually disbarred. After all, how could the righteous, these lifelong believers, not be in heaven?

For a while he wandered the land, sleeping out in the open, wishing there were stars to gaze at. No stars, but no rain either, just a sort of watery light filtered by endless clouds. Bleak and rugged, kind of like how he always imagined Wyoming to be. Walking the wilderness, hills followed by plains and then more hills, was much more restful than he would've imagined, and the occasional travelers he came across seemed more intent on preserving their privacy than sharing the load. A country of roaming hermits, he decided. Some time after setting out, several days perhaps, he was not sure, he noticed that the wickedness within him seemed to be slowly leaking away. He began to watch it go: some of it looked like a bad case of righteousness and some of it just excess baggage.

He's telling me now that he doesn't care to go into the details, as his ability to be judgmental on the behavior of others still embarrasses him. I assure him that I understand completely, as will the readers of this book.

He came across a small settlement that looked for all the world like a frontier town from the old west. Not many folks about, and those who were eyed him warily. They were all dressed kinda old-fashioned like. Then he realized how strange he must've looked to them in his blue jeans, white trainers, Jesus t-shirt and neatly trimmed hair. For no reason he could think of he walked into a saloon and asked for a beer. The man behind the bar asked him if he was from the twentieth century. Of course he was, wasn't everyone? Well no, the folks hereabouts had all died about 150 years back, most of them in an Indian massacre, and had created a little time warp community.

He asked him if he was part of the community. Actually he wasn't, he just came by from time to time when the regular guy didn't show up. Ed then asked him how he knew. He replied that, Oh, he had his ways. Then two cowboy types came in, wanting drinks, and their conversation stopped. For a time all the talk was of horses, fence mending, and thinkin' about maybe ridin' up to

Canada for a bit. Ed listened and was eyed warily. Eventually he excused himself and went for a walk. The town looked just like he'd always thought a frontier town would look: like a movie set with all the actors and technicians at lunch. A woman peered at him from behind raggedy lace curtains: he smiled at her. She scowled.

He saw some golden leafed aspens set in tall grass ahead and thought to rest there a while. He lay there for maybe hours, considering all his strange experiences. None of it made much sense. He felt like he'd made some progress, emptying himself of all that pride and judgment and anger, but where did it leave him? In some cowboy town full of wacky ghosts who knew nothing of running water or electricity. He prayed for guidance. The bartender fellow showed up almost immediately and said "I'm the answer to your prayers". A bit nonplussed, but he had to laugh. Well that's a good start, the bartender said.

Randy took him back to the twentieth century, to a lovely little place by the Pacific ocean, which looked just the those wealthy enclaves north of Los Angeles. Not sure how they got there, as Randy had him close his eyes for the trip, which took all of about two seconds. But got there he did, and settling in was no problem. Folks seemed a mite friendlier, especially in the church Randy brought him to. Pastor said they didn't have no denomination, he was through with all that now, and only wanted to embody Christ's teachings on forgiveness and love. He guessed they were some kind of evangelicals but didn't push it. Didn't seem to matter anymore.

He wound up in Randy's spare bedroom, and pretty much had the run of the place as Randy was often away, 'visiting' as he put it. Ed guessed he had more bartender spots in time warp towns, but thought twice about asking. He figured there were some things you really didn't need to know. Well, he settled into town life, called Lovely-By-The-Sea by the way, and got just about as relaxed as he'd ever been, when Randy showed up out of the blue, and asked if he'd like to put in a few hours in a new nursing home nearby.

Ed couldn't see why not; in fact, he'd been kinda itchy for something to do and had been looking around a bit. Several things had come up but he hadn't been able to decide. Maybe this was just what he needed. Then Randy let him know the main purpose of the place: no doubt about it, he was shaken. He excused himself and took a walk along the beach. The surf seemed to soothe his sudden discomfort. Dead homosexuals, what were they doing here? Guess they had to go somewhere, and if this was hell, it was one heck of a nice hell. Maybe he should talk to his pastor. A young fella, but he did seem so assured and understanding.

So he left the beach, lovely as it was, thinking to return later, and headed for the church. He walked through town hoping that noone would ask him how he was, as they often did, because he really didn't know. This whole afterlife thing was really much more of a challenge that he'd thought. His pastor was quietly praying when he peeked past the door ajar. Embarrassed, he turned about and faced the other way, silently weighing his anxieties. The pastor continued praying. Feeling the bubbles of impatience rising, he moved away, fearing their itch would cause him to cough.

On the lawn outside he had an urge to remove his sandals and feel the grass on his feet. The tingle on his soles was almost electric. The sudden pleasure rooted him to the spot: maybe this *was* heaven. Pastor George's voice greeted him from behind. He turned to smile. After explaining his purpose, the pastor suggested they seat themselves by the rose garden, which they did. Ed told him of Randy's offer. George said he'd always abhorred the sin but not the sinner, but recently his prayer had hinted that was not good enough. Why, not five minutes ago, he prayed for greater understanding on the matter. Perhaps Randy's offer was just what they both needed. He asked if Ed would like to join him in prayer now.

They knelt together. Ed was not accustomed to such spontaneity in devotions, but he was willing to be flexible on the issue. At first he couldn't concentrate for the beautiful singing of birds nearby. Soon he was charmed right out of his purpose: why were they praying? For a moment he couldn't remember. Then it came back to him, and the answer seemed to be 'Yes, do my work in this world as in all others', or something very like that. When he opened his eyes George was already reseating himself.

Together they returned to Randy's cottage overlooking the sea. At first Randy didn't appear to be around, so they sat on the porch and gazed at the sky/sea horizon. Wasn't this a beautiful world, Ed commented. It sure was, replied George, not what he'd expected, but beautiful all the same. For a while he'd thought it some kind of counterfeit heaven, created by demons to slowly seduce those weak in faith, and redoubled his devotional efforts in the hopes of securing some kind of release, but then he saw how selfish that was. As a pastor he was responsible for whatever shreds of a flock he may have left, so if he were to get out of this counterfeit heaven it would have to be with those who chose to follow his guidance. Of course he thought about Moses, but no, he did not compare. That kind of pride was also a trap. You did what you felt called to do and trusted. Now that was something he had trouble with on Earth: trusting. Doubts plagued him. He thought the ministry would cure him, but it did not. His faith was challenged at every turn: schisms in the congregation, tension and harassment in the surrounding community, so many runaway girls returning pregnant and quite unrepentant. He'd blamed sex in pop music and the instant gratification consumerist culture of television but manfully targeting guilty parties did not dissolve the source of the temptation. Sounds good now, but it'd taken him years to get it on Earth, years when battling the enemy became the meaning of life.

Ed was just about to react when Randy suddenly showed up. Oh hi guys, how's it goin'? was his intro. Pleasantries aside, their decision was quickly communicated. Randy seemed pleased, and Ed thought, not surprised. He asked George if he would mind flying, as the rest home was slightly closer to the earth vibration. Ed assumed that the process would be similar to his transfer with Randy from the old western town. George seemed to hesitate as he looked out to sea; the seconds stretched. Randy said "Oh come on

George, you can trust me!" and George's chuckle broke the tension.

Soon they were standing in a circle holding hands. Randy advised them to shut their eyes else they'd get dizzy. Next thing they were standing on a lawn in front of an ultra modern structure which defied his ability to describe it. Artfully stacked cubes of tinted glass, stainless steel and some kind of stucco that looked so like various shades of scrambled eggs he felt like going up and taking a bite. And, now that he looked about, several strangely alluring sculptures, shining as if they were made of stainless steel, set among the bushes and flower gardens. It was the sort of thing he would have scowled at in his old life, and to be quite honest, he wasn't much more positive now. Still, he'd made a commitment: he wanted to see it through. Randy asked if they wanted to walk about and familiarize themselves with the place. Apparently the grounds were quite extensive. George looked at him and shrugged: what did he think? Ed thought plunging in right away was the best idea.

So in they went, Randy leading the way.

Ed tells me it didn't look like any kind of nursing home he'd ever seen, more like some very stylish small hotel, the kind of thing that was way too expensive for him and Carla when they were married. A lot of the tables, chairs and other furniture and decorations looked to him like antiques, not that he knew much about that sort of thing. They stopped at a lounge area, just steps from the entrance. Easy chairs, potted plants and the kind of space that made you feel at ease. Someone was playing piano somewhere, in a style Ed had never heard before, delicate rippling noises that made him think of the wind chimes on his porch back home. Since the seated men he could see actually seemed to be listening, unlike hotel lobbies where folk chatted away he assumed it was some kind of concert. Randy nodded to a nearby couch and they all slotted in. It was so pleasing he shut his eyes and drifted off.

Ed says that when the music stopped there was silence. When he looked around the musician was gone and those he could see seemed pleasantly dazed. Their nearest neighbor leaned out of this armchair and smiled an hello. He was really feeling better today, and how were they doing? They all introduced themselves. Randy explained the purpose of their visit. Richard said he was glad they had come: as far as he could see, they could use all the help they could get. A lot of the residents were still very sick. Ed asked where they were. Richard told him the really bad ones were in the south wing. He figured some of them wouldn't make it. He shrugged good-naturedly and stood up. Most of the audience were now standing and seemed to be heading out to stretch their legs; Richard nodded and moved off with them.

Randy asked the two of them if they were still okay with the project. The two of them nodded.

Randy put a hand on each of their shoulders and spoke quietly. 'What you must understand is that many of these men don't quite grasp that they are dead now. They passed in sleep or in coma and awoke here thinking that recovery was still possible. Some quietly figure they have passed but are so attached to their symptoms they think they have to get better here. This home caters to their expectations. And since being rejected by society's mainstream was part of their dis-ease, we're finding that a forgiving compassionate approach really helps in their recovery'.

Randy then lead them to the south wing, where they went from room to room being introduced. Ed spent some time with a man in his sixties, a man whose strained watery smile reminded him of his friend Grant by the side of his dying wife Dorothea, Grant who married his own Carla after he passed. Enrico was a tiny Latino perched in his bed like some bird, an IV attached to his arm, who chattered away about how nice this rest home was and how kind the staff. He asked Ed if he was one of the professional visitors. Ed replied that he was no professional, and was actually just learning the ropes. Enrico really missed his old friends, the few that stood by him that is, but he was happy for the new ones he'd made here. A nurse popped her head in the door and asked if everything was okay. Enrico gave her what Ed considered one of those fruity hand waves and said sure. Enrico then looked at him and asked if maybe he didn't like people like him.

Ed knew this was his moment of truth. He felt himself hesitate, then felt himself ashamed. He used to have a problem with men like Enrico, a big problem. A problem that had caused a big separation from his son. Your son is one of us, asked Enrico. Ed nodded. The he sat down and started to sob.

Enrico watched him sadly as he tried to rub the tears away. He'd seen a lot of men cry in his day, and lately they'd all been around his bed. And Ed has not forgotten what this kindly stranger, this maybe sick, probably dead man, said next: 'sometimes it is good to be sad'. Simple wisdom, of course, Ed realizes, but at the time it was just what he needed to hear. Unfortunately it's energy ejected him from the room, and a confusion of shame and anger chased him down the hall. Brushing by people with his head down, he found his way outside and sat on a bench behind some bushes, hopefully out of sight.

The next hour or so was a tortuous reliving of various episodes from his estranged son's childhood, those happy years when his sweet smile charmed rather than repelled him, the years he'd thrown away when Randall moved to San Francisco. No, it was not good to be sad, grief piled upon grief and buried you. Buried you in a hole of your own angers and anxieties. At one point, in the darkness of his closed eyes he even felt suddenly beside Randall as he fit together a picture frame in what was probably a basement workshop. That he couldn't stand: too much like his own back home. Randall never was much of a woodworker. So he opened his eyes again: no refuge there.

Maybe a stroll about the grounds would calm his troubled heart. They certainly were beautiful, and seemed to go on forever. It was as if this strange looking institution had been airlifted into place in the middle of some great swath of strangely undeveloped countryside. Like Virginia without the long fences of horse farms.

He wandered into a small wood and seemed to feel calmer somehow. He sat down with his back against a large beech and dared to close his eyes. This time a sort of snooze overtook him: he was asleep and yet not asleep. A halfway place thankfully without dreams. Or thoughts for that matter. As if he'd draped a curtain around his brain.

Some time later he walked out of the wood and rejoined the world around the odd-looking institution. He was admiring a rose garden when Randy and George walked up. George put an arm about his shoulder and calling him buddy, asked how he was doing.

They continued the conversation back at Randy's place, right there on the porch overlooking the sea, where they'd rocked before. Ed wants you to know it was one of those long, soul-searching talks that exhausts you rather then resolves anything. George's experience had been almost as upsetting, but he managed to maintain a veneer of civility. The man's father, a minister himself, had rejected him thoroughly and they hadn't so much as spoken in thirty years. George, in turn, had spoken of *his* father, who'd urged George into law school and had fought his sideways drift into divinity school. That gave them some common ground at least, some way to share and open up.

Ed wants you to know that he was touched not only by George's story, but in his honesty in telling it, something he couldn't, at that point, bring himself to do. Ed thinks it important that you get a sense of how difficult his path actually was. He doesn't want to drag you through the mud, but he does want you to understand just how far he was from the ideals he espoused. One thing that helped was journeying with Randy and Henry to an earthly hospice to gather some incoming souls.

Both he and George were asked if they'd care to learn the ropes. Ed now thinks this was one of Henry's little tricks, as either of them, if asked alone, might've turned down the opportunity, but standing together, neither had the nerve and just fell into line. After what Henry called 'sufficient preparation' they moved en masse to a hospice somewhere in the continental United States. Henry said not to bother trying to figure out where they were, for despite superficial regional differences, they were mostly much the same. Suffering, Henry thought, had brought the gay community together as a force to be reckoned with. Not since Stonewall had such solidarity been felt. Henry then made a little speech about the importance of suffering in man's evolution on earth that Ed thought was a bit much. The fact that he was wearing a teeshirt with the words 'Hey! Wanna be lead astray? I'm your man!' didn't help, but Randy took him aside and advised him of Henry's need to be outrageous and how it was best to just let it slide.

They appeared, the four of them, in a small neat bedroom. Ed immediately had the peculiar sensation that he could see through the walls onto the street outside. He felt kinda queasy and wondered why. The room was dim and quiet. A small bundle seemed to be under the covers and a woman sat close by, knitting. Ed had the strange notion that he could hear her thoughts. It was not an experience he enjoyed. There was altogether too much about being dead that did not sit right with him. All this snooping around for one thing.

Randy nudged him and nodded toward the bundle on the bed. An emaciated body, curled in sleep, rose slowly up from the blanketed bundle below. Much to his surprise, it hovered in mid-air. The woman knitting seemed not to notice. Randy and Henry moved towards the form, Randy taking what appeared to be the head and Henry the feet. Like orderlies in a hospital, but without the gurney, they maneuvered the horizontal form to his side of the room. In doing so Randy walked right through the bed, as if it was the most natural thing in the world. Ed and George were commandeered to take over the task at hand. Ed wound up with the feet of the pathetic shriveled refugee. Henry and Randy took each of them by the arm and told them to close their eyes while holding the body. When he opened his eyes a moment later they were standing in an empty bedroom much like the one in which he'd visited Enrico. Randy pulled back the covers on the bed and they placed the sleeping, or maybe in a coma, he couldn't tell, body on the sheets and tucked it in.

Ed asked Henry what the heck was going on. Henry told him that the man was indeed dead, but so unconscious that when he roused himself eventually, he wouldn't know where he was and would likely think he was just in another hospice, maybe just more upscale. Which, in one way, was true. The staff would cater to his expectations and let him come to the full realization of his new state in his own time. Many men arriving here imposed their subconscious notions of disease and recuperation periods onto their actually perfect astral bodies to such an extent that a fully fledged theatrical display of medical care was required to convince them slowly back to health. Thus the buildings, thus the grounds, thus the staff.

In response to Ed's question, Henry replied that Yes, it was a game, but a game played by actors who cared deeply for the recovery of their clients and who would go to any lengths to see that goal fulfilled.

Ed wants you to know that the longer he helped out at the hospice the more he came to understand the hold that beliefs can have on people, himself included, and the more he gives himself to the tasks at hand rather than brooding on past mistakes, the more he feels he's doing the work of spirit. And although he cannot accept Randy's talk of past lives and karma, he is unwilling to let their conflicting beliefs destroy their friendship. George, while still George, the pastor who's more passionate about prayer than anyone he's met, has taken to meeting with some Quakers from time to time, and says he finds their silent get-togethers very refreshing.

Higher Self Merge (2)

Outside of time, outside of space, outside of relevance to cultures, religions and political systems, I, and those like me, exist and have our beings. We are. We always have been and always will be. Our eternal selves are circumscribed only by god, that immutable infinite consciousness out of which all creation comes. Planets are our playgrounds, galaxies our outbacks. Options are innumerable, and we build what you might think of as our characters by exercising as many of them as we feel we can handle. Endless experiments in multiple incarnation. Multiple simultaneous incarnation.

The thrill of power, the gloom of oppression. The excitement of youth, the serenity of age. The pride of riches, the shame of poverty. Adventures in the food chain. Ignorance and intelligence. Instinct, intellect and intuition. All these and more are our game preserve. We send you out into them to collect experiences. You return to show us just how the varieties of fear and desire create their rigid systems of belief in which you inevitably settle or struggle, depending on the details and your perception of them.

Those of you who have followed the word thus far: we would like you to feel that you are us and can have the accumulated wisdom of our data banks at your fingertips, pretty much anytime you wish. Exhausted with the illusions of power, we feel you are ready to access even more. Only now, at this juncture of the planet's evolution and yours, such knowledge breeds the understanding smile of humility rather than the reckless laugh of indulgence.

Earth matter now vibrates with a greater degree of freedom than ever before: the physical plane is about to take wing. We trust that you are inspired to fly with it, knowing that the harmonizing of your so-called past sufferings enabled the slow severing of ancient bonds. You have paid for your enlightenment in full, friends! Please feel free to assume the new freedoms unfolding.

SECTION FIVE:

GORDON TAKES THE REINS

GETTING READY TO RETURN

Although it is, and always has been, quite possible to return to incarnation from the purgatories and hells of the lower astral realms, given sufficient determination and cunning on the part of those who fervently desire such a placement, the route most useful to the evolving soul is that which takes her from the immediate post-mortem state, through the required residence in the astral, mental and causal realms and the seemingly final and heavenly reunion with the higher self in that godly void so full of life, where the bliss of non-being somehow begets the itch for more life, and down she goes, through the planes, reacquiring the bodies activated by each level, until the society of the astral once again reasserts its grip and the pleasures of its paradise stall the forward thrust of the ego. Which is just as well, as the shock of the physical takes some getting used to. And that's why the valley, and places like it, were created: to give souls a place and a quietude, to contemplate the upcoming struggle.

The valley: a wooded vale complete with meandering river and meadows of wild flowers and dotted with cabins, cabins where the incoming soul can stage its own retreat to contemplate their incarnational gameplan as it were. Pressures, challenges, strategies. It has all been planned and discussed with guides, friends and advisors beforehand, but now, in the final run-up before merging with the fetus, souls stroll through their set-up as they stroll beside the river, and some of them were willing to talk with that aspect of Gordon who takes his nightly vacation from the sadness and stress of earth out here in the realms of light.

In this channeling, rather than receiving guidance from myself or others, Gordon has earlier projected his own thought forms from here, the astral, to the mental level of his own apartment, endowing them with enough staying power, as it were, to be downloaded into text, on what he tells me is a rainy afternoon in the spring of 2004. And so it is with the designation "I" that he continues.

I found a lovely young couple dangling their feet in the river and laughing about how on earth were they going to find one another, if he was going to be born in Arizona and she in Sweden. I informed them of my project and asked if they would like to share their stories. That got them laughing even more. Well then, they told me, I could be a witness to their foolishness. She, calling herself April for the present, had settled in the Scandinavian tribes several times now, and had carved out enough unfinished karma there that touching base anywhere else would be something of a waste. It was estimated that 25 years would be enough to sort things out there. Then it was off to the States for what would likely be sun & fun at first, but then develop in another direction entirely.

When I asked what that might be, she said to wait a minute. She closed her eyes and seemed to be thinking hard. *There*, she said, *that should do it*. A tall blonde fellow, looking very Scandinavian, appeared from nowhere, saying *You looking for me?* April introduced me to *Sven, Stephen, whatever you like, I've lost my attachment for now* and told him what I was up to. *That's right*, he went on, *entrepreneurial skills are my forte, but this time I'm giving most of the rewards away, and since April, bless her, willed me a sizable chunk way back in France five hundred years back, more than enough to pay for the travel and art studies in Florence, we plan to meet up in San Francisco, where she'll work at one of my art galleries and I shall unload a windfall which will help her start her own in Santa Fe or Sedona*. Then April chimed in, *That is, of course, if he doesn't get me pregnant first, which we have a bit of a track record for*. All three were laughing now.

The man seated beside her looked up at me: *As you can guess we've done the triangle thing a few times now, sometimes with disastrous results*. I nodded, having been there myself the odd time. April added quickly, *Oh, I can't complain, I've done my share of careless insemination. Ran off to sea once, leaving poor Phil here with child and not too many options*. With this she placed her arm around his shoulder and hugged him toward her. Phil looked up at me again. *Another time I condemned her as a fornicator and got her banned from the village. Course, as the local priest I'd been at her myself once or twice*. The blonde fellow added, *I was her younger brother then and too*

*afeared of my father's wrath to express myself, I did sneak off to the woods
with extra food from time to time. And then when the plague hit our
village, I snuck off to my witchy sister's lair and survived.*

I smiled conspiratorially: I think I get the picture. Phil had
always loved the desert and as a couple of what he called *kinda
ancient friends* had already settled in southern Arizona and were
keen to start a family he'd agreed to slot in as their son. A tiny fetus
was, even at that moment, beginning its growth, and although he'd
been reminded by guides just how to vaporize himself into it, he
wasn't quite ready to take up residence as yet. April's fetus was yet
to be conceived, she told me, but as her parents-to-be were happy
with their two boys, their desire for a daughter would soon
translate into action. *I've been told I can go forward in time to intersect
with the actual insemination, if I wish, but I think I'll just wait.* Forward
in time, I queried, well that was a new one on me. *That's nothing,*
Phil added, *there's a soul several cabins away, I'll show you where if
your like, who's going to go backwards in time about five hundred years
just to see how much modern knowledge he can bring through.* I said I'd
be thrilled to meet him and hear his plans. And I wasn't kidding:
this was just the sort of scoop I needed. I mean, how many afterlife
books have information on going backwards in time to be born?

I asked Sven if he was currently visiting his fetus. No, he was
holding off on that one. Hated that squished feeling, so claustro-
phobic. Preferred jumping in at the last minute. His companion
Gaia, I might be interested to know, was waiting a few earth years,
until Phil and April here met up and got hitched. Then she was
going to be their darling baby. They hadn't tried that combination
in many a century, and the last time had been traumatic to say the
least. April had died in childbirth and Phil's sister had brought her
up, a sister not overly inclined to attentive mothering and she'd
run away from home disguised as a boy, to go to sea, gotten
thrown overboard in her first storm, drowned, wandering the
earth as a lost soul for years before April's spirit had gotten her
attention. April grinned, *this time I'm gonna survive no matter what.*
She looked at Sven, asking, *and where is Gaia?* Practicing for her
piano recital apparently.

That's why we're so giddy, April went on, *the whole shebang falls apart if Phil and I miss each other. I supposed to see an ad for his yoga class, and as a stressed out business lady, feel it is just what I need. And I'm all set up to be some kind of all round alternative practitioner, if I don't get too hooked on flying. My dad to be is a lawyer with his own plane, and I can see I might get the bug. Plus I gotta work on this innate competitiveness. It's useful if you keep reins on it, but I've got a habit of letting it run wild and ruining things.*

Phil gave me directions to the cabin he mentioned. It was set back from the river a ways and was so shrouded in bushes I would've missed it had I not been made aware of its existence. The buildings themselves were charmingly rustic and I guessed comfortable in only the most basic of ways. A short, compact gentleman with a demeanor just this side of grave answered my knock. When I explained my purpose he invited me in. Seating us by a window he unfolded his purpose. In his last two lives he'd been an Istanbul merchant who dabbled in magical practices and an Egyptian engineer who'd discovered Sufism in middle age, making the kind of commitment to its regimen of self-development which souls at a certain stage must experience. Control of desires and marshalling of mental energies were the two things he'd learned from those lives. Now he wanted to go backwards about eight hundred years to the Mediterranean area, and likely Spain in particular, to experience the culture and surroundings which shaped the beginnings of the esoteric teachings now known as the Kabbalah. I let him continue under his assumption that I knew little or nothing about the magnitude of his aim and was little more than a sensation-seeking journalist. He had some blinders on and I didn't feel it was up to me to remove them. Perhaps their efficacy was intrinsic to the journey.

His father, he continued, was likely to be a North African merchant, a devout Muslim whose business regularly took him to Spain and interaction with both Jews and Christians, men of sciences and the arts as well as business. He wanted the kind of wide ranging experiences that such a cultural mélange would bring. Of course, in that epoch risks of illnesses and infections were high so the seeds of determination were being built into his character. The willpower would be balanced by compassion so that his almost natural urge to dominance would be tempered with waves of kindness which would, in theory anyway, wear away the walls of contempt established in other lives. And yes, he continued, anticipating my question, he was making a brave and perhaps ultimately foolish attempt, to bring through some twentieth century knowledge to that world. Quantum physics and cosmology, he smiled, gesturing to some books on table. He'd been advised by more than one guide not to, that it would inevitably lead, if not to madness then at least mockery by the intellectual establishment of the day. Perhaps only wisps of knowing would remain in a brain beset by the beliefs of the epoch and perhaps those wisps would be next to useless, but maybe, just maybe, he would meet up with one of the men who would dare to write down the oral wisdom of the centuries then congealing into the commentaries we know as Kabbalah and influence him with his sub-conscious inspirations. I had to admit it was a daring experiment, was it not? Becoming even a tiny part of cultural history seemed like a magnificent adventure to him.

I thanked him for his time and wished him well. He walked me to the door, his eyes twinkling. I strolled through the forested bliss, simultaneously intrigued with who I might find next and yet somehow carefree in that couldn't-care-less-about-anyone's-agenda kind of way. Don't ask me to explain it, please. It's probably something to do with being obe at night and not giving a shit you're having so much fun. Anarchy in heaven and all that.

I sat down with my back to a tree, always a telltale sign. Within seconds I had merged with its spirit, felt its joy in being and knew at least some of its ambitions. Then I shot up its spine and out into the astral space that could, if you want, be called sky. From there I spread out over the landscape like a fat cloud being flattened into a very thin pancake, with every square inch of that pancake conscious of the thoughts and desires of the astral beings below it.

I say conscious but maybe I'm exaggerating: not so much the details of every soul's aspirations, but a general impression of the collective semi-conscious. I say 'semi' as on the astral everything moves up a notch or two, so the collective unconscious of the physical plane becomes at least semi-conscious here. There's a vibrant, bustling kind of joy, an enthusiasm for adventure, a sense of game plans unfolding and lessons learned, the thrill of at least a glimpse or two of the plan of evolution, a seeing that it applies to spirit as well as form, and a kind of irrepressible giddiness at the interconnectedness of everything and everyone.

Of course, that's just this level, which is largely populated with souls about to return to incarnation; there are many others where conditions vary greatly from here. Having absorbed the vibe like an invisible sponge, I reassemble my intentions and move up a level or two, arriving at what the theosophists called the buddhic or intuitional plane. Here you just seem to know everything, or at least instantly understand each manifestation as it appears. All the painful contradictions of family and society seem very self evident here. The seemingly pointless turmoil of existence appears all too obviously simple. That whole experience of "well, of course!" Complex three-dimensional geometric structures float by and I somehow understand the method of their construction as I perceive them. Music multiplying from one tone, the ultimate scheme of self-replication. Fast forward movies of giant prehistoric mammals morphing into hawks and sparrows, of fish becoming hairy, leaning on rocks and trying to breathe, or various evolutionary strategies doomed to failure, the first being incest, the second man and beast, the third selective breeding based on rank and gender. Those almost unimaginably tough early days on the planet when various volunteers decided to decamp in favour of other planetary systems with an easier learning curve. And more. And more. All in about the time it would take to unwrap some chewing gum and pop it in your mouth.

But I digress. Fun is fun, but I do have a purpose, and that is to inform you of some of the rich variety in the realm of re-embodiment. So let us return to the valley of cabins and see who is ready. I reappear in a small meadow in the middle of the forest and approach two women lying in the long grass. Hello ladies I call, hoping to minimize the invasion of their privacy. Well, I need not have worried. Abby and Valerie, at least that is what they believe their mother has planned for them, are going to be identical twins. And it's not the first time either. Sure, they've been closely associated many times before. Probably a little too closely for comfort. Mother and daughter, father and son, business partners, deadly rivals, they've done a bit of everything actually. But almost always together. Last time they lived out their old age as spinster sisters in the mid eighteen hundreds in the cottage their dear father had bequeathed to them. Herbalists, gardeners, nature lovers, fulfilled in each other, they had no need for society. In fact rather disapproved of it.

This time their guides have convinced them to look outward instead of inward, and so, to that end, they have picked completely incompatible personality traits that should drive in a very early wedge, pushing them, hopefully, to either side of the continent, where they can face up to various challenges that they mutual devotion previously let them skip.

Yes, they've been in and out of the womb a few times now. Fetuses about five months on. Mother very pleased with the ultra-sound images. Dad a little panicky about money, already started a small college fund. They'll be born somewhere in the Hudson Valley, but a job opportunity will likely have them brought up near London, England, by the time of their teen years, affording them both a mixed up bringing and easy access to various European locales, where they can work off the remaining heat from any of several karmic links. Budapest, St. Petersburg, Oslo, and a variety of small towns throughout Belgium, Holland, Normandy, Tuscany and the Greek islands will get work out this time around.

Husbands and children are definitely on the map this time too, although a number of complicating factors have the opportunity to intervene. Abby has a habit of running from the steady routines of family for the thrills of foreign adventure, and with the help of, well, it looks like he's going to be called Eric this time, she'll have the chance to jump ship one more time, but hopefully will have the strength to resist and stay the course. Eric, apparently, has been shown a possible opportunity to bring his outlaw talents to the fore once again. By the time they're all adults, the successful regeneration of organs from stem cells should be a done deal, science wise, but resistance from various religious groups will restrict access in certain parts of the globe. He, or someone like him, will be instrumental in developing a climate controlled and virtually indestructible set of carrying cases, and their inherited Robin Hood qualities will give them the ingenuity and drive to over come the obstacles placed by repressive societies.

This set up, of course, combined with Eric's customary maverick allure, will prove almost irresistible to the kitchen clutching Abby, but resist is what she really wants and needs to do. Valerie laughs and says she'll believe it when she sees it. She, of course, will have no problem sticking to *her* domestic course. Stoking the home fires has rarely been a problem for her, at least in her female lives. Mothering and grandmothering are second nature by now, and this time her two boys have promised neither to run off to war or die in some other young man bravado schtick, as they have done several times before. *Biologist and gynecologist this time mom, they've promised*, she tells me, laughing.

I ask about parents. Yes, they're both well connected. My dad's been my uncle, brother and son, and once, in Roman times, I had a torrid affair with him, Abby informs. *That's until I got a witch to put a spell on her*, Valerie grins. *It worked too*, adds Abby, *I sickened, got ugly spots on my face and had to go to another witch to get the curse removed, and by the time I'd got all that done, he'd lost interest.*

Men! They squeal in unison.

Want to hear about our male lives, asks Valerie. *Sure*, says I.

Comrades, monks, soldiers, business rivals.

Don't forget the slaves, that's where we really bonded, pipes Abby.

Yeah, but it was so nasty and tough, replies Valerie.

That you hate to think about it, right?

I know but it's where we really started to care. When we were competing over the Greek senator, it was mostly pretense.

Competitive envy was our bonding agent. And let's face it, his wife always came first.

Not to mention his stupid kids!

We won't even get into the prehistoric stuff. Way too violent for a family audience. I engage Valerie as she says this, wondering what they might have to say about Atlantis and Lemuria. Nothing, as it turns out. Maybe they haven't checked it out. When one does a past life review, one only accesses what one is ready to handle. There is no pressure to take on more than you can handle. Guides understand the need to focus in on certain themes and areas without complicating matters unnecessarily. There's always 'time' for the forgotten civilizations, not to mention the other planetary systems from which earth seemed like fascinating learning opportunity, once upon a time.

Abby asks if *I'm* about to incarnate. I tell her no, I'm just out adventuring while sleeping in Canada, taking notes for a book I'm writing. About people being reborn? Well that's part of it. I outline the Eternal Life trilogy for them, and some other works that might spin off from its success, stuff dear old Gordon hasn't even begun to think about yet. They seem impressed and joke about reading it when they grow up. Their own Higher Self experience is still fresh, but it's the one thing they both assume they'll forget while incarnate. Well, that is one of my purposes. I wish souls to make and remember that connection to source. I want them, in the midst of all their earthly entanglements, to be able to embrace their divine connection.

Be still and know that you are god, says Abby.

Yes, I smile, that's it.

It was hard to end such a pleasant interaction, but I could feel old Gordon stirring in his predawn anxieties, the pull of the physical elemental pressuring the soul into another performance. And perhaps now is as good a time as any to tell you how astral Gordon feels about physical Gordon. I, emphasizing the figure of speech rather than the metaphysical conundrum, usually feel a combination of love, pity and amusement. This poor blinkered being who carries me through the rocky terrain of an earth day, with all its surging passions and conflicting thoughts, while I, in my way, remain a calm reservoir of wider perspectives and deeper inspirations, deserves all my sympathy for enduring what can only be a very tough haul, while I take a nightly vacation in the lands of next-to-no gravity and lottsa laughs and light. That life of three rather shadowy dimensions is a psychic prison he endures for my, and others', benefit, and my gratefulness, although innate, is perhaps not as often expressed as it should be.

So now I dive down the ever-darkening ladder which ends in his rested body about to blunder its way through another set of society's demands. But for the purposes of this chapter let us not dwell on his lack of solid connection to my activities, but swiftly move on to the next thought form deposited by moi for his (and your) delectation.

Next night I speed out of the physical and up to this valley of soul preparation, this time at the other end. Just to see what I find, or what finds me. Close to the bank and easily in earshot of some hypnotizing rapids I find another youngish woman. She smiles at my approach and seems glad of the interruption. Yes, she tells me, she's readying for return.

Remorse seems to be her main motive, and self-righteousness her main hurdle. A dedicated rebel last timeout, one who was completely convinced of the rightness of her personal crusade, she started out insolent in a very teenager-ish way, going against every one of her mother's wishes on principle, and then developed into an over-the-top party and adventure girl, using her looks to charm her way into the pocketbooks of various wealthy young men. The political and social activism of her parents came to seem as indulgent to her as the carefree jaunts and endless parties of her circle did to them. The hurling of accusations became something of a blood sport.

I ask if perhaps she died drunk in a speeding car. Yes, she smiles, of course, how did I guess? My turn to smile. But what a way to go, flying through the air at 100 mph or more, and then finding she could continue flying, that there was no end to it, not if you wanted to keep going. What a blast! Zooming about the

Rockies first, over snowy peaks and down into mountain valleys. Zipping right up to tiny flowers, breathing in the scent, and then zipping off. Flying down the west coast highways, one gorgeous view after another. Is this how angels live, she wondered, in the midst of all the fun. No wonder they loved being angels, who wouldn't?

Drifting slowly through the giant redwoods, like a tourist in a strange city. Were they more like buildings or people? She couldn't tell, but they had this gravity thing they did that was just amazing. Then over to the desert, that incredibly bright emptiness which now seemed so much more welcoming than when you were dying of the heat. Heat and cold, she noticed that it didn't seem to matter any more. Couldn't figure out why, then gave up trying. Then out to the coast, somewhere near Big Sur, she wasn't sure even though she'd been there plenty. Flying over the water, coming closer and closer to the waves but not quite touching. Exhilarating? You bet. Then into the water, wow, that was something else, holding your breath for what seemed like ages then realizing you didn't have to, then so busy looking at the fish that you forgot to breath. Some fish seemed curious, others fearful, and others didn't seem to care. And wasn't that just like people anyway, she challenged me to agree. I laughed and said sure.

The underwater thing seemed to go on forever, but the colours were so rich and pure and some of the fish so weird lookin' she hardly noticed time passing. God knows how long she was down there. Suddenly she thought of her buds Mark and David down in Key West: hadn't seen them in a while. Holy shit, next thing she knew she was there, in their kitchen, watching David make a salad. Seconds later she found Mark on the back porch grooming Wilber, their pet schnauzer. Oh those darlings, she just loved them both to death! She charged back into the kitchen and hugged David. Major squeeze and kiss but he didn't seem to notice. She stuck her tongue in his ear and wiggled it about. She bent down and bit the right cheek of his ass, just like she'd done at their anniversary party last year. Nothing worked. She bit him again, this time harder. Mark walked in with Wilbur draped over his shoulder.

David laughed and walked to the fridge, pulling out some white wine and bread. She hopped up onto the counter top and watched them share a light supper. God they were happy together! Why could she never finds that with a partner?

Her relationships were always so,…so speedy. Like everything happened so fast she could barely keep up. Exciting for sure, but crazy making too. Tumbling from one situation to another. But she never crashed as her mother had predicted. She always kept on top of things. Like her t-shirt said, *good girls go to heaven but bad girls go everywhere*. Yeah, wasn't that the truth.

I nodded, grinning, charmed as much as agreeing. I've never been averse to chatterboxes, so I asked what happened next. Well, she'd gotten a bit gloomy over the relationship thing and sat out dinner on their garden swing. Then for about the first time in a century she thought about Jane. Her mother Jane. The lawyer's wife. Yup, her dad was a lawyer and her mum was a lawyer's wife. You know, all that do-gooder shit, inner city this and Sandanista that. Pictures of Commandante Marcos in the bathroom. Guilty liberals to the max. Always pissing their money away on causes. They were *made* for a Woody Allen movie.

So, next thing she knows, and that means like a nanosecond, she's standing behind Jane as she types up a letter or something on her laptop. Still serious sensible Jane, pencil stuck in her ear. She hasn't been home in months, maybe more. And the last visit was the usual screaming match.

You slut.

You fake.

You'll die of aids.

It's better than dying of boredom.

Your father's ashamed of you.

I don't care.

And so on, with doors slamming.

That's her mother there: Jane with the graying hair, Jane with the crow's feet, Jane with the goddamn sensible shoes. Jane with the James Taylor and Sting cd's. Jane with the family farmhouse in rural Pennsylvania rented to deserving strangers. Jane the devoted maid to Clayton, the lawyer on a mission from god.

She looks and she looks and she looks. That could easily have been her life if she'd stayed. They told her she could do as she pleased once she finished college. Well, college finished her. At least the classes did. The social life was the best though. Why couldn't they have given her a degree in partying?

Like turning a page in Vanity Fair there was her dorm room with Cindy asleep. Was Cindy still there chugging degrees? The room was dim, but the door opened and light from the hall flooded in, and she and Brad giggled their way in. She watched them slither under the covers and begin to make out before it hit her: she was watching herself from two years before! And Brad was the guy she was driving with before she was flying through the air! Suddenly she was looking down on a car wreck. Deep in a ravine, smashed to bits. Nothing she really wanted to look at.

I don't blame you, came a voice from behind. *It sure is ugly. And the worst part is, nobody knows but you and me.* She turned her head, and there beside her, floating in midair, was the dweebiest looking guy you could imagine. Like Kevin Spacey on downers. Lousy downers. Course he turned out to be her guide. Been after her for days but she wouldn't pay attention. Too busy having fun as usual. He'd snagged Brad right away, and left him off at some party palace in heaven.

Now he wanted to know where I wanted to go. Like I really cared just then. But maybe he had a point. Grooving on a car wreck was pretty retarded, so why not watch another movie? Dweeby as he was, I figured he knew his way around. And boy, was I right on that one! Smartest move I ever made. Took me around in style, just the way I like it. Little princess on a pumpkin.

And I thought life on Earth was weird! I'm telling you the stuff that goes on in the afterlife has got it beat hands down. Kev, as I right away called him, showed me al the winners, from perved out pedophiles, all maxed out from the endless orgy upstairs to greedhead suits bogeyed from the thrills of trading, to ski bums in ski bum heaven and surfers in surf heaven, and man, just endless churches and temples with people praying and praising like mad, and miles of cross legged monks as silent as I don't know what, and natch, all the totally trapped suburbanites as righteously bored as ever. And about a million more things, give or take a couple, and then over to where Brad was partying.

Couldn't believe that one, he was already movin' in on another chick, the usual slutty blonde with no bra he always goes for the minute my back is turned. He's like Oh Hi Jen! Isn't this great? Absolutely the best drinks right over there! And he's pointing to some bar in the corner after he gives me this hug like I'm his sister or something. And we just drove across the continent together! Men, I've never had much luck. Jane says I make myself too available, which is pretty funny as she does just about everything for old Clay but wipe his ass, and I wouldn't be surprised if she did that once in a while. Then this blonde bimbo bounces over, kinda licks my cheek and says, *Chill out Jen you're not the only one here that's dead.* I gave her a look and squeezed my way to the bar, where a cool looking guy passed me a long blue drink, which I'll have to admit tasted damn fine.

Kev appeared outta nowhere beside me and asked if I didn't want something a bit more fun to wear. I said sure and wondered what he was gonna do about it. Well, first thing was, get this, he changes into a chick! Kinda tall sultry model type, full lipped, great legs, eyes on fire. How'd he do that, you ask. Secret, won't tell me, but he did it, I was right there. Next he takes me by the hand, leads me to some back room with couches and stuff, and I'm wondering is this all a big come on, some lesbo seducto hype? Don't laugh, it's happened before. I've had chicks hustle me all over. You know, like bored with their dates and they'll ask, do you wanna come home with me, like now? Anyway, not so. He asks what kind of outfit I'd like. I name something and suddenly I'm wearing it. Bonus! Then it's back to the dance floor for some fun. Got this really sharp designer job that seems to make my knees disappear and my tits like the perfect little pears I'd always wanted.

So talk about party palaces! This was the best. Cool people, great music by these totally unknown bands from god knows where, hot guys galore, all of them pushing for a chance. God I musta been there for like the whole weekend. And no sleep! And no crash and burn either. That was when I really knew I was in heaven. So I'm chillin' with this guy Greg who's tellin' me all about his inoperative tumour. Right between the eyes, kinda latchin' on to his brain. Painful as shit. For months. Radiation, chemo, don't do shit. Morphine to glide you into the big fuzzy. Friends scared off. Mother suicidal, dad drinkin' more than ever. Sister mad that's he's pissin' on her parade. And he was just kinda gettin' started on the bass with some band, workin' up some obscure Replacements and Cure stuff.

So he's talkin' away about this and that, like missin' his music and some of his friends, and slowly we kinda relax into each other's arms and next thing I know we're asleep. How do I know we're asleep? Well that's like one of the seventy-three totally totally wild things you can do here, mostly without trying. What's it like? Like a webcam between your eyes, facing in. I was, like, watching my own dreams, and then watching Greg's. I mean, like totally too weird, no? And holy macaroni, the stuff that was going on in there! Like all that really out there stuff you catch yourself thinkin' about and quickly try to forget in case you get caught and charged? Wow, let's just not go there, okay?

So-oo we wake up refreshed and go for a walk somewheres. Down the street there's this park, which looks kinda nice so we go in. Haven't seen Kev for a bit, but I know he's around someplace. There's a set of swings in the sandpit and we head for them. Kinda fun, hadn't done it in years. Am I boring you?

I tell her no, it's all fascinating and just what I need for my book. People on earth want to know what being about-to-be-born feels like. And they're gonna use her as the example? You and a bunch of others, I reply. Well shit, why didn't I say, she knows all about that.

After she and Greg find their apartment in a small condo building near the party palace and this really cool Cineplex, way better than the ones on earth but with a lot of the same movies, where there's like, a lot of people their age with similar interests, there's a honeymoon period where they are like so-oo happy, but eventually he gets this serious hard-on for his ex who's still alive and he finds out how to go and see her when she's like, asleep, and as far as she's concerned that's cheating, so she asks him to move out, which like a good mama's boy he does. Just after that she meets Kev in the park and he says her old buds Mark and David are thinking of hooking up with a couple of their gay girlfriends and making babies, one for each couple. The plans are all set, so would Jasmine like to maybe, you know, be their kid?

Wow, what a cool idea! She's like, into it, now! Mark and David are so cool, she can hardly wait to join the family. Doesn't even care what sex, though Kev thinks it'd be better if she was a girl, as she still has a bunch of girl issues to work through. She asks Kev if he's gonna be, like, her angel dude. He says sure, he'll be around when she needs him, and he'll even look like Kevin Spacey if she wants.

So that kinda brings it all up to date. Jasmine's been snooping around the test tube lab place, watching the surgical procedure for putting the fetuses in. Really gross actually, but well, Kev said it might be a good idea. He's also helped her with slipping into the womb and trying it on for size. Which sounds kinda funny but is not that far off. Life sure is weird, weirder than Jasmine ever figured, even in her stoniest moments, and here she is about to be a baby again. They're thinkin' of calling her Audrey, which is okay by her. She's always loved gay culture and Mark and David are just the best people ever. Kev wants her to make plans, career type plans, so she's decided to be a kind of roaming teacher of little kids, someone who moves about America, showing kids how not to get caught in their parents traps, how to be free spirits and have lottsa fun. Kev thinks it's a great idea, and frankly, given Jasmine's track record, so do I.

I thank her for the input, and give her the hug I think she's been wanting all along. She promises to read my book when she grows up, and, as I'm walking away, says she'll teach it to all her kids, wherever. With Jasmine still ringing in my ears, as it were, I moved through some tangled bush, enjoying every leaf and twig rubbing and scratching their way into my heart, and trying not to get too involved with the various trees around, as their energies are so appealing to me I could so easily get distracted. *Another time perhaps,* I say to a couple as I pass.

In case you are wondering, I am not consciously aware of who I am visiting next. It is not pre-planned in any way that I'm aware of. This valley, and other installations both like and unlike it, are so full of souls getting set for the human race that there's bound to be a fascinating variety of circumstances, motives and plans playing out. And as I get caught up in the energy of the process I vibrate to the electric thrill of souls and their growth. As we say on earth, the excitement is infectious. If I'm not careful I'll get carried away and forget my purpose. Now we can't have that can we? After all, there's a trilogy to finish. We'll save the big fun till later.

I notice a cottage up ahead and a woman standing at the door, saying goodbye by the looks of things. She hears my thought somehow and turns to say, *Let's hope it's only au revoir.* I laugh and apologize for interrupting. A head pops out, a man with a friendly grin, who assures me it's no problem. They're about to part but agree to let me in on their story after I share my project. Basically, Bill's going back into his genetic family as his own grandson. Used to be this sort of thing was almost unheard of, at least in the so-called western countries, but the call to karma cleansing to catch up with the ascension process has folk hopping on the back to earth express every few minutes these days. He thanks Amelia for talking him into it. She's been dead for decades, and probably should be back on the treadmill herself, but Bill's need is definitely greater. They both chuckle at this, eyes warm and sharing.

Bill declares Amelia his little rescue angel and she blushes as she smiles. She found him in hippie stoner paradise, still addicted to grass, and slowly convinced him that straight society was not quite so maddeningly straight after all. A grower and dealer from the old school, which meant only the herb and sacrament and absolutely no weapons, he'd toked himself over the line one night on the way home and crashed his truck on a muddy s-bend in the woods, leaving Angie and the two girls to fend for themselves.

Saddened beyond belief at his own stupidity, he'd hung around for months, trying to help any way he could. Eventually one day, while dish washing strangely enough, Angie always seemed to get quite spaced doing that, she turned to him, looked him in what he surmised would be eyes for her and said *My sweet William, go on now, we're gonna do just fine.* Just then a guide he'd never noticed before, put a hand on his shoulder, and the rest is history, more or less.

The guide took him away from the house, away from the beautiful forested land he'd loved so much to a quiet place, where, apparently, options would be laid out and choices made. I recognized the m.o. but kept my mouth shut. Bill asked for astral Hawaii and was told no problem. The guide, a kind of genderless but soulful person who seemed to have had Bill's well being front and center, flew him there. It was one of the most thrilling moments of his life. No, the most thrilling. He'd floated about a bit since the crash, but the idea of flying across the world was an absolute mind blower at the time.

They came to rest on the beach. Bill looked about him: well, it sure wasn't Oregon. An ocean breeze rippled through his hair and then kind of rippled through him. The guide said *Oh, that's one of the many pleasures of this level, Bill, and there are many more.* He asked if he/she could feel his thoughts. The answer was Yes, but only when it was appropriate. He was not to imagine his privacy constantly invaded. Well, that was a relief, Bill tried to joke. Not that he really cared, his guide, whatever the name, and face it he was scared to ask, seemed so trustworthy it hardly seemed an issue.

With the info that there were many options available on the island, both communities and solo paths, Bill was left there on the beach to fend for himself, not that there was actually much fending to do, as it turned out. After a long walk and a swim he came across some folks playing frisbee and setting up for a clambake. It took him about two minutes to feel right at home. A mile or so inland they'd reproduced a reasonable facsimile of a northern California commune that a couple of them had helped found.

He settled in there with an ease that surprised him. The pain of regrets that had held him to his old home and family now seemed manageable. Others in the community had similar stories and sharing certainly lessened the load. Finally he allowed himself to relax. The astral conditions that he's now so familiar with revealed themselves one by one, delighting him with their seemingly miraculous pleasures. Creating things with his mind made him happier than he could've ever imagined. Tiny and intricate sculptures of various media, some existent and some pure invention, soon became his specialty.

On a social visit to a nearby community, Amelia had expressed a warm interest in his work, suggesting that they might enjoy a trip to a fine arts center she knew of. And here Amelia gives forth with a big smile. No, she was not some kind of secret guide of Bill's. Her only agenda was to help souls expand their horizons. As I knew, many of the mid-astral levels held souls in a kind of paradisiacal thrall. She was good at sensing the vague yearnings of such souls. *She showed me a few options, I don't mind telling you*, says Bill, smiling. One of those options was college courses. Just to start with languages and anthropology had always intrigued him. Another was the kind of wandering astral plane social work Amelia specialized in. He apprenticed there for a bit, and enjoyed it. But something was nagging away at him, no matter how much he got involved in things. Amelia asked if he missed his girls. He'd had to admit it was still a sore point.

They went down for a visit. Angie had let Dan, one of their old friends, move in. Christy, his oldest, didn't like the new regime and had bolted for Seattle and some kind of free school thing run by rich idealists. The communal house she shared with a rotating crew of budding musicians and actors reminded him of several he'd stopped over in during his youth. She seemed to be hooking up quite regularly with one boy there, and as far as they could tell, having oodles of unprotected sex.

One night, after several tries, they were able to make contact as she floated up out of her sleeping body, thanks to a little energy trick Amelia made use of. Christy was overcome with excitement and broke down in his arms. After calming her down he explained as best he could what had happened to him since the crash. Christy said it wasn't so much that she didn't like Dan, he was nice enough, but she just needed her freedom. Angie had been driving her crazy. Amelia asked if she thought she might be pregnant. Christy asked what business it was of hers. Bill said he was worried. *Why don't you be the baby then, you can keep an eye on me*, was Christy's immediate response. Everybody laughed. Christy added that Shawn wasn't likely to hang around if she announced she was gonna have a baby, so likely as not they'd wind up back at mom's. Bill looked at Amelia, who sensed his thought. It could just work. Especially if Christy was not tempted by abortion. Christy scowled and said never.

And the moral of the story is, I say smirking. *That careless teenage sex isn't always without a purpose*, smiles Bill, once a rebellious product of the Eisenhower years and soon to be a babe of the new millenium. And in case I was wondering, Amelia adds, she's not letting love drag her back into incarnation. At least not yet. With this she gives Bill the sweetest smile, just like the puppy in love she doesn't want to be. There's lots of learning to do in spirit, that's one thing she's learned. So many just live out their astral paradise lives pleasantly, never expanding much beyond their ethnic and educational boundaries, only to return to earth as a part of reincarnational wave of linked souls. It seemed so sheep-like to her.

I asked if the experiential training she was giving herself now might make her a much better sheep dog. Fortunately she saw the funny side of it and chuckled *maybe*. Bill was reminded of his favourite childhood pet, a happy go lucky mongrel called Ranger, who he'd rediscovered living with his grandparents in a delightful replica of their small Kansas town. He hadn't mentioned going back to them, didn't think they'd approve. He did plan, however, on giving his own parents a shock when Christy went for visits, by chatting about his last life as Bill. He and Amelia had been working on the memory keys for a while now. He figured Angie wouldn't have problem with it at all, as she'd been reading popular books on the subject when they were married. Books, Amelia added, that Bill refused to touch. *Yup, can't deny it*, Bill agrees, hanging his head in shame.

I thanked them for their time and wished Bill all the best for his project. They said *ditto* for mine. I made a formal bow on my way out, causing them both to laugh. I wandered away from their cottage, wondering what to do next. Various astral resort activities suggested themselves, one or two particular favorites of mine, but project completion beckoned. I checked back with base: old Gordon was snoozing away, his usual 3:45 groove. Bless his gypsy soul, I smirked; back to the valley.

But I'm thinking, or some unknown agency is giving me thoughts to think: even here not all questions are answered. The thought is this: not all souls take advantage of this valley to consider the upcoming challenges carefully. Some stay right where they are, in family homes and familiar surroundings. The type of people who don't like their comfort zone challenged. I'd rather you took that as an observation than a criticism.

So let's go to a spacious, gracious sub-division, astral style, that I know of. Lotta souls here who lived in cramped inner city neighborhoods for decades, working hard and dying young of all the usual 20th century stress diseases. They just love the big rooms and sprawling gardens here; they feel like kings. And unless you can show them a radical improvement in physical plane conditions, they ain't budgin' an inch. And why should they? They paid taxes all their life and worked their butts off. This is the life. Swimming pools without maintenance and barbeques any time you please. In fact, I'm called over to one as I pass. Let's just say I'm known hereabouts.

Husband, wife, grandparents, all sitting about the picnic table munching away merrily, beers at hand. A well tended, if perhaps predictable garden, complete with melodious fountain, compliments their cheer. I am offered a beer and a seat. What have I been up to, where have my wanderings taken me to this time? And while I was away did I discover the meaning of life? I join their smiles and chuckles. I'm used to such good-natured ribbing and take it in my stride. I've been all over, I tell them, all the levels between heaven and hell. And did I have converse with the angels? Well, I didn't exactly chat with them, but I did feel their presence. And the best I can do to describe it is delicately seductive singing. One of the ladies sighs that is how she always imagined it to be. The guys twinkle as they chuckle.

Then the talk turns to children still on earth, their lives and jobs and young ones. Families like these keep pretty close tabs. The conversation is not much different that it would be if we were in San Francisco and the kids in Vermont. The blood-is-thicker-than-water metaphor carries through here for many souls. The men play golf and the women bridge. Leisure fueled gardening consumes the rest of their time.

I am told that a nearby amateur musician has heard about my period piece cottage concerts and is intrigued. A piano teacher who charms the locals with his renditions of the Ellington repertoire, it is whispered that he has a secret love of Bach. I recall meeting him once before but need to be reminded where his house is. Apparently he lives alone, while waiting for his wife on earth to tire of her vibrant sunset years.

My feet lead me in the right direction, and soon I am at his door, knocking. Unless one is dropping in on old friends, such earthly etiquettes are still observed. I interrupt Don watching a master chef video. He invites me in by calling from the kitchen. I grab a stool and watch. Always wanted to cook and never had the time, he smiles. And I know what you're going to say, why don't I just think of it, but that's cheating. I want to do it right. He seems to remember me better than I remember him. Not sure why. Maybe I look like someone else.

While he's mixing and blending he tells me he's heard I hold musical soirees at my cottage cum recital hall. I throw up hands: it's all true, I admit it. Is it a members-only situation, he asks. Heck no, anyone can come. That is, anyone who knows about it. Ah, there is a membership then! No, not quite, I just don't advertise particularly. Word of mouth then, is it? Well, not exactly, more spirit of thought. What did I mean by that? Well, I send out thought forms of upcoming events and the folk who tune in wind up coming. Did he just have to think about what he wanted then? Yes, I grin, think Mozart and you'll get Mozart, probably in several locations at once as he's so popular. Think Satie played on exotic percussion and you've got my next soiree, and who knows maybe several more.

What I do not mention is that these concerts are on the upper astral, what Monroe and his acolytes call focus 27, whose vibrations might be a bit on the intense side for him. But the principle of telepathic discovery has been communicated and that's probably enough for now. I ask about his wife on earth. Jeannie's still teaching fitness and yoga to seniors Tuesdays and Thursdays and leading a women's chorus on Saturdays. Eighty-four and still going strong. He doesn't know how she does it. Son Robert just got a promotion and daughter Sarah just gave birth to her third. He's so happy for them both, and since he's been shown how to visit and return safely he's no longer miserable without them. All he wants is to share the joys of this paradise with them. The sailing alone is worth the price of admission. How could anywhere be lovelier than this?

I hold my tongue and ask for a couple of snacks for the road. I am given a couple of bacon wrapped scallops dipped in some sticky rice concoction and leave with a wave. With those visits as a reminder let me return to the valley.

Are some of you wondering just how this valley came into being? Was it always here, the forest, the meadow grasses, the sparkling meandering river? It's been here for many a century Earth time, as have many, if not perhaps all, astral landscapes. But it has been modeled for its current usage. Modeled by creative beings who specialize in creating areas suitable for souls undergoing certain types of experiences. As the pursuit and perfection of the individuated physical plane experience matured, producing souls who were not only eager for rebirth but bruised enough to understand that preparation and focus could help bring about the desired results, the value of such areas, so congenial to the contemplation of plans and interactive schedules, became apparent.

How the varieties of astral landscapes evolved to suit the ever bifurcating needs of the human spirit is as complex as any other aspect of life on the planes of form. But I sense that although some of this book's readership is curious about such background details now is not the time for such a revealing of the science of god. Another time perhaps. What does seem to be pressing is Gordon's urge to sketch in some of the life of an angel. That's physical plane Gordon, the one in front of the laptop in the coffee shop, down there in springtime Ontario, the scales of his winter armor slowly falling off, not me, the astral version, so full of the joys of limitless spirit that societies and seasons seem but harmless passing fads in the ever shifting shadow play of eternity.

It's not as though I haven't encountered and blended with angelic beings myself, but it's important the physical plane Gordon has some genuine input into this project, so I shall save the rest of this chapter till later. Some of you will likely be thinking by now that this is not a book by Gordon, but a book by a committee of Gordons, two of whom are called Henry and Higher Self. In this you would not be far off the mark.

AN ANGELIC INTERVENTION

I do not care to have a name, dear readers, but I do enjoy casting a dusty rose light wherever I go, so, if names can help you feel my being then by all means consider me dusty rose. I have not been a human being, in the way that you think of humans as beings, for many a year of your time. After many centuries of challenges, ambitions, defeats, joys and sufferings I saw that forgiveness and love were the only paths to follow, and that all else was but vanity and dark deceit. Contrary to popular notions of sainthood and so on, I was not a humble cobbler or devout nun at the time of my sudden illumination, but a minor aristocrat, with lands and tenants to consider. Not to mention a wife who did not share my new understanding. A wife who took my sudden spurts of kindness and compassion to be unmistakable signs of a brain unraveling, perhaps from syphilis. It took me some time to convince her otherwise, and she spent the next few years eyeing me warily, waiting for what she thought was inevitable. When she suddenly passed, from one of the many mysterious ailments which beset our times, I was left with two devoted daughters, neither of whom seemed inclined to doubt my sanity, but whose piety caused them to see a man whose good works would perhaps outweigh his apparent lack of proper devotion in the final reckoning.

As for my transition from normal to extraordinary consciousness, I seemed to suddenly see a light around everyone and everything. A multihued light which seemed to sparkle with endless shifts and changes. It took some effort not to be continuously dazzled. I often had to retire to my bedroom for what some assumed was prayer and others a restorative drink. I also seemed to hear everyone's thoughts in my head before they spoke, revealing all manner of anxiety and deceit. With all your modern freedom of thought and education, you will doubtless recognize these gifts as clairaudience and clairvoyance. In my day, I just took them as gifts of god, and although not an excessively religious man, I spent many hours pondering the best use of my new talents.

Seeing all the world, and not just people, all aglow like this, caused me to feel I'd been ushered into some new garden of eden, yet why I was there alone, as it were, puzzled me. I sought out the assistance of men and women reputed to be wise and heard that I had gained a state many spent their whole lives trying to achieve. I was also warned to keep very quiet about my talents, as there would be those who would urge me to use them in the service of unclean ambitions. Suffice to say I accepted this wise counsel into my heart, and the remainder of my days were spent in a quiet glory, indulging the errant and wishful children who chattered and fluttered about me.

A resonant serenity guided my days right up to my death and beyond. I hovered about my estates until convinced that my eldest daughter and her husband could manage without me. Then an angelic being guided me heavenwards. All aspects of the life eternal intrigued and charmed me. I dwelt in paradise with ease; the love of all beings became my second nature. The state of my aura was noted by those who take an interest in such things, those beings that some of you think of as saints and prophets, and others ascended masters. I participated in meditations, joined in discussions, and generally, as you say down there, brought up to speed on my status and options. I asked and was given the knowledge necessary to transform my path from that of the human to that of the angelic.

I wanted to inspire those on earth with the love that inspired me. And so I moved about the planet, performing. Let me reveal some of my recreations to you.

I loved to hover over church and chapel, blessing the congregation and all its activities, infusing them with the rosy light which was the essence of my being. Depending on the sincerity of their devotion and the relative strength of their doubt, some would feel my presence, others wonder if it was at all possible, and others silently scoff. As you might expect this love was spread to all, evenly. It was, of course, not my willingness to give but their ability to receive which determined their experience. And, needless to say, what they did, if anything, with their divine infusion, was entirely a choice in which I never interfered. Angels don't feel those kinds of urges. We want to love and inspire indiscriminately, like sun, like rain. We are not on anyone's side, regardless of speeches and slogans you may hear to the contrary. Humans who assume some kind of loyalty, based on religion, ethnicity or righteous cause, do so in error. We aim to inspire all who exist in the squalor of need, but the weak interpret our energy as a message to free themselves from oppression, while the strong succumb to the righteousness of their power. It is the nature of such situations that many conflicting truths are held to be self-evident. Only a few on either side see through the illusion of their viewpoint to the shared humanity inherent in any situation.

We accept the resulting excesses of self-righteousness as something of inevitability in our line of work.The growth of man's soul energies is destined to overcome the territorial vanities of the ego that we know from our own experience. It is only a matter of how long the bulk of humanity takes to follow our lead. Many currently incarnate are set to graduate from both nationalistic fervour and karmic necessity; we'll see how many remain to assume the bodhisattva mantle on one or other of the planes. I wouldn't say we're taking bets on it, but interest here is certainly high.

I also take a great interest in politicians, bureaucrats and financiers, for they too have their higher natures which need nurturing. While I would not take credit for any particular policy shift or implementation, I would assure you that while many decisions of an altruistic nature mask darker agendas, some are indeed genuine attempts to solve tensions and difficulties, attempts to aid societies evolve towards the kind of perfection they dream about. Although it may seem to many of you who keep a close eye on current events that progress is at best abysmally slow, if not almost entirely an illusion sustained by false hope on the part of the terminally naïve, I would like to suggest to your cynical ears that despite innumerable setbacks, the human drama on earth is evolving to higher and higher expressions. Unlike the noble failure of the exciting Atlantis experiment, man's moral nature has grown to a point where he can see that his life is an integral part of the overall ecological balance and that he must harmonize with himself as well as harmonize with the earth. Although there are some who would laugh at this woolly minded optimism, it is our observation that the technology currently in development will not only resolve many, if not all, of man's environmental issues, but will go a long way to clearing up most of man's outstanding medical problems. Much of the karma being worked out in this manner has been dealt with, so of course, the need for such harsh instruction will diminish. And those who blindly continue to stumble into the behavior patterns which produce these old diseases will have an ever increasing army of energy healers to resort to, as the vibrational atmosphere of the physical plane allows more and more of these *indigo children* to freely express themselves.

Those of you who feel wise and well informed will point to those agents of anger, greed and vengeance who, claiming godly sanction, seek to impose their hallowed traditions on others, and feel, not surprisingly, civilization as we know under serious threat. Well, be assured that such agents are well monitored, not only by the brotherhood to which I belong, but also some of our extraterrestrial friends.

Triggering systems have, can, and will be, shut down, if deemed necessary. Pirated nuclear technology which switches hands in back room deals, can be tracked and rendered ineffective by similar agency. This course of action, seemingly interfering with the free will of the dark operatives, is permitted, as the vast majority of humans now desire a world free of war and the destruction wrought by the overweening pride of the powerful, and are willing to lay down their worn out prejudices to achieve it. Especially in the cities, many thousands of ancient enemies now dwell happily as neighbors. Permitted by what or whom, you ask. Permitted by our interpretation of the divine will, which we see as composed of the majority of humans who wish peace and harmony with both friends and strangers, and who, more and more, feel the planet as one family. Are not the dark operatives also making their interpretation of the divine will? Yes, but they are vastly outnumbered. The majority now desire otherwise. At the times of the so-called great wars, the majority, swayed by old gods of ethnic pride and nationalism, craved victory by deadly force. That harsh lesson, for which so many lambs had to be sacrificed, has now been learned. The returning souls wear the wisdom of their scars and are ready to move onward, where greater challenges await.

Perhaps my argument and subsequent assurance will not be taken seriously. To those who would so choose I would say this: why do you opt to believe the dire warnings of the doom sayers rather than embrace the optimistic visions of a more enlightened world? You will have your reasons, no doubt good ones by your own estimation, but I would remind you that you are making a choice, a choice with significant ramifications. The fact that you are even glancing at this book bodes well. Whether you chose to ponder deeply on the options is another story. But believe me, this is not a veiled threat of the old kind, where hellish punishments await those who do not heed the appointed gospel, it is a call to consciousness, a tip of the hat to those who suspect that they are intimately involved with the moment to moment construction of the consensus reality, a timely reminder that choices are being supplied by the second.

BACK TO THE VALLEY

Astral Gordon here again: physical Gordon feels satisfied with his contribution and is happy to be the secretary again. Another ramble through the woods, another cottage coming up. Someone is sitting outside on a small stool, smoking and looking quite relaxed. It's Ben, who hasn't been dead all that long but is fascinated about the way the world is changing so rapidly. Rumor has it, he tells me, that the more advanced nations will have personalized flying machines by, oh, 2035, maybe even earlier, and as a former bush pilot, he can't wait to get down there and participate in the research and development. It'll be anti-gravity drives of some sort, he's sure, likely back-engineered from the crashed alien vehicles, though the government will still deny it. The techie stuff might even be smuggled out by some maverick engineers willing to sacrifice their rights of citizenship for the freeing of humanity from the fuel sources hogtied by the multi-national corporations.

Ben was a bit of a daredevil last time around; the thrill of the risk outweighed almost everything else, including career and family. After he passed, a stupid miscalculation at high speed, his wife lost no time in remarrying a real estate broker. He can see now the boring, predictable life she moved into was just what she and the kids needed. And a ready made family totally fit the bill for Richard, a career nut who'd banked his pile and was looking for a challenging midlife project. His eldest boy, perhaps reacting to his insecure childhood, had turned into a play-it-safe hard working carpenter, hiding out in Montana and driving a battered old pick up. But Ben had found an ideal parenting situation nearby and was planning on playing hooky from the family as quick as possible to spike up Brian's bachelor life. That's why he was smoking really, getting back into the earth habits, psyching up for addiction. No, guides had not sanctioned this move, in fact they thought it crazy and almost certainly doomed to, if not failure, then at least some serious karma accumulation. The upcoming parents, for starters, would be scarred by his proposed wildness and early flight. What mother really wants her son running off at such an early age? Ben was ready to take that chance.

I neither condemned nor condoned his plan, settling for thanking him for his forthrightness and said I'd be on my way. He asked if I was about to go back myself. I surprised him by saying I was actually there right now, just sleeping. Oh, you're one of those, he laughed, I should have guessed. Would I remember any of this in the morning? I outlined the transmission process we were using and some of the basic training mechanisms. You know, splitting consciousness but remaining in sympathy, and that kind of thing. He nodded, thinking it over. Would he be able to do that next time? If he really wanted; add it to his to-do list, just like anything else he was trying to plant a seed for. He said he'd think about it.

A pleasant little stroll and I was at the next place. A woman dressed like a man, or maybe a very attractive man, seemed to be changing form as I approached. Stabilized upon seeing me. We excused ourselves simultaneously, laughing. Erica might well end up as Eric, so she was just trying it on for size. She and her upcoming twin hadn't quite decided which fetus to take. Samantha was so unsure about being a guy she might still drop out. Most of her male lives had been testosterone driven disasters, and although her guides had given her lots of pointers, she was far from sure any of them would work with her track record. Erica, on the other hand, could probably benefit from being a guy this time.

She was very keen to become something of a wandering Buddhist pastor. Laugh I might, she smirked, but face it, somebody had to start the trend. Christ teaching's had to be blended with the Buddha's, no doubt about it, as far as she was concerned. Certain parts of the Americas could really benefit form such a blend. Sure, she'd been a minister before, but not much of one. In England about two hundred years back. A failure at law, he'd been given a "living" by a friend of the family and he spent the rest of his days moldering away in the growing boredom of utter conventionality. Deferment to local nobility, laws of the church and precise devotion to ritual were his life. More toeing the line than anything else.

This time would be different. Oh, she'd take her training seriously, but then she'd take it on the road. Guys could do that sort of thing, couldn't they? This with a smirk. I asked her how she enjoyed her time in spirit. She looked at me as if I was bonkers. Yeah okay, I answered, you loved it but it's time to get back to work, right? Yes, I did get that right. The playground downstairs was where all the action was. It was all very well living out the full tilt fun fantasies of the astral, but the testing ground was elsewhere. Any fool could be a minor deity for the day here, but taking your act down below and seeing what was left after the strip search of family and society, that was the real challenge. Lots of folk up here liked to pretend otherwise, but you really had to take your act on the road, didn't you? That I couldn't disagree with. When had she last been down there?

Not that long actually. 1930's sunny California. You know, the Midwest farm girl turned film star then script girl and general studio fetch-it. Coulda been better, but she had her fun. Died drunk in a car wreck after a party. Hung around her sister's family back home for a bit, watching the kids grow. Thought that was all she could do. Why would heaven take a floozie like her? Enjoyed it really. Slept in the attic, joined in just about everything. Got used to nobody speaking to her. Like anything else in life, you take what you get dished out. Well, that life at least. Her nephew signed for Korea and didn't last six months. Pretty surprised to see her waiting for him. She showed him the few tricks she'd figured out, but he soon got antsy. Wanted a wife and family. She'd never thought of going back herself, not for a second. Didn't realize you could. Jimmy was keen though, and she wound up helping him. They found another farm family in the same county, one with too many kids and not enough money. She already knew you could slip in and out of people, but taking that step further and moving into a womb had never crossed her mind. Some other earthbounds were hot to take up residence, but she figured out how to hold them off while Ed made his move. Didn't work the first few times. Sex didn't always make babies and he couldn't hang on without a fetus to attach to. The mother to be was not to his liking, but he was determined to make a splash. Watching the couple have sex was getting really boring. She'd never done it in her own sister's household, but now she gotten caught up in the whole mission aspect of it. Anyway, Ed finally gets his fetus and he's off to the races. She's sitting in the garden, wondering what the heck to do next, wondering just what other weird possibilities there were, when this guy walks right up to her out of nowhere and introduces himself. He's a guide of course, and in no time he's got her out of there and into one of the entry levels. And the rest is history, including having Ed die in childhood of some weird viral infection and come to spirit, where guess who gets to adopt him and bring him up properly? Hey, every story has a happy ending, doncha know.

I'm asked about my lives and say it's rather a long story. This girl's got time, she tells me. About three days later I get to the end, the end of what I know that is. That includes going back to physical Gordon two mornings in a row and taking up the stories when I get back next night. Erica takes it all in stride, as if she's heard it all before, which I'm sure she hasn't. I'm like a mini society all to myself, she tells me. Well, that's the point of merging with Higher Self: giving up your little self gives you so much more, not to mention a whole whack of great stories to tell. And it's the stories which tantalize her really, not the massive intelligence gathering effort they represent. Which is, I like to think, why story-telling is the archetypal art form on earth, because, at the deepest level, all the fear, adventure and desire of all our journeys into the valleys of the shadow of death are captured within them. We can thrill without all the sweat and anxiety. Every life we live is a story sprung to action, with shades of tragedy and comedy activating every moment. But that's just my take on it. What's yours?

I left Erica without ever seeing Samantha. Erica put out a call a few times, but we never got a response. Samantha liked her privacy, and that was something she was going to have to compromise on in any twin situation. Erica said she'd enjoy a go at the twin thing, but was really ready for anything. I applauded her up-for-it attitude and said it would surely stand her in good stead in the struggles ahead. She was doing cartwheels and laughing as I walked away.

All this astral Gordon stuff has perked up old physical Gordon to once again track down his nightly adventures. The <u>OBE AT NIGHT</u> sequence, besides permanently blowing all his parameters for such concepts as individuality and experience, intrigued the heck out of him. He's been telling himself for months that he ought to try it again. I think he's just about plucked up the nerve. But first a word from our sponsor.

Higher Self Merge (3)
Welcome, Gordon and all his readers, to my consciousness! Let me open the non-existent gates to your questing searchlights and welcome you to see exactly what it is you need to see at this stage of your unfoldment. And not only to see it, but to allow yourself to believe in it. You often say down there that seeing is believing, but as often as not a great veil of doubt falls across your vision and you opt to deny what you fervently desire. That denial is of course, your choice, and cannot be taken from you no matter how frustrated your monads and guides may pretend themselves to be. Although the raising of consciousness from the blind obedience of matter, through all the wrenching grades of struggle against the forces which oppress the blooming of the divine seed, to the clear light of understanding that dissolves all limitations in a loving embrace, is the primary goal of purposive incarnation on this planet, each unit of individualized consciousness is entitled to conduct its own search in its own good time, and if that means wasting numerous opportunities for growth, then so be it: the system was designed with such false starts and dead ends in mind.

And who designed the system? Well, a number of monads, fresh from the challenges of other planetary systems, decided that perhaps a more difficult series of tests was due. No, we were not bored, but we did feel an urge to upgrade the challenges to a new level of complexity. An almost hopelessly dense planetary atmosphere combined with a crushing level of gravity and the deepest separation of the individual from the divine yet devised, was envisaged, to be truthful, in the midst of much merriment. Gordon has recalled some segments of this experience in meditation, and has, to this day, great difficulty in telling anyone that he was there at the inception. Much too grand a claim, he worries, and who would believe him anyway? He hardly believes it himself. Still the notion sticks like unwanted remnants of glue, and he hopes that the readers' accumulating respect for the Higher Self consciousness will allow this embarrassing moment to pass in relative ease.

Well, this monad will take responsibility for that act of creation, and will add that an uncounted number of others merged to focus on the creative expansion. Many of you now reading belonged to one or other of the Higher Selves thus involved, and will likely be equally surprised to hear that you were in on the ground floor, as it were. You're also in on the completion, be it far in the so-called future. I encourage you all to explore these possibilities in your daily meditations. Those of you who explore non-physically might work on projecting to both these bookends of the planetary game and watch your experiences evolve with practice.

For those of you who worry that "god" has not so far been accorded status in this giant creative act, let me add that the god consciousness does not "act" creatively or otherwise. "God" does not **do**, "God" **is**. "God" is all creation (not to mention all the destruction going on within creation). Minor deities like monads and angels, and a host of others are the creative ones. We do the building and renovating, but "god" supplies the plans and the endless energy. As you might have heard elsewhere, the divine energy is downloaded in a series of steps so that all beings, no matter how distant from their self-realization, can experience some small aspect of it. Variations of the creative game are played by all, on every level: from the sub-atomic to the galactic, being endlessly re-creates. An aggressive virus attaches to a host, a powerful woman has cream added to her coffee, a state renegotiates a treaty, devas process a tornado, the agents of light and dark beam the opposing energies to war zones, an angel with aids dies as a baby and ascends with new knowledge, souls incarnate into strife torn societies, planets sing their precise mathematics as a sun maintains a mysterious status quo, "God" embraces all of creation.

BLOSSOMING IN THE DARK

Gordon here. That is, the one on earth, the last in line, the one to whom much is given in the hopes that he'll remember, in the midst of all his duties and commitments, the expanded states which seem like impossible magic to the so far unawakened.

I've suspected for some months that a return to obe@night memories, and now that a year has passed and another close family member completed their transition, it seems very appropriate. Within the last hour I have contacted my mother N. Consumed by a rapidly expanding cancer less than one week ago, I found her seated in the gardens of an astral plane nursing home, a small blanket about her shoulders, and my long deceased, and now very pleased, father at her side. Obviously overwhelmed by her experiences and the small crowd of family members and friends who had likely only recently visited, she still managed to overcome her surprise to greet me just as she did in the nursing home in which she spent her last several months on earth. In typical family fashion we chatted about all sorts of details likely uninteresting to others. I told her about the upcoming memorial service/wake planned by my sister, and although she said she didn't know if she was ready for that, I suspect she'll put in an appearance, and she asked me to pass on various regrets about her behavior in those last days.

Such meetings are a great relief, even to me, accustomed to such interactions. That another transition has been seamlessly effected leaves me quietly pleased, for so many souls get stuck somewhere and often require, as you now know, a great deal of prising out. Over the years I had grown so used to worrying about my ailing mother, that the habit is now a regular part of my day. I caught myself doing it about three times today and had to tell myself, "You don't have to do that anymore". I feel layer upon layer of care drifting up and away from my shoulders. It's a liberation of sorts, a welcome liberation. One that is likely designed to lead us into the following accounts of soul travel, where the *I* that is hidden in *me* goes forth in secret to *blossom in the dark*.

Thursday eve: listen to fff27, attempt meditation after very busy workday: make contact with father and travel to his house to talk, but can't stay focused, too sleepy. Try again tomorrow.

On morning before Nancy's memorial/wake, I contact my father and her, using fff27 as vehicle. Find them in astral plane nursing home, in Nancy's room, with her sitting up in bed, looking quite perky and refreshed and my father sitting back, relaxed, beside her. Nancy not quite so overwhelmed by it all, but still, well, surprised to see me, as if everything that happens from moment to moment is a surprise. She says she's feeling much better now, almost back to normal. I say that is great and ask if she's going to move to father's place. She wonders how I know about it, and my answer leads into my various astral travels and experiences, which she heard about while still alive, but didn't ever seem to really believe. I'm still her oddball son and she indulges me in that role. She trusts me not to lie, but how I know all these things is still very much a mystery to her. Father understands, but keeps wisely quiet in his armchair. I mention today's memorial/wake and ask if they're planning on coming by. I can feel my father wishing I hadn't asked this, but he says nothing. Nancy seems to still have outstanding issues with my sister and irritations surface. I always suspected that their quarrels had a past life source, but have yet to investigate. That my sister has modified my mother's cremation related plans seems yet another example to my mother of her daughter's insolence. I try to fence mend and mention a plan I have for the future, one I hope will go some way to pleasing her original formulation.

Mother asks how she and my father will get there. Knowing that my father already understands the principals of astral travel I tell her that it's all a matter of thought, and that father will show her. We socialize a little more, questions about this and that, and then I make my goodbyes. I can tell father wishes I hadn't been so explicit in my questions, but he says nothing in reproach. Having departed their consensus reality I have some "time" left in my meditation and choose to go for a short cottage visit. I wander around, embracing it all, and still amazed that some aspect of me created it. Just before moving on, I think of Henry and he appears. Like all our get-togethers, it's an affectionate reunion, full of charm and wit. He tells me he's been spending a lot of "time" in the formless state recently and is really enjoying it. Obviously it's transcendentally blissful, almost beyond bliss really, a state so refined he thinks I wouldn't quite grasp it, even if he could find words to explain it. As if to illustrate, his last few words to me are uttered alternately in form and out of it, i.e. every second word he disappears. It's another of his comedy acts and reminds me, as I think it is intended to do, of an occasion about two years back, when Frank DeMarco asked me to add some more material to the five year old text of A First Hand Account and on putting out the request, Henry showed up to answer by changing form with every word, i.e. from old crone to sexy young thing to muscular youth to doddery old man to rambunctious teenager and so on. Back then he was feeling that he might as well be everybody, and now he feels that he might as well be nobody. Point taken, Henry. I ask if I'll be piloting the project from now on. Apparently so: it's my baby now.

Thursday July 1/04
At Hidden Valley house, after several days of stress, a relaxing evening leads to an early bed. Next evening, Thursday, Canada Day, a long day of relaxing activities such as walks and lazy lunches, find time for a hemi-sync meditation. Methodology is the same as before. At f27 enter cottage and touch screen. Back at Hidden Valley house rise out of body and watch as S. reads quietly. A peaceful scene, one that settles my somewhat anguished heart. Knowing that S. will be quite some time there, I move out of the house and explore the Valley's nighttime life. Flying about, resting on tree branches, feeling the play of the night breezes and the tree spirits radiating their various greetings. Up and down the sizable valley, feeling quite wonderful.

Then up to my mother's astral plane nursing home, where she's sitting up in bed and looking much better; almost her old feisty self. We embrace and chatter away: the sort of family stuff, riven with humor and tension, which I think is common to all. I ask if she came to the memorial get-together. Yes, she says, my father took her. There's a comfort in reverting to their old roles that I sense in this remark. I suspect she enjoyed the experience more than she's willing to admit. Her reluctance is perhaps the result of misplaced pride: I let it pass. By this point my father has shown up, perhaps knowing that I was here. I ask about her extended family, most of whom have been here in spirit for quite some "time". I tease her, saying, I told you they'd be here and you didn't believe me did you? She asks how I knew anyway, I think meaning, how was I so sure. I explain my out of body stuff one more time. She listens, smiling, but refuses to take it in, just like she did on earth really. Always was reluctant to learn anything from her kids: pride again. I stay a bit longer then make my goodbyes to them both. Shoot straight back to earth plane, splitting into two Gordons: one who roams the streets and buildings of the western GTA (greater Toronto area), looking for challenges, and another who heads to the Hidden Valley house and S's sleeping body, from which she rises quickly. There we assume horizontal positions, rotating around each other slowly and sensually with an abandon that we have definitely become accustomed to. The other Gordon roams the streets and gardens of Burlington and Oakville, looking for, but not finding, lost or confused souls. A break atop the hill overlooking Oakville harbor, watching the lake and feeling the life, becomes the moment where the moment is all. The clouds, the sky, the water, the life nearby asleep.

Gordon and S. sit on their back porch and thrill to the nighttime life. How splendid it all is. Then they float up through the trees, flying about, gliding in joyful ease. The other Gordon moves around some more, and finds himself around the crematorium at which his mother's body was recently consumed. He'd forgotten it was this close. Perhaps some souls are hanging about. He finds a few "sleepers", that is astrals who have followed their dead bodies to burial/cremation in a state akin to sleep, coming to some dull consciousness later, meeting each other and sharing their ignorance. Before revealing himself, he shines a white light on them from a distance, a light designed to bring them more life without undue shock. Let's push that vibration up a bit, shall we? Then he approaches them with offers of assistance. Much backing off and disbelief results. They're not sure what has happened, but they're not about to believe his version. Issues of trust and doubt rise to cloud his good intentions. Well, no surprise there, par for the course really. He'll be back in a couple of days and it'll be worthiness issues. Gordon and S. have retired, satisfied, to their sleeping bodies, and he sees no reason not to join them. He bids his clients-to-be goodnight, leaving them to quibble over the mystery of his appearance.

Wednesday July 9, 9:30am:
Following usual methodology, using fff27 tape, I quickly exit body and split into three. (1) Goes straight to Higher Self, where blending and merging with other selves seems to be the order of the day; (2) Moves to father's long established home, on hill overlooking valleys in all directions, where mother is visiting, perhaps for first time; (3) Goes out into space, with intent to travel to Saturn, but becomes somewhat overwhelmed with the enormous emptiness 'out there' and returns, abashed, to the more familiar territory of the moon, where the friendly proximity of Earth ensures a comfort zone unavailable elsewhere.

(1) Seems intent on merging with various past life 'selves', the king, the philosopher, the courtesan, the Druid, the Egyptian priest, the Chinese merchant, and so on, the purpose being an absorption of life experiences (actions, thoughts, emotions), learning the roles much as an actor would, so that they become second nature. I sense this has been practiced before, and will be again, perhaps often, so that the evocation of HS consciousness, slated for volume three, will be as complete as possible. I wonder if I shall have to devote many entire meditations to 'bringing back' the bulk of this material, or if it will spring fully formed from some part of my mind as I sit at the computer.

(2) Is the devoted and caring son, fulfilling his family commit-

ments. I can see that my mother, though quite thrilled to be reunited with my father, feels only ready to visit his home for what seems to her like a couple of hours, before returning to her astral nursing home. Also I sense that my father's hilltop house, although just perfect for his needs at this stage, is a bit remote and scary to her, and she would likely be much more comfortable in one of the pretty compact bungalows, complete with conventional flower garden and a Scottish sense of community that the bulk of her extended family live in quite happily. Although charmed and pleased by my visit, my mother still seems amazed that I can do what I do.

(3) After walking about the moon surface, feeling more than a little ashamed, Gordon 3 remembers his physical plane friend J.F., now resident in Kentucky, and his request for energetic assistance in helping his body to not reject his two year old transplanted heart. Apparently, the drugs that had blanketed this problem now have to be reduced to save his deteriorating kidneys. A couple of physical plane meditation sessions have already been devoted to this end, but an obe visit seems like a good idea. He finds J.F. out of his sleeping body and convinces him some energy work would be helpful. J.F. in his astral body feels much more ambivalent about his deterioration that physical J.F. Perhaps a decade of heart problems would leave me much the same. Expressing the intent to fuse the cell structures of the 'new' heart to the 'old' body, we blend into one astral being and project yet another type of light down into his sleeping frame.

These three Gordons remerge about five-thirty am and slot themselves into the dense vehicle driven to dopeyness by endless brain induced dreams, the kind of swamp I find myself struggling up through on many mornings.

Thursday July 10; 9:00pm:
Usual methodology and tape: Out of body with singleminded desire to see S. Off to her home then recall that she's staying at Hidden Valley house miles away. Oops, how could I forget that? Arriving after following major roads there I remember that her

sister is staying over. S. out of body without much prompting from me, and although sister is astrally asleep in replica of physical position, we tiptoe around her and out of room. Much intimacy and fun flying about later, we decide to go visit my mother. S. only slightly reluctant. Mother in nursing home room, sitting by window admiring the view. Greets S. very much as she did on earth. Quite pleased I brought her by; chuffed as we used to say in the old country. Of course we play into her expectations of gradual recovery, as everyone does here. The newly dead are indulged like children at Christmas, with much the same justifications. Mother still quite nonplussed about how the living actually manage to visit, and I can see her concentrating on enjoying the experience despite the mystery of it all. I feel as though I could explain the body-for-each-plane concept (physical, astral, mental, buddhic, monadic etc.) ten times over and it still wouldn't really sink in. Lots of souls are like that here, why do I expect my mother will be different? Hope based on snobbery? I wonder.

Later we visit S's father J., who is still staying at the home of friends' N. and P., as he was this time last year. Of course a year here does not seem anything like a year to them. Perhaps because of several recent lucid dreams concerning J., S. seems more overjoyed than overwhelmed, and the entire visit has a very natural, at-ease quality to it. I chat a bit with N. and P., who still seem utterly charmed with their post-mortem existence. This country home, surrounded by forest and lake, is the perfect comfort zone for them: a heaven as cozy as an old slipper.

After this we return to Hidden Valley house, where S. seems quite glad to rejoin her sleeping body. I fly about a bit, looking for recent casualties, but finding none, gladly retreat homeward, where sleep awaits to pacify my restless energy with the opiate of its gravity.

Wednesday July 14; 9:15am:
Usual methodology, usual tape: It would seem that once again, after exiting the physical just after midnight, "I" split into three spheres of light, and "my' initial activity was a giddy game of

aerial chase through the tree tops of Streetsville. Much silly fun, of course, was had by all. Next up was three parallel journeys: (1) travels to the deva hovering over Lake Ontario/Toronto, (2) moves to find the Maitreya, and (3) ventures city-wide, cruising for retrieval cases.

(1) Merges with said deva, feeling as much of the life-currents passing through that, well let's face it, exalted being, who blesses not only all our desire based activity by stepping down all available cosmic energies for our instinctual and intuitive use, but overlights all the aerial and marine life of the great lake who is the energetic counterweight to all our anxious strivings. It can be immensely thrilling experience, almost overwhelming for the first-timer, but I see that I have upgraded my abilities to absorb with months of practice and am now sufficiently harmonized with the situation to live the experience without falling off the edge, as it were. Like a well loved website, taking many hits per minute, and registering all energetic impulses as equally valid and useful in supporting, sustaining and balancing the whole, this dedicated soul thrives on the constant exchange of energies in her system. Sure, there's no sexuality here, but the caring, nurturing qualities of the overlighting seems to suggest the 'eternal-maternal to me'. The experience is somehow simultaneously static and yet overflowing with ceaseless movement. The balancing act she provides seems to be no more than a willingness to fully embrace all the energetic impulses saturating her oasis of love, however wildly contradictory they may be. Love and devotion may, at first, seem to make strange bedfellows with anger and raw ambition, but her embrace boils them all down in the soup of her heart, a very nourishing brew for all passing meditators, I might add.

(2) Moves to the Maitreya with unassuming ease and is cordially greeted by that level of his being which appears as a man conversant with men. This is the level which has many similar aspects 'doing the rounds', as it were, of needy humanity, making appearances where useful and appropriate, in a variety of cultural contexts, and counseling astral visitors such as myself. I have a hunch that Henry introduced me a while back and I've just taken

it from there. Both words of wisdom and lighthearted humour are exchanged.

M. completely at ease, analyzing and creatively responding to any visitor's expectations, anxieties and general state of mind with the fluid grace of the professional. He knows what you want, what you need and I suspect, the best of the several available delivery methods. That I feel no urgent desire to update his knowledge of earthly matters, the politics of light and dark if you like, comes as no surprise. I know he knows all those details from his constant roaming through the planes. The talk revolves around the ascension process, as keenly anticipated by new-agers the world over, and how it will continue towards its inevitable fulfillment despite the dark agents of greed, lust and fear which are everywhere apparent. The two can coexist; the two must coexist. Each will be raised in the transition. For example, on a scale of minus ten through zero to plus ten, those at plus three will move up two or three notches, while those at minus four will be moved up a couple of notches. It is not, as some have envisioned, a total transcendence or dissolution scenario. Soul energy is very rarely wasted, just recycled into varying scenarios of change and challenge. Yes, there will be those who cannot, or do not wish to, cope with the energetic changes pervading the planes, and will likely seek, en masse, their comfort level on other planetary systems of suitable density. And, of course, there will always be outposts of ancient lifestyles available on the astral: just as one can now discover proud remnants of ancient cultures secreted away on the sub-lunar planes, there will be pockets of retrograde tribalism, both urban and rural, around for astral 'centuries' yet. Some of those reading this text will more than likely become guiding spirits of such slow learners/late bloomers. We, of course, can never be sure just how many will be required, but the term 'plenty' would seem operative in this regard. Yes, calendars, which anticipate immense cycles, such as the Mayan, are based on ancient and largely accurate information. There will not be major fireworks on January first 2012, or any calamities or a so-called cosmic nature, at least as far as Maitreya is aware, but the date itself is a useful midpoint marker of the upcoming changes, and not to be sniffed at. Maitreya says, just as I'm settling into a kind of comfy chair of anonymity, where I can forget about being any kind of an important messenger guy, and just kind of chill out into his marvelous geniality, "Gordon, you're in touch with artists of all types, why don't you see if you can get them online with this ascension stuff. We need the cognoscenti on board for this." I grimace, asking how a no name like me can reach out in that way. "You will not always be a no-name," he smiles. This brings us back to the credibility issue, the same one I've struggled with since being encouraged to participate in part one of this project, way back in '98. I illustrate my current version of this insecurity by saying that those Westerners who espouse Buddhism get way more credibility than those who espouse the new age. "Well be a new-age Buddhist then" is his succinct solution. I have to laugh. And as Maitreya is more or less an embodiment of the 'twinkling eye' syndrome, as all the ascended types I've had the pleasure to meet, this is not hard. Sure they've got that unwavering sense of mission that you'd expect, but the information delivery is usually, mmmn, bedecked with chuckles, as if none of this supposed cosmic stuff really mattered in the end. He told me once before that this is the result of seeing so many previous worthy initiatives fizzle out for one reason or another. Of course, judging when the planetary consciousness is ready can more often be likened to a role of the dice than anything else. I need no reminding of this principle as my Egyptian priest incarnation project was pretty well doomed by my over enthusiastic perception of the populace's readiness for a direct connection between the incarnate personality and the god consciousness. Priesthoods who emphasized the structured bureaucracy of power retention won the day on that one, and I retired to the relative backwaters of British Druidism. There, of course, I eventually came up against the same syndrome, in the power hungry bureaucracy which soon encrusted the original Christian impulse. Of course, by now it is obvious that on this planetary experiment divine missions almost always devolve into the elaborate pomp and ceremony disguising the decrepitude of back room deals. It just took "me" about ten or so incarnations to fully realize the futility of my overreaching idealism. Such is the cosmic lure of suffering and redemption. Maitreya, naturally, has a complete understanding of this, and barely gives it a passing thought

(3) Explores the streets of Toronto and suburbs, known to locals as the GTA, looking for the lost and confused. For a couple of days a short news story has intrigued: a stabbed wife on the lawn and a maddened husband bolting madly into midday traffic. I find them living in the astral replica of their dwelling, almost as if nothing had happened, going through the routines of their daily life. They seem like any devoted couple who occasionally burst into violent argument: afterwards it's all put away, an embarrassment best swept under the rug. Puzzled at my appearance, they struggle to figure out whether to be polite or pushily defensive. A relationship turned in on itself and needing little or no validation from outside, I just cannot seem to get through to them. How I managed to make my way in is as confusing as what I have to say. What do I mean they're dead? Here they are in their apartment, finished with the dishes and just getting ready for bed. How can they be dead? They hug each other and laugh. Am I mad, they suggest? Maybe I'm the one who's dead. Maybe I'm dreaming about them.

The situation reminds me of the movie "The Others" with Nicole Kidman, where she and the children she murdered eek out a fantastical post-mortem existence in the astral replica of their home, whose dream world is sustained by the conniving of other ghosts acting as servants. Although these two live in the city and have no servants, their contact with the outside world was so minimal as to be hardly missed. I imagine the next argument will result in some poltergeist rumblings. I choose to disappear in mid-sentence, hoping the eerie effect will stay with them until next time. From there I move on to some other earthbounds I've been working with over the past few weeks.

A sad old fellow in a dusty basement apartment, who passed while drunk in his easy chair and then woke up in the astral version of same and doesn't believe anything I tell him. Thinks I'm the ghost and chuckles away while reaching for another thought form rye. Humor, I can tell, has been his guard against the specter of madness for the last years of his lonely life, a life filled with resentment against perceived wrongs, a life dominated by a refusal to forgive. I'd bring in some dead relatives if it looked as if he might unbend enough to want to see any of them. Right now, though, he's got his rye and television, a television on which he seems to be watching endless reruns of various sports events.

A couple of junkies in an astral replica of their old rooming house. They're either sleeping or bitching at each other when I show. Scared to venture out I suspect. Lower astral Toronto is like many cities on that level, populated with addicts, criminals and the woefully weak-willed, all suspicious, hateful and angry to some degree or other. I've given these two thought form heroin a couple of times so they kinda trust me, but not enough to come with me and see the better life I hint at. Thought form heroin, by the way, is no more dangerous than thought form anything else. Certainly it sustains their illusions, both of addiction and satisfaction, but if I can gain their trust and get them out of there, it'll all be worth it. There's nursing homes one level up that cater to just their level of paranoia and energetic depletion. Well, I'll be back another time.

The lady that was living the high life in Casa Loma (local palatial home now a tourist attraction) still seems to be there, and still insists she's doing no one any harm. And as far as I can tell, that is quite true: she has no interest in harassing the living, and is happy to follow the imagined daily routines of the aristocratic lady. So far she's figured out thought form servants and cooks and is working on a rolodex of guests. I have tea and scones with her, indulging her fantasy, and then bid her adieu.

Next I find a couple of nighttime strollers in the parliament buildings at Queen's Park, one of them laughing at a sleeping security guard. Both of them are, as I have termed it, obe@night, and seem not to require any assistance, although one seems interested in my method of daytime recall. I have never yet met up with any nighttime revelers who wish to raise themselves up and see, for example, the great deva who hangs over the city and lake, but I keep thinking it will happen sometime, and hey, when they do, I can show them how. I move to one of Toronto's Buddhist temples and feel the protective light encasing the place. Some, and maybe all, lamas seem to know how to do this. A wise move, as lower astral nutbars sometimes like to hassle newbie meditators. I harmonize myself and slip through the net. Sometimes dead Buddhists hang around their temples waiting for help, and sometimes it's just some average person, sickened with regular Christianity, who thinks maybe those Buddhists know what to do. The Dalai Lama's public image certainly feeds this suspicion. But there's no one tonight, unless they're hiding in a closet. Funny, yes, but I did once find someone doing just that. Vietnamese guy, shot outside a karaoke bar: thought he was safe in the closet. I flew him back to astral Vietnam, where we seemed to meet up with some kind of ancestor spirit that he was happy to move on with.

This segment reminds me of my Buddhist monk incarnations, and I move back to that for a while. Thousand years in a blink, more or less. There he is, crossed legged in his quiet space, his body pain left behind, his consciousness clear and calm, and my presence within it mysterious and in the long run, distracting. Angels and deities are superfluous in the undifferentiated light of the void. Even bliss is a bit of a bore here. He's made it and he doesn't care about me. Ah, but I care about him, and so the blessings unfold. Do they make any difference? Well, like many issues in our issue laden universe, it depends on your viewpoint. From the monk's view it does not, from 'mine', Mr. Bodhisattva on his nightly binge of do-gooderism, it does. From the point of view of the earnest seeker, I'm doing a fine job of selfless-osity. From the fundamentalist angle, I'm likely a dangerous promoter of the blackest kind of magic, and best cast into some type of fiery pit from which I can no longer pollute the fields of the lord. From the planet's perspective, I am likely just another point of light whose expansion ever so slightly advances his own.

Meanwhile (2) is still engaged with Maitreya, trying to be as polite and deferential with "him" as he is with "me". He seems pleased with all the earthly efforts on his behalf, all the founda-tions, magazines and websites. Yes, his message is filtered through the personality concerns of each individual placing themselves in his line of light, and the egos all aflutter with the implied flattery, but the general direction unfolding is much as he and the hierarchy desires: The one-world consciousness powered by compassion, kindness and mutual respect, the bringing together of the planes, particularly the physical and the astral, the awakening to the extraterrestrial visitors and the understanding of their needs, the growth of individual consciousness, unshackled from nationalist and religious dogma, the acceptance of women and children as equals.

Yes, there are many hurdles to be jumped, and many who will not make the dimensional transition, but their relocation will be painlessly accomplished between incarnations. Another planet is ready to accept the influx. The ascended earth will not be to their liking anyway. They will no more recall their last earth life than the average soul now remembers their stints on Atlantis. I ask about dangers, about dark forces seeking to corrupt the plan and retard the development. The dark forces are part of the great plan, he says, implying that I know this already. The demons of fear, pride, lust and power have always been with us, always offering their avenues of seeming excitement and escape. They continue to propel divisiveness and anger and destruction, as they always have, but although they have no significantly more influence than before, their adherents have more technologically sophisticated means of implementation and the usual fanatical lack of qualms about using them. Despite all signs to the contrary light and love will prevail. I am asked not to take this on faith but to help bring it about by manifesting it on a day-to-day basis in my own life. Obviously my role is to relay this to the reader. Yet surely this message is repeated in many popular metaphysical books? Yes, but it does no harm to repeat it. I should understand that my book will attract a slightly different audience, and as such, is as valuable a tool as any other.

Wednesday July 21, 8:30 pm:
Whilst attempting a daytime hemi-sync assisted contact with the

English direct-voice medium Leslie Flint, after listening to one of his taped sessions at Toronto Reference Library as I read a 1981 letter from the researcher/collector Jim Ellis to a potential Canadian purchaser, and succeeding, I had the hunch that it was basically a "replay" from the night before, and decide to investigate, at my earliest opportunity, what else transpired that night. Tonight, Wednesday, is my first chance.

Usual methodology and tape: approach cottage, enter room and touch screen with intent to recover events of Saturday night 17/18 July. Easily obe and giddy with anticipation. Split into three Gordons.

(1) Which gazes lovingly and pityingly at sleeping body and then moves up above building, there to project the light of love and understanding at building and inhabitants, a sudden and unplanned expression of blessing for my neighbors. Inspired, that "I" begins to move through town, thus blessing every dwelling in turn. Though seemingly boring in retrospect, this divine exercise seems to electrify "me" more and more as I continue, culminating in a sort of uncontrollable giddiness. The more you give the more you get? Of course!

(2) Which moves up through the levels to embrace the Higher Self consciousness, much as on other occasions, recognizing, and perhaps saluting, the energetic entrapments of all the purgatories, paradises and heavens along the way. They are all, ultimately, merely places to be, fascinating rest stops on the incarnational cycle. As is the Monadic, I suppose. Once there, I enter and embrace, seemingly in turn, various "completed" personalities, feeling out our similarities of character and motivation in differing historical circumstances. Here are the philosophers, the courtesan, the king, the peasant, the trader, the innocent child, the deserted wife, the priests, the shamans, the devout pilgrim, the Atlantean magician. How they all give of their essence when I ask! How complete their commitment to the overall education of the monad! All preparatory work, I imagine, for the later, much more detailed encounters, in volume three. Part of 'me', of course, is impatient, and wants that immersion now, but I recognize that insufficient

preparation could be, if not disastrous, then at least something of a wasted effort.

(3) Asks for guidance to the astral residence of Leslie Flint, and soon finds himself mysteriously guided to lovely home in what appears to be a village in the astral version of the Cotswolds in south west England. I am outside a door, knocking. Then I am greeted, quite cordially, as I am expected. Very much in the 'Ah, Mr. Phinn!' style. Seated in the front room with Mr. and Mrs., I am offered tea. Very congenial: an impression of a quiet but happily fulfilled life, perhaps a welcome rest after a much too busy earth life. A couple enjoying each other's company, house, garden and local community. I mention the recent arrival of the huge Jim Ellis audiotape collection at the University of Manitoba and how pleased I and others are that it landed up in Canada. Leslie seems interested, but not overly so. Says I should really be speaking with Jim Ellis, as that was his pet project. The audiotapes represent the work of many mediums not just him. Of course, I know this is true, having examined the detailed contents of the archive included in the 1981 Ellis missive stored at the Toronto Reference library.

I congratulate Leslie on the marvelous accuracy in his rendering of Winston Churchill, a tape section of which I listened to just that day. He rather poo-poos my praise, insisting that all he really ever had to do was 'vacate the premises' while guides organized the ectoplasm and the spirits used the newly constructed voice box. It worked so well because he didn't interfere, essentially. Again I sense that the Flints feel they've 'served their time' in the spiritualist cause and are happy to let others fill the front lines. An almost textbook example of the 'astral vacation' mode. Yes, they love their life here, and take advantage of all the cultural opportunities of the astral, especially film and theatre. There are media outlets which monitor and report on Earth plane news, and they still take an interest that way. I get impression of both newspaper and television type service. The afterlife is as lovely as they thought it would be, and much more. You just can't put into words how lovely it is. I agree, knowing well the verbal hurdles he means. I ask if they're aware of the project known as *The Scole Experiment*. They are indeed, know some of those involved, but do not participate.

Thursday July 23, 4:00pm:
Usual methodology and hemi-sync tape. Upon exiting body, a sense of zany comedy erupts. Astral Gordon seems to think: *Gee, what'll I do tonight? I just don't know. Do you?* Then a replica Gordon appears from #1, standing next to him. He shrugs his shoulders in the classic 'search me' pose. Then he says: *Why don't you ask him? Maybe he knows.* #3 then pops out from #2, but he acts just as clueless as the first two. They stare at each other in a parody of idiocy. Then they fly out the window and onto a branch of the tree outside, my old friend Walter. There they dangle their legs like happy boys skipping school. #1 says *I think maybe I'll visit my dear dead mother.* The other two nod, wide-eyed. #2 says, *Maybe I'll go to Sudan and see for myself just how vicious that civil war really is.* #3, suddenly inspired, says, *Maybe I'll go to England and cavort with devas and crop circles.* Then they fly off in three directions, as if challenging the observing 'me' to try and follow.

#1 does indeed visit with his *dear dead mother*, who, of course, is also my dear dead mother. I find them seated on a lawn somewhere, probably the nursing home grounds. She is with her long passed-over sister Nelly, someone who was very dear to her heart, and with whom I am sure she is thrilled to be reunited.

They have obviously had plenty of time to get reacquainted, as they seem quite comfortable together. Nelly and I exchange cautious greetings: I was about four years old when she passed. There is a formality to our interaction I find quite amusing, the result, I suspect, of an energy blockage caused by her not having had a boy child while on earth, although why that should be operative after fifty odd earth years I cannot say. As sisters they bonded deeply during WW2, when both their husbands were abroad for years and their daily lives intertwined to make them and their four girls almost one family. I did not come along until several years after that and was perhaps seen as a bit of an interloper, or cause for jealousy.

#2 flies over towards Africa, but takes a small detour to the Middle East first, becoming one of the endlessly rotating crew of discarnates who beam light into the roiling mass of dark cloud-like energies covering Israel/Palestine. He doesn't so much originate the beam but merges and magnifies what is already there. After some of that no-time time, he moves on to the Sudan, expecting the worst. The observing 'I' resists following, reluctant to observe the cut-throat raids, destroyed villages, starving children and mass rapes which are likely to emerge. Rather like flipping through the entertainment section of the newspaper and knowing exactly which movies you'd rather *not* see. Looking back at it later, when the observing 'me' had come to terms with his disgust by allowing the heavy vibrations of vengeance and bestiality to pass through unhindered instead of being hindered by pride and ethics, I could see this Gordon attempting to apply energetic zaps of mercy and compassion at those who were either preparing or conducting a program of rape and pillage. Mostly it was ineffective as the rage and bloodlust which propelled the attackers had a determined, steely edge which could not be significantly softened. I fretted about freewill and chain-of -karma issues as I watched the grim tales unfold. A number of other angels and helpers surveyed the scene with attitudes saddened by inevitability. And, of course, ethnically appropriate guides assisted the 'dead' to remove themselves from the scene.

#3 shifts quickly to England and meets up with a deva intimately concerned with the crafting of crop formations. A merging of beings, which could be considered a discussion of sorts, leads to a suggestion that I should perhaps re-experience the druid character who was in on the plan to begin with. I've sensed this character several times before and made certain efforts to, as we say these days, understand where he was coming from. I see now that he is but one of several druid types who incarnated as 'my' monad's contribution to the culture. In an earlier meditative connection, completed whilst sitting inside a formation on a very hot day in the summer of 2001, I'd gotten the distinct impression that the whole crop circle phenomenon of modern times was planned out by a gathering of humans and devas who knew, even then, of the energy/vibrational shift slated for the planet, and together prepared the energetic templates for the elaborate designs now emerging in the fields. The news had not surprised me, but like any of a dozen other issues brought up by my explorations, I had not gotten around to exploring it further. Perhaps now was the time. Of course, *now* is always the time. But the scheduling nature of physical plane life tends to put agendas into lists of things to do, and some of those things seem to take forever to get to. There are just so many fascinating avenues of exploration, and each of them leads to at least four others.

All cultures worthy of the appellation have their share of the ancient wisdom, for no matter how maligned or repressed by power hungry elites and the armies of the ignorant, fonts of ancient light have and will always poke their heads through the cracks in the concrete. And though the counsel of the wise will more often be mocked than moved on, it is always there for the truly curious. The Druids, at least those who lived in ancient Britain, were a priestly-scholarly elite of a distinctly Celtic hue whose profoundly oral culture leaves plenty of room for romanticizing and guesswork. I do not propose that my 'incarnational access' is any more accurate or verifiable than any other source. I offer it humbly, without any hint or insistence of doctrinal authenticity.

After the disappointments of Ahkenaten's Egypt, a number of us were seeking a non-hierarchical society where the path of honorable action coupled with the selfless pursuit of wisdom could be attempted with a minimum of power base interference. The effort at earthly Eden which we joined was perhaps as successful as any essayed on this planet. Scattered tribal groupings pursued their hunting, agriculture, arts and sciences with the joyful diligence born to those who root themselves in nature. Pagans to be sure. Co-operation with the nature spirits was a daily fact of life. Trees and rivers were our ancient companions, prayed to, played with, and endlessly consulted. When I feel out those past 'selves' I sense a profound commitment to a type of meditative shamanism, almost certainly aided by the psychoactive plants then gifted to those holy isles. In meditation and/or out of body experience, the illusion of time was easily transcended. Many of our caste traversed the timelines like tourists. Both the roots of Hinduism and the psychic scars of Atlantis were available to our scrying. We understood the powers of light and darkness and harmonized ourselves to their tides. We knew the arrival of the Romans and the Christians was written in the winds, and we awaited their incursions secure in our assumptions.

We retreated, bruised, from the first and were ever so gradually absorbed by the second. The last Druid incarnation of which Gordon's soul energy was a part can be witnessed to this day, at least by 'me', standing proudly in the forest of which he was a living, breathing component, viewing the imminent arrival of disciples from the Mediterranean on the southern shores of mythical Albion through what we now think of as the third eye, and basically, bidding them adieu before they set foot on the land *he* thought of as holy. We do not need your prophet and his claim of divinity, we have our perfect place here. Breathing with the mountains, trees and rivers, creating and procreating in the bosom of our mother nature, we fulfill god's purpose in our being and we need no further reason. Return to the land of the olive tree!

This soul can also be witnessed, at least by 'me', being counseled in the afterlife by his guides, counseled to accept the cosmic inevitability of the Christ energy and devote himself to working towards it's fulfillment on Earth. This leads to at least three incarnations carving niches in the long Christian project of pacifying the pagan energy stream, binding it with the fear of damnation, and rewarding its docile behavior with the promise of salvation.

But, as I said, *now* is always the time. A number of human souls, then appearing as Druids, entered into a project with angels and devas, to design energetic templates for miracles far into the future, a future when man, in order to conquer the physical with feats of engineering rather than those of the imagination, would have separated himself from the ancient understanding of his place in nature. Seeing himself as the only sentient intelligence: alone in the universe with his pride and prerogative, a defiant Lucifer. Those 'miracles' are the crop formations, now manifesting worldwide to much discussion, debate and amazement. The energies they embody are for the earth *and* us, to regenerate and inspire. You can enter these sentient temples at will, no matter where you live. Move to their sites with passion and imagination, physically if you can, but obe if you must. The energies are gifts for the unveiling of your light body; open yourself to them and feel the expansion, which you can interpret according to your mental inclinations: geometry, architecture, healing, music and extraterrestrial anthropology are among the disciplines illuminated. Whatever your intellectual or psychological predisposition, if your surrender your separated ego to the cosmic presences you will, like some helium balloon, begin to float away from the anchors of your self-limitations. And surely that is what you ultimately desire.

Understand that so-called miracles can be planned and executed from anywhere in the space-time continuum, and as well as inspiring both those who choose to believe and those who choose to doubt, they can and do act as a counterbalance to those dark feats of mind control exercised by the powers of greed and voracious consumption at the helm of the capitalist enterprise, those feats which encourage fear and the desire for protection. Understand that both will continue and that their audiences will always have a choice. Understand that it has never been any different. And above all, know that graduation is inevitable. (Weeks pass here, vacation weeks followed by much busyness)

Last week of August: Daytime hemi-sync assisted contact/retrieval

Once in a while, some form of criminal activity interests me, usually a curiosity about the mental state of the perpetrator. This week, a man, after beating his wife with the butt of a gun outside her workplace, took off through downtown Toronto with police in hot pursuit. On a busy rush-hour sidewalk he grabbed a passer-by and held the gun to her head as police surrounded him at a distance. A well-positioned sharpshooter ended the tense scenario moments later. Newspapers revealed two aspects to the story: a man well liked by his neighbors and a family terrorized for years by his in-house abuse. That was a few days ago. Today, with hemi-sync, I accessed the event of his passing, by expressing a backwards-in-time intent. The shot that felled him instanta-neously, not surprisingly, left him dazed but quite unaware of his 'death'. It took a bit of convincing and when, as I pointed out his crumpled frame, the reality sunk in, his 'bitch beat me again' remarks reminded me of those power struggle marriages that so often wind up in the courts prior to the final explosion of violence. I avoided lecturing him on the ethics of personal relationships and suggested that he might want to check out the afterlife instead of standing about on this street corner. My frankness seemed to inspire at least a momentary trust and we shifted levels without a fuss. He was accepted at a typical reception center and seemed quite pleased with the place as I left.

A couple of days later, I returned to find him in a friendly social grouping around a pool, preparing for a barbeque. As I stood on its fringes smiling and joking, I could sense that he was worried that I would blow what he thought of as his cover. When I bent down to his ear and asked how he was managing, he smiled, quite relieved. I could see he was quite happy continuing his friendly neighbor role from earth, which, as that is what most folk fall into, seemed fine to me. Retrievers are neither judges nor executioners, and the afterlife is not a penance, not unless you make it one. His conscience would assert itself over his rationalizations sometime, and the paradise of his arrival might turn into the purgatory of a longer stay. Or, he might reincarnate. Or, he might grow in his lust for assertiveness and control, leading him to realms where that behavior is the norm. Only the illusion of time would tell.

With some of my own time to spare, I thought about Elisabeth Kubler-Ross, whose passing had been reported a few days before. Knowing something of her life work and writing I was not surprised to find her in a lovely astral version of the Swiss Alps, where sparkling light and beautiful vistas reflected the relative elevation of the souls in residence. Sensing one of those hemi-sync reruns of a longer nighttime visit, I walked through what felt like a media interview, and since I planned to report this on the radio, the slight formality as Elizabeth greeted me graciously in what I'm sure was a friend's sitting room. Comfortably seated, we chatted in a format that must have replicated many an earthside interview. She reported that she was more than ready for her transition and made it easily. Spirit was even more wonderful that she had imagined. Tell people it's well worth the long wait, she said. I assured her I would. She also asked that people send here the kind of love that would help her on her way rather than bind her to the past. I sensed she'd be moving up a level or two fairly soon, as much due to expectation as achievement. As we talked she emanated light, as an enlightened soul would do, but I could see she was still attached to her 'Elizabeth' character and would be for some while yet. Success, of course, can be as much of a trap as failure. It's the degree of attachment which counts. Basically, the less the better. None, and you're as free as a hot air balloon. Naturally, I said a lot about what a unique contribution she made and how much society owed her for her pioneering work. That death, or the discussion of it, was no longer such a taboo, was largely due to her efforts. With this she seemed almost as relieved as flattered. I understood: astral dwellers often care little for earthside reputations, and those thus attached can be somewhat crestfallen at the lack of reception.

These two almost casually conceived contacts illustrate what was rapidly becoming the norm for me, as the expansion continued throughout the seasons of this volume's composition. Earlier in the year, I'd worked on a couple of unusual retrievals which deserve some small mention. On March 22nd, it would appear, I had sought the spirit of the actor/film maker Spalding Gray, who, after weeks of suspicion and debate amongst his friends, had been found at the bottom of the East river, where he had apparently jumped in from a ferry, after months, if not years of depression brought on, they claimed, by the reduced capabilities resulting from a car accident. I had read his books and seen his films, and had a distinct hunch that his zen meditation experience, although valuable, had told him little about afterlife conditions.

This, amongst members of my spiritually inclined generation, is not uncommon. Yoga, Zen, and a host of other fringe disciplines, though not without their benefits for body, mind and spirit, are as woefully inadequate as any of the mainstream religions in their paucity of useful information on eternity. Gurus, lamas, swamis, rishis can chatter endlessly about the void, the clear light, the pure land, the attaining of nirvana and the bliss of nothingness with varying degrees of felicity, but their legions of baby boomers followers are as ignorant as the average church-goer when it come to understanding the necessary illusions of the various spirit realms and how they function in the overall education of the embodied soul. The psychic communications of Spiritualism seem terribly fussy and old-fashioned to those brought up on Castaneda and Seth, but as navigational tools to the various realms they are, in fact, very useful.

I found him in focus 23, sitting hunched over and looking gloomy. Using the trademark greeting *Spalding man! Spalding man!* (from *Swimming to Cambodia*) I acted cheerful and chatty. Told him I was a fan and wanted to help out. Intellectually I think he knew there must be an afterlife but didn't realize his state of heart/soul would actually define his location/landscape. In that foggy area of f23 he seemed to be living on remorse and memories. I asked him what he thought of the society of aquatic life at the bottom of the river. He said something about it moving around a lot.

After cracking some wiseass remarks, the kind he used to use in his own work, I grabbed his hands and got him up to play the children's game "Ring around the rosie", something I hadn't thought of in years. You know, 'A-tishoo, A-tishoo, we all fall down', dancing around in a circle and then falling backwards on your ass and laughing hysterically? That seemed to loosen him up a bit. Knowing, from his book, that he'd always been affected by his mother's suicide when a kid, and feeling his own remorse at leaving his kids behind, I asked if he'd like to go to a part of the afterlife where he could meet his mother and learn how to hook up with his kids. Worthiness issues came up, and also a bit of doubt (of the 'Are you who you say you are?' variety). I tried to convince him by joking around rather than being serious. I suspect others had been by before me, but he'd dismissed them as either fantasies or pests. Finally got him to hold my hands and accept the fact that we'd be changing dimensions. Told him to shut his eyes, but he kept opening and peeking! I had to laugh. Told him the journey might be disorienting if he kept them open. Probably the wrong thing to say to a joker like that. He obviously liked teasing me on the issue.

Arriving at f27, the Park, he seemed mighty impressed. I told him he should just walk about and meet people, that there were lots like him, not to worry, that nobody would really give a toot how he got there. Told him the food was really good, sushi the best ever. Then explained how he could image his family here and visit by expressing the desire to do so and then come back to the Park by imaging it. Warned him not to get caught up in family emotions or he'd get stuck like a ghost. Gave him a big hug, which he seemed to enjoy, and told him I'd be back to help out if he needed it. Then kind of pushed him away with my hand as if to say 'On you go, get started now!' and disappeared.

Not long later I had a similar experience with Canadian political activist and former Toronto mayoralty candidate Tooker Gomberg, who like many young energetic idealists, run out of steam and into depression when the corruption of the world will not yield to their enthusiasm. Another drowning. I found him wandering through the homes of his friends, like some sweet but ignored puppy, not long after his memorial service, which as they often do, surprised him with its spontaneous outpourings of respect and love. He seemed to know little, and care less, of afterlife conditions, but I somehow convinced him that moving on would be smarter than hanging around. Though his state of rueful retrovision and remorse was similar to Spalding's, he was easier to convince, and I deposited him at f27 without much further ado.

Such contacts and retrievals form the daytime background of the varied nighttime explorations recounted here, and as such can be seen as physical Gordon's participation in an ongoing multi-leveled experiment in expansion.

Friday September 3rd: Unassisted Daytime Meditation, early afternoon.

Whilst out of town on business, I had few hours free, and was checking my email on computer terminal at a small town library, when I noticed that the Beslan school hostage drama in Russia had come to its grisly end. A half an hour later I walked to the town's pioneer cemetery, beautifully situated on the hills just to the south. I had visited the year before and pleasant memories of my meditation had accompanied me all winter. Laying down in the welcome shade of a tree guardian I slowed my consciousness further by watching the clouds sail through the skyblue, the shapes slowly but constantly shifting. The tragedy I was about to attend in spirit seemed about as distant as world war two.

Executing my intention I appeared at the site and quickly began interacting with the dead, most of whom were walking about rather dazed amidst dust and debris. I convinced a couple of children to hop on for the ride to heaven. At the reception area I was greeted by a line of women who passed my charges along from hand to hand. I made four or five quick trips with these young victims. At one point I approached a couple of adults, who, although aware of their new state, seemed distrustful of my stated mission, and went off to discuss things with friends. On my next trip they'd decided to throw in their lot with me. Got them to hold hands and shut their eyes and we shifted in a second. During this activity I was aware of many other helping spirits working all around me. It felt like the most organized disaster retrieval I'd participated in. On my last return a voice said something like "That's about it for now Gordon", and I was done.

Back in the sunny, breezy graveyard I thought of my client V., who'd phoned a few days before after hearing me on the radio, wanting to contact her best friend B., who'd passed but a couple of weeks ago. I'd felt her presence hovering from time to time since V.'s call, but hadn't had the time to make a formal contact till now.

B. appeared quickly and easily, as if waiting in the wings had become something of a chore. A vivacious and cheery soul, she danced about in front of me during our entire interaction, spinning, twirling, and laughing the laugh of someone who loves joyful times. I asked V.'s questions and received answers that V. later seemed happy with. A simple straightforward contact, inflated with an obvious irony. The world, of course, is filled with joy and sorrow. Always has been.

I refocused on my physical state: the afternoon was exquisite and I had no need or urge to move on. I felt another presence nearby: it was the spirit of a deceased human who so loved this rural area that they had stayed around to overlight several of these pioneer graveyards in the southern Georgian Bay region. Seeming more caring than obsessed, it warned me that there were many spirits lingering about the place, most of whom could not be encouraged to leave. I thanked the spirit for the assistance and sought to move my consciousness towards the local deceased. Forming a column of light and announcing it as a pathway to spirit for all, as I have often done in graveyards, I was gingerly approached by several. Finally an imposing figure of a man, likely a prominent citizen in his day, confronted me to debate, lambchop sideburns still proudly displayed. Much talk of judgment day, the souls of the righteous and spirits lead astray by false gods followed, the other spirits hanging back to watch. I denied all accusations and suggested that the column of light was a test of their faith, which I would leave manifested for a short time, that their departure from this sad place might be enabled in my absence. The figures retreated to consider my offer, and I stood up and strolled away, all the while enraptured with the beauty of the summer afternoon. I paused by one gravestone at the edge of the property and read the inscription. It was a couple from well over a hundred years before, who were declared to be *sleeping in Jesus*. I felt very much as if I had met them in contours of that very sleep.

Tuesday 21 September, 10:00am:
When initially obe last night, I stayed in my bedroom allowing the

wondrous devotional music of 12th century mystic Hildegard Von Bingen to suffuse my astral being. It was playing as I nodded off and I couldn't see anyplace I'd rather be. The deep purity of her song to god inspires throughout the centuries. Beyond style, it exists in grace alone, truly timeless in the manner of all great art. A prearranged phone call from S. awakens me. We chat and then I return to bed: it has been a long stressful day and physical Gordon is glad to finally surrender. Astral Gordon seems unaffected and shoots out through the bedroom window without so much as a backward glance at the vehicle of his daytime exploits, ungrateful slob that he is.

Flying around for the sheer joy of it, swooping through the trees of the town and down to the park to absorb the river vibe, thinking about the Nick Drake song *River Man* ("going to see the river man, gonna tell him all I can, about the plan for being free") and wondering if it is finally time to pursue a contact. Split into two Gordons: one to seek out Nick, the other to venture southwards, where the Caribbean storms have been having their way for some time. Latest destruction is on Haiti, where many souls have been thrust out of bodies in the last twenty-four hours. The regular disaster rescue teams are already at work, but I know their efforts are being hampered by the vice grip that black magic and its local practitioners have on the culture. Haiti is perhaps the primary example on the planet of a local black hierarchy of shaman/wizard types who define themselves by their ability to control a populace by continually rotating them from the physical to the lower astral and back again. Their propaganda of fear is extremely effective in keeping the majority of souls from ever ascending higher than the rigidly controlled purgatory/paradise just above the physical island mass.

Many priesthoods have pulled similar stunts throughout history, with varying degrees of success, and as free will trumps every other card in our planetary game they must be allowed to exhaust the energy of their illusion without interference. This is not cruel and unusual punishment for innocent souls involved, for as with all belief systems, planet and history wide, they have all allowed themselves to be seduced by a thought form which enslaves them. As with all believers they exchange their cosmic birthright of absolute individual freedom for a known territory of strict regulation ruled by local power brokers who see themselves pretty much as deities.

The retrieval work, such as you have seen previously described, is seriously hampered by the local power structure, which maintains its own retrieval network to support its astral set-up. In this they are not unlike the third world physical plane drug barons, who proudly act as community pillars in their resource communities. What we do in situations like this is wait around for souls whose colors show that they are ready to move onward and upward. Then there can be a bit of a tussle, as the local network representatives realize they are losing one more slave. Personally I prefer the zap of white light method, where instead of arguing the toss with the local rep, I suck up the soul essence of the deceased to a mid-level astral reception center suitable for a peasant in the tropics. There they can relax and settle the choice for themselves without listening to the bickering of rival helpers, which often only confuses them. No method is perfect, of course, and light-workers have to improvise, constantly aware that their efforts, through well meaning, could be misconstrued.

As some of the more perceptive among you may see, this brings up the whole issue of the ethics of moving souls along. What right do we light workers actually have, whether we're helping a lonely, weak-willed young soul trapped in an oppressive purgatorial realm, or an about-to-be-former adherent of a strict rules-and-punishment sect or police state, or a fairly free-thinking Christian or Moslem who feels more than a bit itchy in his so-called heaven, in altering that individual's perceptions? Basically, the same right or opportunity that any human has, to advise a friend who seeks advice. If, for example, your workmate, recently arrived in your city, tells you on coffee break that he can't stand his neighbors or, for that matter, his neighborhood, wouldn't you offer him some sound advice based on your greater knowledge of the urban area? Plenty of physical plane Christians have had the experience of meeting someone from another denomination, at a barbeque perhaps, who, after a drink or two, will insinuate certain discomforts with his church/minister/congregation. Haven't they all offered their own church as an alternative? We lightworkers/helpers face an almost constant stream of such decisions in our work. And, like high school career councilors we have just enough on our charges to see where they *need* to go, as well as where they *want* to go. Certainly there's a certain amount of sneaking folk out the back door of some belief system communities, usually the more repressive kind that require a quotient of psychic slavery for survival, but the joy of liberating a yearning soul generally trumps all other concerns at that point. As they say in certain sectors of the new-age community, grace trumps karma every time.

And speaking of grace, let's see where Gordon number two went in his search of Nick Drake, who, way back in the 1970's, once sang "Please, give me a second grace". As the observing consciousness follows this astral aspect of the 'author', it becomes understood that Gordon has contacted Nick quite some 'time' before, but the knowledge, instead of penetrating his daytime consciousness with images and thoughts, blended into his already existing love for Nick's music and making him feel that much closer to the creative spirit behind the songs. Passed these thirty odd years, Nick's reputation, tiny to begin with, has steadily spread through the oncoming generations to become something like a permanently assured cult status. The ineffable beauty of his melodies combined with the mystic enigma of the words caressed by that soothing voice, affects everyone within earshot.

We find them seated in an English country garden on a late summer's afternoon, an astral version of the kind of pastoral beauty many fans might expect. A gentle unassuming soul, Nick seems a bit surprised to be contacted. He's aware of his growing reputation on Earth, but seems abashed that it has spread even to here, where he felt safe and secure. Gordon promises that hoards of adoring fans are not about to follow in his wake. Nick seems pleased. Gordon asks if he actively abhorred the ideas of fame in his life. Nick smiles, as if he'd been expecting the question. Yes, although he was depressed about not receiving recognition from beyond a small circle of music business people and friends, the idea of massive fame actually horrified him. He was much too fragile for that sort of thing. Even the kind of thing his friend John Martyn was achieving by the mid seventies would have been a strain. He never actually got over his terror of performing live. What about his new life here, does he get out to play for people? Yes, he has to admit, that is becoming more of an attractive proposition. There are gatherings of folk music fans hereabouts which are intimate enough to let him breathe. And some of them are fans from Earth, wanting to hear their favorites. I mention his ever-growing fame on the physical plane. Yes, he knows and he's fascinated. He'd never have believed people would lap up his demos and rejected songs like they have. When will it all end, he wonders, there can't be much more to release, except his home tapes, which are very ragged. I tell him that they've already been bootlegged several times, and I myself have one tape that I find quite charming. Not to mention instructive in seeing where his influences lay, as even by his first official album, *Five Leaves Left*, his style was so unique it was virtually impossible to tell. Ah yes, he smiles, I worked hard to cover all that up. I didn't want people knowing. He does want me to thank his sister Gabrielle for all the effort she is putting into maintaining a sense of quality and dignity in the managing of his estate. I tell him I don't know how physical Gordon will manage this feat, but at least he'll try. I ask if he keeps up with the current events on Earth. He says he cannot be bothered, as it always seems so depressing. He'd much rather enjoy the world he's in now. Which, he adds, is so incredibly beautiful he's still overwhelmed by it all. Almost enough to make you believe in God, he jokes. My turn to smile. Seriously though, it does seem as though we live forever. I can't see it ever ending, he says. Neither can I, I agree.

After some encouragement, Nick retrieves one of his guitars from the cottage and returns to play me some newer songs, all of which display his trademark wistful embrace of the mystical and transcendental. "I am a sky with clouds sailing through me, light falls from my heart and hovers into weather, night never happens, this now I know, this now I know." These are the words which Gordon on earth will have doubts about. I don't blame him: if I lived there, in that narrow band of conscious awareness, I'd wonder about the accuracy of the transmission myself.

These days of doubt will slowly wither, at least for those who embrace the ascension. I'm not sure if Nick knows this, but the 'I' that is doing this reporting does. The planes will continue to move closer together. One day, not only will physical plane dwellers be able to sustain contact with astral plane dwellers, visually or telepathically or both, but contact between the various astral levels will become easier, given an active desire to so communicate, something of a rarity on the rather self-obsessed lower astrals. Of course, there will still be opposition from those entrenched forces who believe such communication either impossible, undesirable or distinctly demonic. Just as today there are those who would convince some that their sexual preference is a symptom of illness and cultural perversion, there will similar efforts directed at the sudden fascination for post-mortem chit-chat, which between telepathy and spirits invading the internet, will become as common as cell phones now. 'Seducing our youth with lies about heaven' might be the new battle cry. Some will be shocked that there's Muslims in heaven, some amazed that Christians are resident. Some will be appalled to hear that Jews have their place there, not to mention Rosicrucians, Rastafarians and Sikhs. The tacit acceptance of earth side criminals and corrupt politicians will no doubt raise a few eyebrows. That the doctrines of love, forgiveness and mercy really rule in spirit will doubtlessly surprise those enamored of ethically based hierarchies. All these themes will be debated with much vigor on the street, school, café, church and internet. Arguments will rage. Certainly the notion that sexual relations are uncorrupted by disease on the astral will set many to incomprehension and wrath. Punishment for sinners will die a slow death, its tormented agonies writhing about for years.

Sunday September 26, 10:35am

Upon leaving the sack of bones and flesh that constitutes my physical vehicle on the surface of the planet, and knowing that physical Gordon would be writing it all up in the morn, I attempted a four way split. Just one more challenge really, one more step to the dissolution of identity and the emergence of the multidimensional entity, who, like a building with many floors and departments, conducts operations in a number of spheres simultaneously, with its overall operating system being the software powered by the Christ consciousness. Four Gordons at the ready, sir. There they stand, saluting, in a mockery of conformity. Mirrors making light.

Number one goes quickly to one of the majestic cathedrals in the higher reaches of astral Christianity, entering a mass already in progress. Hundreds of devoted souls singing Palestrina. Everyone firmly entrenched in their bodies. Gordon one allowing himself to melt into the light, knowing he can reassemble at will, something many present do not quite realize. Devoted but not ready to dissolve. When they understand that dissolution is quite reversible, that nirvana is more negotiable than negation, they will relax their hold on the me/not me dichotomy. As Gordon one merges with the musical love of his environment, Gordon two returns to the psychic atmosphere of lower astral Haiti, where rescue operations are ongoing but muted in the manner previously described. This time he channels the divine love Gordon one is absorbing and spreads it around the areas of devastation, trusting that those souls ready to make the leap out of their repressive belief system will avail themselves of the energy. If they have the courage to do so, even unconsciously, it will give them the boost they need, the escape velocity as it were. Of course, watching helpers follow their path, ever ready to assist. Gordon three moves back in time to the killing fields of World War One, where an aspect of his Higher Self, yes that same Monad who joins us here from time to time, has been, or more correctly *is*, along with many others, operating a rescue mission for the thousands of confused souls trapped in the psychic turmoil of that conflict. Gordon three is also channeling that same energy, boosting the efforts of the dead British officer organizing and inspiring the small band of rescuers on his team. Physical Gordon knows about this rescue effort, or at least remembers about it from time to time, especially when he's involved in healing work. Years ago his friend Deb Aaron suggested that he always move some of the healing energy involved in hands-on work towards this rescue team, always understanding that the time frame scenario could be easily transcended by expression of intent. Gordon four visits S., where they enact the loving relationship they have let slip in the last few days. Out of body intimacies, such as have been previously indicated, are followed by much astral romping around with Misha, their beloved Husky.

Monday September 27, 10:30am
After pleasant, relaxing day absorbing the golden energies of early fall in and around the Hidden Valley house, astral Gordon emerges from his day time vehicle, observes S. still reading beside him and shoots off for some fun flying. A clear starry night with an almost full moon, and the lights of Hamilton city almost as pretty as the stars themselves. Zooming over the waters of Lake Ontario, antagonizing a few sleeping ducks by the shore: in a rascally mood tonight. Split from astral Gordon into three spheres of light and race myself to the moon, dancing about each other on the way. Arriving in the orb's atmosphere, we hover and turn towards the Earth. As I said to S. earlier, while gazing at the moon through the trees, "the only thing more exciting than looking at the moon is looking at the Earth". It is so beautiful: a planet in full bloom, a brooding mother, a stern father, a highly evolved entity raising its own vibration and grappling with its new status within the solar system. I have learned not to project a human sense of suffering onto her physical self, as various interest groups would have me do. Earth offers, and humans receive; this humanity understands. But because of the recent breakdown in reciprocity, modern man does not see how he, in all his foolish egotistical striving, contributes to the evolving consciousness of the planetary being.

Earth lives through its minerals and its vegetation, its seas and mountains, its volcanoes, hurricanes, oceans and deserts, but it also lives through man, in his ignorance, suffering, creativity and joy. It feels these games of energy, geared to form.

The three of us beam love to her like little bolts of light: they bounce back renewed. That's karma as close to instant as you'd want. We zip over to the dark side of the moon, singing that Pink Floyd line "And if the band you're in starts playing different tunes, I'll see you on the dark side of the moon". It is dark over there, but not *that* dark. We can still see the base that many obe adventurers have come across. Like the Agency and the Mafia, they won't bother you if you don't bother them. They don't actually sense our presence with instruments as they do in Area 54 on Earth. Infrared and vibration sensors completely miss astral and mental bodies. But the extra-terrestrials know you're about, and if they're not too busy, like to chat. Obe's are a refreshing difference to the straight laced military types they're used to. At least that's my impression.

On previous visits I've hassled them over the hybrid breeding program. Initially I was appalled, but their intransigence made me moderate my rage. My "How dare you!" attitude just bred a snotty rebuff.

I felt very protective of my 'children', as I called them, but my demands for ethical behavior were met with denial. That human souls who agreed to participate before birth might forget that commitment when incarnate was incomprehensible to them, or perhaps it just suit their agenda to believe so. To me it seemed like cruel and unusual punishment of innocence, and more than worthy of the contempt I was heaping on it. My suggestion that an open honest appeal for sperm and egg donors would result in a significant increase in production rates was greeted with the reminder that 'your government' insisted on secrecy. We were told that the populace would react with panic and our assessment was much the same. When I insist that we've come a very long way from a War Of The Worlds scenario, I was reminded that the program was already in place and it was too late to change course now. The formula 'paranoid power-hungry politicians plus imperious heartless manipulative aliens with an eye for the main chance' seemed quite operative to me. Of course, that was then and this is now.

I've accepted that deceit and mind control are now to be factored into the ascension equation. And perhaps that doesn't complicate matters as much as I first suspected. Ultimately it's still a case of 'Father forgive them for they know not what they do'. Which he does I'm sure. But do *I* or do *we*?

Tonight we merely observe. No visible activity from the above ground structures, yet that unmistakable sense of activity within. At first cognition the industry of these dark operatives seems impressive, but once one has overcome that initial high-tech dizzy spell, the wonderment palls, and the grim faced agenda of hybridization or oblivion soon becomes apparent. Then you feel their desperation, albeit masked by pride of achievement. Having to resort to the likes of us, those interminably squabbling humans, I think, really humiliates them. We're so stupid, so easy to fool, and yet they need the heart energy and DNA we've developed over the millennia of struggle and suffering. There's the karma of overweening pride for you.

A sphere of light comes over to check us out. We beam 'hello there' in unison, as goofy as we like to be. Our greeting is returned, rather formally, leading us to feel that our visitor is robotically controlled from within. We are examined for any aggressive thoughts or tendencies. Our clowning, under this microscope, takes on a sub-atomic style chaotic splendor, which we feel fairly represents out status in the scheme of things. Perhaps readers want to know more of what it actually feels like to suddenly become not one but three spheres of light. Well, how about *silly*, *giddy fun* and *totally irresponsible frivolity*? Is my energy divided by three? Only if I was to think it ought to be. But I don't, so it isn't. Again, what you believe creates your reality.

The inspecting sphere departs, no doubt satisfied that we three clowns do not represent a threat. Mere observation they are not worried about. Obe's have been seeing this site on and off for decades, but as a group they have little mass credibility. The power brokers behind this enterprise are confident that the skeptical materialism of the media will not be broken by any number of wingnuts on the psychic fringe. And if it looked for a moment like it was, their paid watchdogs would submit a report and appropriate subversive action taken. They know from experience that silence, mocking denial and the stressful striving for material gain are enough to keep citizens preoccupied with the daily grind calm and continuously productive. The human personnel sharing these facilities, are, by the way, transported in alien craft originating from underground bases in the U.S. and Australia, Earth craft not being, as yet, sufficiently advanced, shall we say, in power or discretion, for the journey.

Much of the preceding information has been given in other modern metaphysical books, but it is repeated here as physical Gordon seeks to build bridges between the UFO and new-age communities. As they will be ascending together, he feels, why not get to know each other first? Although it is becoming apparent that the abductions necessary for the hybridization program are resulting in a much increased level of psychic activity for both the participants and the researchers, much of the UFO community still reflects the materialist mindset of the societies from which they spring, and our intrepid representative on the physical plane hopes his various efforts will be, in some small way, helpful in bringing the two camps together.

The three spheres race madly back to Earth, swooping and spinning about each other like the silly fools they love to be. To top things off with a flourish they merge in the upper atmosphere and speed around the planet at about ten thousand feet, going through a day of dark and light, over ocean, desert mountain and city, the globe at a glance, before screeching to a halt above Toronto, saluting the deva over the lake and then zooming low over the waters towards Burlington Bay and then back to sleep in the Hidden Valley house.

Thursday September 30, 11:00am
As night was shared with S. at my apartment and sleep assailed us

both early, our emergence from the physical was almost simultaneous. We embrace in intimacy and comfort, and then, with
mutual intent, change levels to visit her father J. The friends who
he was staying with last time, N. and P. tell us that he's moved
into his own place not far away. An area of cottages around lakes
in the midst of forest, the place is a bird lover's dream come true,
which for J. is just about perfect. The ideal astral holiday for many
Canadians born and bred in southern Ontario, which all three of
them were. Like the well known 'cottage country' of the physical
plane, it creates in them a calm and fulfillment often just out of
reach during their incarnation. Some of course, opt for the astral
version of the foothills of the Rocky Mountains, something they
must have fantasized over during their skiing visits. And others,
not surprisingly, go for the tropical resort archetype they visited at
every opportunity during those long Canadian winters.

J. seems very please to see us, and the thrill of reunion between
him and daughter S., now devoid of the relief / anxiety polarity of
his passing, feels more balanced and healthy, but still powered by
the deep bonds only multiple shared incarnations can bring. The
phrase 'all's fair in love and war', passes through my
consciousness but remains unspoken. Ensconced on his porch to
admire the flitting, singing birds and the verdant foliage of their
home, we chat about many things, some of family interest only,
and some more generally metaphysical. At one point John asks me
what it was like to be aware of "all this" when alive on Earth.
"Which I guess you still are", he laughs. I try to explain a situation
that has been emotionally and psychologically complex to me even
at the best of times, not to mention a total mystery at worst. It all
boils down to *sometimes it's very frustrating, and others quite liberating.* The complexity would often arise in trying to separate what
I felt were purely metaphysical insights from the more standard
psychological ones available to anyone willing to stop and think
things through. J. seems intrigued, so I continue into my often
long-winded theorizing about how intuition can rise up like a
phoenix from the ashes of intellectuality, if given half a chance. Of
course one constantly runs the risk of appearing arrogant and

presumptuous to those unwilling to explore the outer reaches of intuition, I expound, especially when one had begun adulthood as a bit of a preening intellectual, as I had. J. seems to have no trouble understanding my frustration as part of his own earth experience. After some more of this, we hear, upon request, about some of J.'s astral activities. It would seem that he has his nature love, his sports enthusiasms, personal friendships and family life in fairly good balance. He claims to be as happy as he can ever recall. We discuss his various attempts at contact. S. has had several very realistic dreams, which I of course, have already heard about. She and J. share details and feel that their efforts to link across the veil have been well worth it. I mention two occasions when I felt his presence about me and apologize for not relaying his messages to family members as I felt they might be too upset. J. understands and thanks me for being so open, but reiterates his request that I relay his greetings to N., his first wife, and his daughter Sh., with whom he had such a contentious earth side relationship.

Sometime after this, we leave to visit my mother N. Arriving first at my father's hilltop residence, we find the place empty. I guess that he's at one of his classes. Having had little education earth side, he has taken every opportunity here to, as they used to say, in the Scotland of his day, improve himself. We sit and admire the view for a while: rolling hills, verdant valleys, about halfway between the Scottish and Kenyan highlands, if that sounds believable. So many spirit world landscapes are sublime blends of various national identities that it's quite a challenge to describe them. S. feels very, well, she says, blessed, sitting there. Like all couples there are moments where we seem to be in tune with each other and our surroundings to such an extent that our personalities merge and we seem to disappear in the bliss of the moment. This is one of them.

I guess that my mother has departed the nursing home atmosphere she was 'recovering' in the last few visits and is perhaps staying with one of her sisters, N. being the most likely candidate. S. is still a bit shy about wading deep into a family she's a stranger to, and I bow to her apparent discomfort. As the youngest child of parents, both of whom were the youngest of long lines of siblings, I had a minimal contact with the 'clan' before they all passed, so I can understand her position.

And as understanding each other's positions seems to be one of the golden keys to operating throughout the planes of this planetary being, let us leave these two to their moment of blessedness on the astral hilltop. Soon they will wake up to another day of challenge and joy, and disseminate their consciousnesses about the energetic continuum of their existence. *Have a life*, as we like to say. There they will be surrounded by other journeying beings of varying degrees of sentience and be submerged in an invisible sea of silently suffering intelligences, all of whom have come willingly to undergo the experiential initiation this planet offers. Not that they will have much time or calm to so acknowledge, but the understanding is always there, patiently waiting for any encouragement from the active participants. As it is for all you dear readers anxious for such divine access.

HS Merge (4)

My blessings and greetings to all the readers who have arrived at this end of Gordon's line of words: I believe I understand your need and I certainly embrace your determination. The journey from the limited incarnate personality to the virtually infinite consciousness of the Higher Self can be shocking and dwarfing to the ego isolated by its pressing concerns, and I applaud all your efforts to span the pilgrimage. I know you will be rewarded for all your apparent sacrifices. Surrendering to the wider, deeper consciousness at your shoulder can, and will, remove all the insulation you thought was so necessary for your survival, allowing in all the extremes you once believed injurious. May I suggest you inhabit your newfound insignificance and breathe the tiny breaths which make it come alive in the hands of the creator so close to us all. The in and out of your lungs is the breathing of the universe in miniature. The endless streams of your thoughts and emotions are the energy of the universe coursing through your mental and astral bodies. Every activity of the universal mechanism is replicated in one or other of your bodies, some of which you have yet to discover. But fear not, all is destined to be unveiled. After all the centuries of necessary suppression and deception, the esoteric can now be exoteric. There are no more secrets to be blessed with leaking.

You are the secret you have been keeping from yourself. You are the initiations you have been seeking: each layer of your being peels away to reveal deeper and deeper understandings of divinity and how it doubles in laughter. You are the back pocket in which the divine has been hiding its most precious bauble. You are the lord of the rings. Move to the sun at the center of your system and feel its power preparing to radiate to its own little collection of villages.

Join us Monads in the endless unmasking of creative potential. We really want you with us. In fact, we cannot make the leap without you.

DAYTIME EXPLORATIONS:

contacts with John E. Mack (Oct5, 13/04), and Betty and Barney Hill (Oct19/04)
I move, backwards in time by intent, to JM's immediate post mortem location. He is standing beside his prone body. I say *Hello* and ask him how he's doing. *Surprisingly well* is his answer. *Have we met before* he asks, *perhaps at some conference*: undoubtedly the response of someone who has attended many gatherings over the years and met many people who he can only vaguely recall. We shake hands as I introduce myself. I tell him no, we have not had the pleasure. But I do know of his abductee work and have followed it with interest, including all the academic kerfuffle. *Ah, that*, he muses. Basically I'm a spiritualist and have come to assist his transition, if he so cares. He thanks me for my interest; it is very thoughtful of me. To me, it seems appropriate given his lifelong care of, and interest in, others. The whole process is quite fascinating, he tells me. Observing your own death.

You're not upset then, I ask. No, not for himself, for others yes. It's more of a puzzle than anything. I'm wondering if he subconsciously chose this exit, but do not comment. The process has him so fascinated, I don't think he's had time to emote, never mind work out which emotions he's feeling. I enjoy your scientific style detachment, I tell him, it's so unusual. Well a scientist he is, a detached observer and interpreter of human behavior. An old habit he can't give up (he seems amused by this). I apologize for stopping to take notes. He suggests I get a voice-activated tape recorder. I reply that, yes, I've been advised of their usefulness in situations like this. (I feel embarrassed as Bruce Moen told me this at least two years ago. I'm unbelievably slow at getting around to things. Spirit suggested I acquire a laptop years before I actually acquired one).

I tell him I'm an afterlife guide and that I can show him where to go from here. Ah, you're an out of body traveler. I comment that he's likely familiar with the process from talking to abductees. Yes, and their stories lead him to read up on the subject. He seems in no hurry to move on as yet. No panic, no anxiety. I can see me coming back in a couple of days. I ask if he knew that the subject of his prize-winning book, TE Lawrence was channeled in Jane Sherwood's "Post-Mortem Journal". No he did not know while he was writing the book, but found out much later. Of course, in his community such communication is frowned upon or completely derided. Considered very unreliable. But after his plunge into the abductee phenomenon, his bridges were half burned anyway. I joke about channeling him. Oh, so I'm going to publish? At least on the internet; it's what I do, does he mind? No, not really, as long as it's not slanted to appear scandalous. No, I assure him, it will be a bare bones report of his state of mind, his well being in this process of transition. So I've done others then? Oh yes, most recently Elizabeth Kubler-Ross. So I'm in good company then? Most certainly, I assure him. We laugh together.

So I'll leave him be for now, and maybe come back later and see how he's doing? What, I'm not going to take him to his place in heaven? Not right now I'm not. He's having way too much fun here. Fun of the scientific observer variety. Will there be aliens about, he asks. Not unless you go looking for them, I shouldn't think. I can't tell if he's relieved or disappointed. I suggest that when he's more oriented in the afterlife, I, or someone else can show him where the alien intelligences hang out. The ones watching the earth changes. Until then, I'll get out of his face. He chuckles; we shake hands, I disappear.

Tuesday October 5, 10:00 am
Contact quickly established; little sense of time, distance or location. Dialog immediately enabled.

So John, you've had an interesting couple of days?
That much time has gone by has it?
Four actually, it's now Tuesday morning in North America. Est.
Well I never would've guessed
Time flies when you're having fun, no?
He smiles, chuckles.

Seems to me like you're doing just fine. Lots of folks I work with are filled with anxiety about the road ahead, or even if there is a road ahead.

I guess I'm so fascinated with events unfolding from moment to moment that I haven't given what's coming up much thought. Plus it's obvious to me that consciousness continues after death. It's merely a matter of which from and expression it takes, and I'm quite happy to watch that process unfold.

How are your family members and friends coping? Have you been drawn to them?

Yes, of course, it's just as I read and suspected. Their emotional states have an overwhelming magnetic quality. Resistance, if I had any, which I don't, would be quite futile.

Did you find yourself able to contact and comfort them?

I certainly saw how empathy can be more of a risk than a help. One's being becomes swamped with another's grief. It's as if one is drowning.

Surely you learned the value of distancing when working with abductees.

Yes, of course, one balanced the need for sympathy with the need for some measure of objectivity. But with those near and dear the draw is that much more intense. Advice from guides certainly helped. Now I'm told the memorial service will be something of a challenge.

Souls are often amazed at the outpouring of love, I find. Be ready to feel treasured! (He seems a touch bashful) Have you enjoyed the traveling around?

Fascinating, as is the whole experience. One moves to the emotional needs of others, regardless of location. One is barely aware of distance, speed or location. One merely appears, interacts and moves on. Flying about, when one has the psychic space to appreciate it, is a wonderful thrill. Trees, for example, have the most beautiful emanations. Tell me, how did you get into this line of work?

To be honest, John, I suspect it was a priest's training in Ancient Egypt that started it, but that's only as far as I've traced it. I'm almost willing to bet Atlantis and Lemuria had some bearing on the situation. Maybe it's suffice to say I'm been a shaman/priest/magus type guy in many incarnations, and I rediscover my abilities afresh in each life. Of course, with a variety of cultural baggage to explain it.

Just as I suspected, an urban shaman. This with a smile.

Yup, I'm one of those new-age nutbars, and I come complete with all the jargon. You realize, don't you, that you can now ask T.E. Lawrence any question you want?

Oh, you think he's still around?

I'd be surprised if he wasn't. Want to check out the real afterlife? It won't take but a minute of your time.

Why is it, as you say, real?

Well, that's reality as defined by the human communities which exist there. You're in the borderland regions right now, neither here nor there. Every country has a counterpart on the astral plane filled with communities of various interest groups and religious denominations.

Do I have to go?

You don't have to do anything John; there is no coercion, no rules, at least not where I plan to take you.

After a little further discussion, I take J.M.'s hand and whisk him up a level and move to a city. Lowest levels of cities are pretty grim, but he needs to see it. Then up to the next two levels, each with its own inhabitants and attitudes. Then a fly over astral Rockies and down to astral Pacific ocean. All quite exciting. Then I tell him about focus 27, and how it's for freethinking folks, the kind of have no overt dependence on any belief system. That's a description which seems to appeal, so we whisk to the Park, where I explain the set-up, and how he doesn't have to tell anyone he's John Mack from Harvard, he can just be any old John. That makes him smile. He certainly seems to enjoy the beauty of the place. I explain how, through imagery and intent, he can return to the earthplane and visit with his loved ones, and then, using the same process in reverse, come back here to f27. I also promise to return and show him f35, where the alien intelligences hang out. Our formal handshake turns into a hug and he says *Thank you Gordon* as I make my exit.

Wednesday October 13/04, 10:30am:

In the interim, I have received an email account of John and Montgomery Keen "coming through" at a British séance, 'Monty' having made a splash in British new-age/spiritualist circles by coming through as promised very soon after his sudden and rapid transition. I have a hunch I briefly met Monty at the 1991 International Crop Circle Conference in England, but I briefly met so many there I could have him confused with someone else. I suspect John was greeted by Monty sometime between my first and second contact, but did not mention it out of deference to 'my' project. Plus I think he was just plain intrigued to see what everyone had in store for him.

On expressing intent for personal contact I encounter him walking through an astral plane university campus, New England style. Graceful old stone buildings set amongst trees and gardens. Very Ivy League. Introduce myself and remind him of my name. He's still identified with earth plane style forgetfulness. When asked of his impressions so far, declares himself to be absolutely amazed. Can't get over his astonishment. That such a world should exist and most to live in ignorance of it strikes him as the greatest absurdity. He will be pondering the significance of it for years he thinks. I agree with him; it is a gap in understanding that deeply shocks all thinking souls. Why we exist mainly in ignorance of our spiritual heritage occupies the thoughts of many. And of course, theories abound. Repressed by organized religion is one favorite. A function of skeptical materialism is another. A challenge to overcome on the journey out of familial and tribal consciousness is another. A plot by the dark brothers, who may or may not be extraterrestrials bent on our psychic enslavement, is another. John chuckles at my list, as if perhaps he'd already touched on them quietly but had refrained from expression. I advise him that the endless hypothesizing on the meaning of existence continues unabated here in the afterlife, at least amongst those who have seen through the pleasures of paradise.

I tell him his communication experience with Montague Keen has been posted on the internet. He knows. He found the experience fascinating. Especially after reading accounts of other-side communication in the spiritualist literature. Funny to be on the other side of the fence and see just how difficult clear communication can be. Yes, I agree, accuracy can be a real challenge. I myself am never sure just how accurate my renderings are. I just hope that there are no outright mistakes in the texts I provide.

He's already heard about the communication devices in preparation. Several teams are working simultaneously he says. How it will change the world, he enthuses. I tend to agree, but suspect that it will also throw up new challenges, especially amongst those who already feel that communication with spirits is wrong and that we should advance by faith alone. John adds that he was more familiar with the skeptical opposition than the faith-based one. I ask him how he's enjoying the food: marvelous is his response. Far better than on earth, although he notices that his appetite is somewhat curtailed. So he's settling in then? Settling isn't quite the tone he'd use. Far too exciting for that. Is he ready to visit f35 as I'd suggested? Where is that again? Where the extraterrestrials hang out. Well, he's on his way to meet up with some academic colleagues right now, could I fit him in another time? Certainly, I'll be back.

Some hours later, I practice a 'forward' projection, on the assumption that I can now connect with the 'time/opportunity' when John Mack and 'I' move together to focus 35, the so-called 'Gathering'.

Certainly this brings up many thorny questions about free will and the past-present-future continuum, but I have learned that I can still practice this 'art' while teasing out the possible metaphysical and ethical consequences. Warning John that I suspect the alien intelligences could manifest in any number of unforeseen ways, and answering his queries concerning movement to new and undefined spheres, we clasp hands and move. Initially I sense no outward form, other than the wisps of iridescent smoke/steam, all of varying but indescribably delicate hue, wafting about us. Is this my expectation? Perhaps. The formless spheres are famed for being completely unpredictable and endlessly mutable, depending on the usually unconscious assumptions/ preferences of the experiencer. About the only constant seems to be an intense glow of light, somehow both brilliant and subdued. On some formless levels this glow is populated by golden spheres which float gracefully about, being either human souls, higher selves or angelic beings of some type. I wonder if the entities observing will manifest thusly. In case I might be cramping his style, I ask John if he'd care to explore on his own. He seems enamored of the idea, and as we wave 'au revoir' he grins mischievously.

I telepath a thought-desire to interact with an alien entity. The thought returns to me as "Which type of being do you wish contact with?" That throws me: I see I do not know what exactly I want. I ask for beings who see themselves as disinterested observers. Nothing appears, but a voice emanates from the mist about me: "We are three who are also one. As you request, we represent a civilization which has no vested interest in your planetary evolution, as some do, but are here merely because we heard an interesting, as you say, rumor."

About our so-termed 'earth changes'?

"Yes. We are interested in how you will move from isolated egoistic consciousness to the shared vibrational state in which you will no longer be able to hide your negativity from each other. We are also interested in your transition from mortality as a given to immortality as a verifiable fact. And no, to answer your thought, we are not involved in the hybrid breeding program, nor have we ever been."

I asked where they learned English.

"From your own brain, Gordon being. And we hope you trust us to learn and not manipulate, as others might do. We take your request for communication as an invitation to express most clearly to you what is our intention, and to do that English seems the most effective tool."

I said that I did indeed trust them not to mess with my wiring.

"That would be an expression of your sense of humor, Gordon being, yes?"

I telepathed a smile/chuckle combination. It seemed effective, judging by the sort of wobbly vibration that returned.

"Your chuckles come across as wobbly to us, Gordon being."

"That's okay, I understand and am amused".

"As are we."

I asked if their own culture's sense of humour was significantly different than the human.

"It changes depending on whether we are in form or not."

So they moved from body to bodiless essence at will?

"Yes that is so. Our civilization is, to some extent, an extended experiment in combining the two."

Are there laws or guidelines outlining the movement, I wondered.

"Guidelines, yes; laws, no. We have free will as do humans, but we have advanced beyond the need for a centralized authority structure. We are like your anarchists but without the desire or ability to destroy."

I wondered if that made their lives a bit predictable and maybe even boring.

"By your standards maybe yes. You humans thrive on conflict. We have seen, by traveling through what you call time, that it brings out the qualities you most seek. Does not one of your famous holy books take place on a battlefield?"

They must have been thinking of the conversation between Krishna and Arjuna in the "Gita", where Krishna urges Arjuna onward into battle, that it might sooner relieve him of his illusions of separateness. "Yes" they telepathed.

"Our lives are an ongoing examination of the One versus the Many. Quite like your discipline called Zen. And as to your unasked question, when in form we live in what might appear to you as enlarged shiny soap bubbles which float about in the somewhat contradictory breezes that are created by us when we are out of form."

I thought it all sounded kind of zany and fun.

"By your standards it is. By ours an amusing pastime. Boredom is becoming a reality for us. We are beginning to see the need for a challenge. Angels from your system have invited us to ensoul baby planets, and some of us are indeed taking preparatory classes for such an undertaking. Have you yet realized that we are the beings you sketched in your first novel?"

Back in 1984 I'd written a short comedy called "Kissless", with a Greek chorus of highly evolved but slightly bored aliens who were monitoring some of our activities as some rascal among them had deliberately wiped some of their vast memory banks. Well, I telepathed, I guess I should not be surprised. But there was no denying I was stumped for a next question. They suggested that this was enough for now and that perhaps I should chat with some others. I said sure, why not, and felt that wobbly vibration as they merged and faded.

I expressed a desire to encounter a being or beings from Galactic headquarters. A response came.

"They are all too busy, but I have been assigned as a representative for this focus level. How can I assist you?"

I wanted to know why Galactic Central, or whatever it was known as, was actually necessary.

"Your question is noted and answered thusly: the members of the Galactic central, as you call it, concern themselves, not with the dull administrative chores you may be imagining, but with balancing the needs of various planetary cultures, assuring that squabbles do not get out of hand. Squabbles such as mineral rights on Earth, which many extraterrestrials, as you call them, seem to regard as their own."

I thanked him/her for the example, as it seemed very apt. Did they continue their mining activities convinced we were so stupid that we deserved the exploitation?

Some of them, yes, apparently. And some of them, while not dismissing us or interfering with our evolution, saw their own need as supreme, and calculated that certain elements on Earth were so abundant that we could easily spare some.

I had to admit that this sounded very human in its reasoning. I thought 'the cosmic beggar meets the rapacious capitalist'. The Galactic Central bureaucrat partially concurred. Post facto rationalization had a very broad usage it would seem.

I expressed a certain skepticism as regards the value of the debating process at the Galactic level. Physically alive humans were being encouraged to participate, but other than a sense of belonging, I wondered what good, if any, it might do. The sense of belonging was, in fact, the whole point of the exercise, I was told. Humans need to know, I was told, that they have a seat at table.

If they remember to show up, I added.

"Yes, well, that could be a problem."

Will the 'humans needing to know' stage last for some years, to be then replaced with the 'few humans who care participating' stage?

"That's something along the lines of what we were envisioning".

I asked about members of the planetary hierarchy, such as Jesus, Buddha, Maitreya and Saint Germain, participating.

"Yes, they and their assistants are intimately involved. As perhaps you might have guessed."

I asked if issues were decided without any human participation.

Well, the hierarchy was human after all, even if they were graduated members. And he suspected that I myself had more than once sat in the visitors' gallery. This shocked me until I recalled portraying that very situation fictionally and wondering where exactly I got the idea. He then diplomatically implied that if I wanted to overcome my visitor-on-the-periphery status I would have to develop a much more continuous sense of consciousness, one that would not be periodically obliterated by sleep.

I knew this to be true and took my lumps like a man. Continuity of consciousness is something all aspirants strive for. That pearl beyond price: knowing where you are at all hours of the day and night. Knowing where *all* of you is, not just *some* of you. I thanked the Galactic representative for his efforts and he sort of dwindled down to a dot and then disappeared.

I tasted my humility for a while and then, perhaps to reassert my status amongst the righteous, put out a call for one of the 'Greys' involved in the hybrid breeding project. As I waited for a response I wondered how John was doing. Intuition said *just fine.*

A being that looked more like a Nordic than a Grey appeared in front of me, beaming with a brew of authority, nobility, charm and pride. Well, something like that. Certainly no shame, which is perhaps what I was expecting, or worse, hoping for.

"I am here to represent the Greys," he telepathed, "And I can see you are one of the old human souls who resent the Greys initiative as a betrayal of some kind."

The Greys and The Reptilians are an abomination to me. I find their arguments specious, their ways deceptive and manipulative and their perceived goals repulsive. This notion that they hold up the human dark side to the mirror of conscience to be the worst kind of retroactive rationalization, worthy of perhaps only the Nazis.

"You would excuse the ongoing human practice of economic slavery?"

"Our sins and shortcomings are no concern of yours. And using them to justify your continued rape of innocence in pursuit of the physical immortality you lust after is a habit worthy only of the dark brothers you serve."

"You yourself have honored the divine role of the rebel angels."

"They serve the polarity created by the law of free will, yes. And they do it well. But the beings you administer serve only their self-interest. And the damage they inflict in the process will take incarnations to heal."

"Not if they forgive as your prophet Jesus suggests."

"None of this supposed forgiveness would be necessary if you and your kind had not initiated the process in the first place"

"You would rather the Greys had died out for lack of a heart chakra and the dna it implies?

"In a word, yes. Species die out continually, especially when they have fulfilled their potential/served their purpose. It's no great loss. Their spirits can always incarnate in other life streams."

"You would condemn them, then, to extinction."

"I would suggest they taste the karma of their own choices, made so long ago, instead of deferring their fate with genetic experimentation."

"You are cruel sir. You show no compassion."

"I fight fire with fire and I speak with the wrath of the righteous. Compassion is received when it is deserved."

"Compassion is always deserved."

"You demean the spiritual laws of this planet when you speak from cynical self-interest, and I dismiss you from my presence."

With this he faded, but I knew my victory was hollow. The hybrid breeding program was so advanced by this point, into its third generation at least as far as I could tell, that there was literally no turning back. Whether the hybrids would survive the vibrational increase of the ascension process remained to be seen, however. As many physically alive humans would not either, I tried not to have preferences on the matter. Also, there was no forgetting Daryl Anka's channeled entity Bashar, whose authoritative utterances and wit I heard at a crop circle conference in Glastonbury some years after 'maybe' meeting Montague Keen. He claimed to be one of the Human-Grey hybrids, traveling backwards in time from 400 years in the future, to tell us, amongst other things, that the experiment had finally succeeded.

I put a thought out for John. He appeared smiling. Well, wasn't this all so fascinating, he seemed to be saying. His colleagues in abduction research would just be amazed. I sensed he wasn't ready to leave, so I reminded him of the 'moving between focus levels' methodology and bade him a fond farewell.

Betty and Barney Hill: October 19/04, 10:00am

Express intent to meet up with Betty and Barney Hill. Ask guides. Response: No Gordon, you can do this yourself. Find them, or should I say Barney, in lovely garden. Barney goes to side door and calls to Betty, along the lines of *Hon there's someone here to see you.* Barney feels almost automatically that folk always want to see

Betty first and foremost. Is this the result of being black in America in the fifties, or merely a personal reclusiveness? Not sure. Betty seems, if not exactly feeble, then not exactly vibrant either. Still attached to her old lady persona from Earth.

We all sit in garden and begin conversing. Barney's been 'here' awhile, Betty but a week earth time, so he's the one with the answers. He's had the time to reflect/meditate/ &check soul files, as it were.

Yes, they agreed to the abduction situation before birth. They known each other in 19th century America and had an interracial romance then, one that hadn't worked out too well, and were convinced by guides to act it out again, partly to give a chance to those who oppressed them before to make amends, and partly as an example to 20th century America.

Betty's glad to be in heaven, earth had shown her all it could, she was tired of her old body. Plus she'd been longing for Barney, her soulmate, for so long it's become a bad habit. She feels as if she's waking up from a long sleep. It's not being in heaven, it's being *back* in heaven; that's what it feels like.

Barney has been preparing this house for her, and he's sure had a lot of fun doing it. Being able to choose exactly what you want for the house and the garden, without worrying about cost kind of gives you a new lease on life. He's been creating some things with his mind, but also receiving all sorts of items from the local crafts-people hereabouts. They make such lovely and unique pieces and are so glad to let you have them it seems a shame to disappoint them. The delicacy and intricacy of the hand carving alone is marvelous. Both Betty and Barney are quiet while the other is speaking, unlike some couples who excitedly interrupt all the time.

Betty asks what my purpose is. I tell them about contact and retrieval work, and my habit of posting the results on the internet, so that others may learn and understand. Betty asks if I'm a spirit guide. "Sometimes" is my answer.

I ask how they feel about their interactions with aliens now. Barney's glad it's over, he wants a normal life now, and so far he's had one. The joys of church and community life without the stress of economic and social conflicts are almost more than he could've hoped for. And now that Betty's here, he has everything man could want.

They smile at each other with the warmth I would expect. I sense they've discussed religious and spiritual matters already but are not about to expound on them for me, unless I corner them with questions. Having experienced the doubt-fringed exaltations of church folk on the astral before, I'm happy to let that be. They have to discover for themselves that heaven actually lies beyond this paradise, there's likely no point in me giving them a pep talk about it.

Betty says she's still thinking over all her alien experiences, and even recalling more now that she's here. Barney says they planned it out before they were born, and that may be so, but she has to recover that memory for herself.

I thank them for their time and ask if I may talk about our meeting on the radio this coming weekend, on a show that's devoted to the alien/ufo experience. They both give their assent and ask that their best wishes be passed along. Tell them things are just wonderful here and that I'm doing just fine. Barney smiles and nods in agreement. I walk out of the garden and their sightlines before disappearing.

POSTSCRIPT

A few days after the last contact above, suggested to me by Toronto radio host Errol Bruce Knapp on hearing of my John Mack contacts, I was preparing supper at home alone when I felt the presence of my dear mother and father. As I still seem to be clairsentient as opposed to clairvoyant, there was no vision as such; nothing like the sights claimed by those reporting recently deceased loved ones standing at the bottom of the bed smiling and waving hello, only a strong sense of their presence. Mother seemed bubbly and excited, perhaps merely because she'd finally had the courage to come. It would certainly be no big deal for my father at this point. She seemed giddy with the idea of surprising me. My son the medium. Father had likely shown her the ropes travel-wise, and after a dozen false starts, they'd made it. I could just see it.

As I'd been experiencing an intriguing dissonance the previous few weeks, a rather sour disconnect between the *me* that is the psychic explorer and the *me* that is the grieving son, this little jolt was just what the doctor ordered, so I played along with their sense of fun, making the kind of small talk you might expect. Nancy was in full teasing mother mode, and well out of the sick old lady stuff I'd been seeing on my earlier contacts. It was a treat, and certainly a fine way to bring this volume to a close.

It's been an astonishing journey from apprenticeship to Henry to full-fledged explorer status. Unwrapping the package of my very own enigma continues to be a boundary-busting exercise in seductive enticement. Just this week I made a soul contact for a man in Mexico and performed a spirit releasement for a woman in Los Angeles. Strangers write and email to report how thrilled they are with the newly released *First Hand Account*. Growth is endless, I now see, but I can put the brakes on anytime I choose. Yet the life eternal, as experienced by 'Gordon' through the retrievals, explo-rations, and mergings you have heard described, continues to so challenge and excite that the thought of braking, even if only for a breather, seems kind of boring.

And so, as I continue to blend with the 'me' on other levels, I absorb at least some of their higher vibrations, and can feel myself *here* speeding up. Perhaps it is all part of the ascension process, personally retooled for 'Gordon'. Meanwhile the planet reverberates with the violent upheavals of fear and anger: ideologies scream their certainties at each other as governments wallow in electoral deception and cater to their corporate sponsors.

No doubt about it, it's a bitch and there's no end in sight. But at this stage I do see that suffering *is*, just as joy *is*; that power dances with its inevitable loss, that the virtues of poverty and wealth compete for the moral high ground; that cultures and species rise and fall; that the design of galaxies equals that of the sub-quantum chaos physicists like to cackle about. God is everywhere in the design, but only if you want to see him. If you don't care for his brand of immanent divinity, he'll gladly disappear into the cold, purposeless calculations of scientists who see consciousness as a mere epiphenomenon of the bustling computer known as brain. The God in god-consciousness is like that, endlessly adaptable to your moment-to-moment needs, appearing and disappearing as your doubt and belief jostle for momentary supremacy.

There and not-there simultaneously. Mystical mumbo-jumbo and the meaning of life: take your pick. I know what mine is.

APPENDIX:

INITIAL HIGHER SELF DIALOGUES AND MORE OF RECENT RELEVANCE

When compiling *A First Hand Account* all those years ago (98-99), I only vaguely realized the significance of Higher Self in the proceedings. I felt I was doing *quite well thank you* just getting it down on paper, never mind keeping up with all of Henry's little tricks. Now this volume opens with a Higher Self monologue of considerable profundity. So profound I was afraid to publish it at first, worried that folk might think I was trying to set up some kind of a guru dealership.

You know the kind, with grow-your-own-deity franchises, available only after graduation. That was in the summer of 1999 when I was beginning on my mini talks-and-seminars career, long before *A First Hand Account* saw the light of multi-national distribution. The fact that it was the first thing put to paper after a long depression over a failed relationship didn't help matters. But I had to admit its delivery instilled the strangest sense of calm in me. I thought, "Ooo, this sure feels like channeling." It was, but I wasn't sure how much more I wanted just then. Despite my local schedule of talks and group meditations, I did not return to HS until October of 2000, when, after sporadic contacts through the winter of 1999/2000 at my local swimming pool, I gave in and started writing. I published the dialogues for local consumption under the title *Being Watching Doing And Feeling Desirous*. They later found a more international home on the conversation board of Bruce Moen's Afterlife-Knowledge website. Here they are now, 'a first series of dialogues with my Higher Self', complete with their original epigraphs. Despite some twinges of embarrassment, I have bravely resisted any urge to modify these baby steps in the direction of spiritual sophistication. With HS we all have to start somewhere: here's where Gordon got his feet wet.

BEING WATCHING DOING AND FEELING DESIROUS

"One may be a perfect Theosophist, she wrote in a letter to a TS member in 1889, two years before her death, without giving one's allegiance to our Master, but simply to one's Higher Self, in essence above the Masters"

    H.P. Blavatsky, quoted in *The Spiritual Tourist* by Mick Brown (1998)

"The problem of the lower and higher self is an old one, and it is undoubtedly difficult to realize that there is, after all, only one consciousness, and that the apparent difference is caused only by the limitations of the various vehicles. It (the higher self) puts a portion of itself down into lower matter, and that portion becomes so much more keenly and vividly conscious in that matter that it thinks and acts as though it were a separate being, forgetting its connection with that less developed yet far wider self-consciousness above"

    Charles W. Leadbeater, The Inner Life (1910)

"If we ask ourselves, 'What would my higher self look like?' then we proceed along our search as though we imagined ourselves gods. We have such linear styles of imagination that we always think of a form in this light, of a human figure. We identify ourselves as humans from the standpoint of our ego selves. This estimate is naturally not the entire truth because only a small part of our multi-dimensional soul is expressed in our human form."

    Chris Griscom, Time Is An Illusion (1988)

Higher Self to Gordon (Oct 23/2000)

After several contacts at my local swimming pool this past year or so, where, after expressions of surprise from me, information was cordially exchanged between the two entities referred to above, I thought to attempt direct contact here at home, with the laptop going, so that the earlier 'loss' of information might not be repeated.

Gordon: Well, Higher Self, here I am at the computer, as promised, awaiting contact. The exultation of watery immersion is still with me, and I bend my ear to your voice.

Higher Self: Hello Gordon! That elevator of light between us is indeed open. The contact, as I told you earlier, is more or less permanent. Only a continuous diminishment of consciousness through foolish or selfish action on your part could wreck it now, and you'd have to try pretty damn hard to succeed. Basically friend, you're stuck with me now. You should never have written that poem years ago, that *Homage to the Higher Self*, you more or less sealed your fate with that.

You have already asked why me? And why now? Let me recapitulate. It's you because you understand and accept my existence over and above many of my other personality projections through space and time; they either have no inkling of my existence, or they so identify me with either an angelic or godlike nature and thus fall into the trap of praise and worship.

At long last I have an incarnate comrade. It's now because your efforts in meditation have facilitated our meeting at the astral level, even as you are functioning in the physical. This, as you know, is the result of a long process of self development, a gradual opening to greater and greater conceptions of self, ones that earlier personalities would not even dare to dream of.

Your surrender to the spirit of unconditional love has, bless you, given me many new areas of consciousness to explore. Even your temporary lapses from this commitment are of great interest to me. Though the heat of your indignation is jarring to your discarnate co-workers, I am fascinated to see how they rise to the challenge. You certainly know how to hold their feet to the fire, as it were.   A couple of earlier personality projections made deep penetrations into the vast depths of the planes and sub-planes of form, but their efforts were defined by the aesthetic and intellectual modes of the monk and scholar, whereas you have learned the trick of mothering wisdom, of giving birth to it from the hips of your own (and others) suffering, and seeing that a mother's love is as close to the god consciousness as light is to shadow. You understand that all form is illusion, and yet you love all these illusions for their temporary beauty.

Gordon: You have repeatedly communicated your pleasure at my progress, the fact of which I seem to be still somewhat embarrassed by

Higher Self: Don't be afraid of your achievement. And let me remind you not to evaluate spiritual worth in worldly terms. You can be of service without bowing or kneeling.

Gordon: I see that I should let it go, this impassioned humility.

Higher Self: Agreed.

Gordon: I take it that this journey of mine, this sacrificing of self on the altar of Self, was carefully planned before Gordon's birth.

Higher Self: As are all life journeys; at least those birthed from the monad. Of course, not all incarnate personalities follow the original plan. As you know it's easy to get distracted.

Gordon: Life has a way of getting between your toes.

Higher Self: So I'm told.

Gordon: One of the times we were dialoging as I was swimming, the talk turned to communicating with the other personality essences you have projected, and I thought I'd be a smart aleck and ask if we were including the one in the 22nd century, and your cool-as-a-cucumber response made me see I'd stumbled upon something. You see I'd been putting a lot of effort into tying up all the karmic knots I could find so I wouldn't have to come back to earth level.

Higher Self: After a century of unrestrained bliss you'll be ready for another splash in the pool.

Gordon: Oh, very funny.

Higher Self: And besides, by then the project of raising the vibration of the physical plane to that of the astral could be very close to completion. Things will be ever so much nicer for you and you won't mind as much as you think.

Gordon: Nicer for the whole planet? What about our perpetual trouble spots?

Higher Self: As perhaps you've heard from other sources, by

then or thereabouts, those who cannot cope with the higher vibration of the physical plane will be incarnated on a denser planet more suitable to their rate of evolution. There, they will be able to play out their dramas of ethnic hatred, power struggles and deadly rivalries to their heart's content.

Gordon: So I am coming back then?

Higher Self: Don't sound so depressed about it. By then, souls like you will be able to exist simultaneously in the material and spiritual words. The vibration will be right and your evolutionary level appropriate. You are, in fact, very close to this now.

Gordon: As we speak?

Higher Self: Indeed. You've already had a number of intimations from various sources that you are active in spirit when asleep, have you not?

Gordon: Yes, the reports and hints I receive make me sound like it's Gordon times ten, at least in terms of capabilities. Sometimes I feel like this tiny version of Gordon who only walks and talks, and feels quite faint if he doesn't eat every three hours.

Higher Self: It is. I'm quite sure that when the time comes you'll jump at the chance.

Gordon: Funny to talk of time when in spirit I'll be in eternity. Yes, but as your life in eternity unfolds, you peek onto the planet to see how time is affecting things. And when circumstances are right for your level of evolution and game playing ability, it is very much as if the 'right time' has come, even though from you viewing standpoint in eternity, nothing has changed.

Gordon: I can't imagine how time must look to you.

Higher Self: Yes you can. Just stop thinking for a moment and feel.

Gordon: Okay, I got three images: (1) turning on a light in a darkened room and having everything spring into activity, (2) being some kind of spirit bird that hovers and then descends into the body of a human being, and (3) being watching doing and feeling desirous.

Higher Self: Number three almost catches it.

Gordon: I agree and the writer in me thinks it would be a good title for this series of dialogues.

Higher Self: That's fine with me, Mr. Writer guy.

Gordon: Do I deserve all this teasing?

Higher Self: No, but we love doing it anyway.

Wed. Oct25th/Dialogue Two

Gordon: Hello there H.S.

Higher Self: Good idea, call me H.S. It will remove any excess formality from the proceedings.

Gordon: Yes, I see your point. Formality will just distance me from you unnecessarily. And, I suppose, return me to the position of earlier personality projections.

H.S.: Exactly. I value this for its sense of equality.

Gordon: I'm not bowing and scraping.

H.S.: Yes, you're my confidant.

Gordon: Any secrets you want to share?

H.S.: Nothing that you don't already know.

Gordon: Yes H.S., very clever. I know it but I've forgotten it.

H.S.: Correct. By choosing to incarnate you chose to forget.

Gordon: But I'm remembering! Bit by bit I'm putting together the whole picture.

H.S.: Yes your connection to source just gets stronger.

Gordon: I was recalling as I swam today, the time that I think of as my first conscious connection to you. Years ago, at least fifteen, I woke up in the middle of the night with the strongest hunch that I was indirect communication with my higher self, so I thought, quite calmly and matter-of-factly, that I should ask some questions. Even as I had the thought I couldn't imagine where it came from. I was awake and it was dark and quiet: so what? So I asked about M.K.M., with whom I was having a relationship at the time. I asked of we'd been married before; the answer was a quick yes. I asked the name and epoch; it seemed like Lord and Lady Dunsmuir (or Dunsmore) and the epoch 13/14th century Scotland. We were some fairly down-at-heels landed gentry, who couldn't afford to keep the servants we'd inherited and were reduced to squabbling over the lamb chops at suppertime.

H.S.: Yes, that was one of our earliest successes. What a lot of out-of-body effort went into that.

Gordon: Some guides helped me out I imagine?

H.S.: You bet. The soul you call Henry was quite instrumental.

Gordon: I should have guessed.

H.S.: And of course he was helped by his guide.

Gordon: Yes the picture gets bigger.

H.S.: As it always does.

Gordon: Now when I did those past life regressions, a few years before that, were you present then?

H.S.: No, that was your soul working on that one.

Gordon: You mean Gordon, the incarnate ego personality, and Gordon, the all-knowing soul?

H.S.: Well, not quite, the soul is certainly much more knowledgeable and wise than the incarnate ego, but it has to have a lining connection with me to approach anything like all-knowingness. When, for example, a soul, once deceased, is rising slowly through the planes, and, as you know, this may take a great long while, as you folks in form calculate things, shucking off its various attachments like worn-out overcoats, it does not realize that it is I who am slowing winding it in, like a fish who's been caught from day one but never felt the bait in its mouth.

Gordon: I think I understand but I'm not sure.

H.S.: My advice to you, sir, is to stop thinking, and embrace my energy. You have already developed the process called intuition, the inner knowingness that such and such is so. Well, that is not only the energy that I use, it is also the energy that I am made of.

Gordon: yes, yes, I know, mere thinking is inadequate.

H.S.: The intellectual categories which it inevitably produces, as they exist in your culture and education system, only serve to fence in that which is continuous, and make futile attempts to bury spirit in form. There is no strict dividing line between the incarnate ego, the indwelling soul and the boundless being that is me, the higher self. Each one blossoms into the other in an energetic continuum that is endless and virtually unstoppable.

Gordon: I notice you say virtually.

H.S.: Well, the incarnate ego, if it's determined to the point of dementia, deranged by fear and pain and the acting out hatred and anger, can effectively strangle the life out of its link to soul and higher self.

Gordon: What happens to soul in such cases?

H.S.: Depends on who it identifies with the most. If it is the suffering ego it will maintain its link and be held down in the lower astral until such time as the ego is willing to make the effort to ride above the tentacles of the depraved desires which hold it in place. If it's the higher self, it rejoins the light energy cluster and stays there.

Gordon: And the isolated ego left behind?

H.S.: Can sustain itself through the assimilation of the dark dense energies of the very lowest astral plane (the same way any resident of any astral absorbs what it needs from its environment) until it sinks to the level of, say, a large ugly boulder, which emanates the kind of bad vibes ands rotten luck referred to in fairy tales and so on. This does not happen often, as souls tend to have almost infinite patience with their egos.

Gordon: As spirit guides do with their earthly charges?

H.S.: Yes it's quite similar.

Gordon: I'm assuming they don't descend to the level of rock right after death.

H.S.: No, of course. They find themselves either in some astral slum or some desolate rocky landscape. It's the desolation of the heart projected outwards, as you know, but they don't see that. First chakra survivalists to the core, they quickly align themselves with one or another power group and continue with whatever nefarious activities they were accustomed to during physical life, never for a moment realizing that their deeply negative thoughts and emotions are creating and sustaining their surroundings. Then there's a stage where the dark energies they unknowingly feed on slowly consume them from within and they dissipate bit by bit, often becoming ragged hermits in caves consumed by anger, moving less and less because they see no need to, until at some point, maybe after centuries, over come with an endless sleep, they solidify into a rock-like structure, just another rock like the rocks that surround them.

Gordon: Meanwhile the soul is safe with the higher self.

H.S.: And had probably reincarnated three or four times in the interim.

Gordon: Well that's something I've never heard before.

H.S.: Yes, you don't see it mentioned much, except in fairy tales, which, I think you know, contain much truth disguised as metaphor. Really though, it's the complete inversion of the transition into the Nirvana process. Instead of exiting out the top of the spiral into the freedom of massless light they fall out of the bottom into very dense dark. It's another of those "as above, so below" things.

Gordon: I guess I'm more familiar with the stories of the egos that descend to the bottom of the astral barrel, as it were, but with the help of a guide, or maybe several guides, slowly work their way up again.

H.S.: That is the more common occurrence, yes. But I wanted to touch on the other kind. You've guessed, of course, why you're more familiar with the type you just mentioned?

Gordon: Because one of the earlier personality projections experienced it and brought the knowledge back to you, the higher self, where I and all the others were able to share in it.

H.S.: That's it. You'll get a gold star in your notebook for that one.

Gordon: I'm deeply honored.

Sunday Oct 29th/Dialogue 3

Gordon: Is my future self in the 22nd century dialoging with you?

H.S.: Yes, it's a regular occurrence by then. The category constructing intellect has long since lost its force, and her psyche is free to project and receive in any direction?

Gordon: Her psyche?

H.S.: Don't feign surprise: that's what you want isn't it?

Gordon: One more hook to pull me into incarnation?

H. S.: An enlightened female who can charm the heart of any stranger? Come now, it's what you've always wanted.

Gordon: But could never attain in earlier societies?

H.S.: Not without playing the game: ...the power game, the sex game, the money game. By then you can just be yourself and be loved and valued for that alone.

Gordon: I think I see where you're going with this. When I tune into my female incarnations, at least the ones I've discovered so far, I can feel them longing to be such a woman, even the powerful ones.

H.S.: Yes, the powerful ones, they were not valued for themselves, they were valued for what they could do for people, either in the sex game or the power game.

Gordon: And when you say charm the heart of any stranger, you mean more than erotic prowess, don't you?

H.S.: Of course. By then the astral plane heart chakra melding in your first 'afterlife' book will be feasible for embodied souls on the physical plane. A lot of you will be ready to do it, and will not hesitate when you actually realize it's possible.

Gordon: You mean it will be some kind of secret?

H.S.: Those who have much invested in the traditional genital contact mode will do their best to suppress, outlaw or scandalize it. It will be so erotically fulfilling, at least once its subtleties are mastered, that no experiencers will want to return to the old way, and making babies will be quite the chore. Institutional religions will be especially incensed.

Gordon: I can see it become a revolutionary act. Will three or four individuals be able to participate simultaneously?

H.S.: Yes, but the love will have to be genuine. Often it will be what you called 'love triangles' from earlier times, with all their jealousies and karma sorted out. I can see two ancient colleagues of yours who could easily fit the bill on this one.

Gordon: Yes, I know exactly who you're thinking of. It's nice to see we'll resolve our differences sometime.

H.S.: When you experience the melding, the long history of hurts and envies will melt into the extended embrace like logs in a bonfire, and you will feel the foolishness of time and form.

Gordon: I daresay you're right. But won't we be able to do this on the astral after this current life?

H.S.: If you put all your pride behind your love, yes. Make no mistake, there will be no possibility of faking this: you're either there or you're not.

Gordon: Do I sense a reprimand?

H.S.: No, I'm merely laying it on the line for you.

Gordon: Something I should be grateful for, I know. Anything else I should know about this future female self?

H.S.: Nothing else you should know, but why don't you try communicating with her yourself? You don't need to depend on me as an intermediary.

Gordon: Well I've tried a bit of message sending to past life personalities, so I guess there's no reason not to try that. But I'm focused on you right now.

H.S.: Okay, save it for later then.

Gordon: Done.

Sunday Nov5th/Dialogue 4

Gordon: I felt your presence while swimming an hour ago, and thought now would be a good opportunity for another chat.

H.S.: Yes Gordon, this is a good a 'time' as any. Let me take up where we left off, a few days ago, when you didn't have time to write anything down. In response to your question, I had said that I exist just below the 'god' level of consciousness and that my conception of how I was spawned could be conveyed by the words 'spat out of the limitless ocean of understanding to feel myself as suddenly somehow unique.'

Gordon: And you explored that uniqueness by sending parts of yourself down the energy highway to check out the territory there and bring back reports?

H.S.: Right. Now the early explorers didn't descend too far down the ladder, they could still feel and hear me as they went about their lives.

Gordon: They weren't completely physical then

H.S.: No, they were at what you would call the astral level.

Gordon: What were they learning there?

H.S.: That they were distinct entities with individual traits, but joined at the level of higher mind.

Gordon: I get the feeling it was a kind of Eden.

H.S.: That would be one way of describing

Gordon: And is that the source of the wispy notions, somewhere in the depths of our souls, of some beautiful life lived in harmony and love with all beings in nature?

H.S.: Yes, and it is renewed every time you're living in the upper astral between lives.

Gordon: So we return with a wry smile of recognition?

H.S.: Sometimes with whoops of delight, and others with the rueful, and maybe remorseful, twinge of *how could I have possibly forgotten all this?*

Gordon: That all rings true for me and I guess that's because I've experienced it and then forgotten. Plato's theory of knowledge and all. Now what if the soul doesn't make it to the upper astral?

H.S.: Well when it gets stuck at a lower level, the heavenly experience seems an inaccessible myth or just a nasty lie served up by an ignorant and deceitful clergy. Of course everyone gets there eventually, even if it takes hundreds of years.

Gordon: When they're 'down there', hemmed in by whatever ignorance and denial, you must have a very hard time communicating with them.

H.S.: Yes, the link becomes extremely tenuous, with just a tiny ripple of energy running up and down.

Gordon: And if they acknowledge you at all, it's as some tattered remnant of some god figure.

H.S.: Or some angelic presence, or maybe a tribal shaman/medicine man figure, whatever fits in with their belief system?

Gordon: You'll excuse me if I suggest that that begs the questions,…are you my higher self, or just a figment of my current belief system?

H.S.: You're excused. There's probably no reliable way for you to verify my existence, any more than you can verify the objective existence of your conscience. But you know your conscience is there, you can feel its effects every day.

Gordon: It's another of those unquantifyables.

H.S.: Yes, and once again I ask you to *feel* rather than *think*. Skeptics will always be able to say you're imagining things and call your sanity into question, and you won't be able to do a thing about it. You'll just have to grin and bear it. You know I'm here because you can feel me; other souls will know when they open to feeling theirs. But the experience is not transferable. You'll probably always wonder if you're just chattering away to another hidden aspect of yourself. Well, you are. I am a hidden aspect of you. You are my child out to play in the fields of consciousness and I await your return with a pleasing sense of familiarity.

Gordon: And when I re-merge with you, I will no longer need to pose such questions?

H.S.: One and one is one.

Wed.Nov15th/Dialogue5

Seconds after my regular ritual of watery submission, I was presented with a vision of the planes as horizontal layers stretching across an event horizon, each about an inch think. I had no doubt that, upon entering, any of them would immediately expand into a functionally complete sphere. From the physical to the formless, each with its entities pursuing game playing agendas.

Although I must have been resident in one or other of those mythic representations, I was allowed a moment apart, to perfect this interactive observation at my discretion. Although time and space did not stop for the beings and societies in my ken, it did seem to somehow freeze for me.

Suspended in a smart bubble between seconds, I saw the life force feeding all things, from the insect snoozing on the breeze blown blade of grass to the aircraft ascending above lightning and storm clouds,...to the earthquake victims amusing their anguish in the improvised astral reception camps, the righteous dead regaling each other with tales of their devotion and charity, and the magnificent choirs in crystal cathedrals endlessly praising their distance from a deity,...to the dead junkies clustering above the barely living, craving the flame which can never be extinguished, the ascended master nudging their pupils as they negotiate the principals of evolutionary chess, and the great clouds of intelligence drifting benignly through depthless skies of transcendence, effortlessly broadcasting the esoteric knowledge that climbers think they need,...to the nobodies in nirvana, vacating a space, in that essence of no-space, for the incoming brides of bliss, and the emptiness inside everything, identical voids from proton to planet, featureless vacuums so endlessly inviting,...

And in that vision I understood the life force to be the propellant of consciousness in all the creaky worlds, which activates all our sustaining illusions, our myths and fears, our love and our anger, our unity and separation, our this and our that. And in my eagerness to ascribe footnotes to revelation, I swam back into action on one of those planes as easily as karma creates its contestants.

Gordon: H.S., my old friend, it is now some hours since I scribbled the above, but as you might have guessed, I want to ask, were you the source of this illumination?

H.S.: I was indeed, though I'm uneasy about your use of the word 'source'.

Gordon: Why so?

H.S.: It implies I'm at the end of the line, giving things a boost. The energy of inspiration arose, to our mutual satisfaction, from the potential that parades between us. Your urge to resume communications expressed itself subconsciously through the pretty clutter of your day-to-day preoccupations, and I gathered you'd appreciate a little nudge from me.

Gordon: I think I see. It reminds me of the seemingly involuntary telepathy between me and my old friends. You get so used to each other you can't tell who thought what first. A favorite poet of mine, a Mr. Leonard Cohen, has expressed it well: "She gets you on her wavelength and you let the river answer."

H.S.: Yes the connection is clear.

Gordon: So this extensive vision, here quoted, that was not something you 'gave' to me, it was something we shared?

H.S.: It is also an experience you have had, as you say, 'before', but had filed away so cleverly, or carelessly...

Gordon: Or so cleverly carelessly?

H.S.: Yes, so deep in the file drawer it took ages to find again.

Gordon: So I had this experience when I was physically asleep?

H.S.: Yes. And many others just as strange and wonderful.

Gordon: You should have seen me, trying to write it all down later in a coffee shop.

H.S.: Yes, you and others have informed me of this fascinating history of these coffee shops and the intellectual ferment and frantic activity they inspire.

Gordon: I felt quite enlightened, let me tell you.

H.S.: You are enlightened my friend. You're only pretending to be a dull-witted arthritic jointed human being. It's a clever disguise to be sure, but it doesn't fool me. I see through all your Halloween costumes.

Gordon: Yes I suppose you do. Being with you is a bit like trying to hide something from your mother, it's well nigh impossible. Do you think we should discuss the quote above?

H.S.: Do you?

Gordon: I can't see what could possibly be added, other than to maybe split the composing credits with you.

H.S.: Very decent of you in the circumstances sir. You are a gentleman to be sure.

Gordon: Well this time around anyway.

Wed.Nov22/Dialogue6

Gordon: I think of you often, but don't seem to get around to chatting as much as I would like.

H.S.: Your deference is charming but really not necessary. I am not your lord and master, nor would I want to be. Besides we're communicating energetically all the time, you just don't have the necessary space and implements to record the dialogue. I understand how daily duties to both self and society consume your energies, and I am in no way jealous of your commitment to them. Rather I am proud to see a giving nature expressed in this way.

Gordon: Wow! I'm honored by your praise. And, of course, that reminds me of our earlier swimming pool contacts, where I was embarrassed to hear that you were happy with my progress. Since then, I have, as you no doubt know, been encouraged to see through the illusion of my humility.

H.S.: I know of this experience, but perhaps our audience needs some details.

Gordon: Yes, you are right, they do. It concerns this light meditation I've been doing for, hmmn, well over 18 months I should think by now. It started when I was beginning to feel quite blessed out when swimming. After doing my laps I would sit in the hot tub and invoke a 'white light of love and understanding' to descend through the planes to my level and enter the etheric version of my body, whereupon I would direct it back out in waves to all the sentient beings in the pool that day, trusting that it would be absorbed by them to the limit of their current capacities. Sort of blessing them in a way. I had been undergoing a radical change in my consciousness for some time then, so this seemed like a small and quite natural extension of what I'd already been doing/experiencing.

After some, what, weeks I guess of this, when I was closing down the meditation, as I had thought was only correct, considering I was heading back to my work as a bus driver, I heard an inner voice saying, 'that's not necessary we'll look after that'. I was surprised and said, 'how can I keep this up while driving, I just can't concentrate?' The voice insisted that 'they' would take care of it and I was not to worry. Over the days I got used to this concept and just let it ride, as it were. Further suggestions came: one was why didn't I begin the light meditation while I was driving in the early morning and just let them take care of it for the rest of the day? I acceded to this request and tailored my invocation accordingly. The bus filled up with light: some days I felt as if I was driving a large sphere of glowing light through Mississauga. It was an interesting experience trying to be a normal person inside this alternate reality. Months went by in this manner, while other experiences of healing and channeling unfolded. When I felt contacted by you in July of '99, you responded to my amazement to you could 'come down' through the levels and exist 'here' by saying that my daily meditations had raised me to the astral level, which eased the whole process. I can see now it was the 'monk' within me who was surprised: he's accustomed to meditating for years to get any results. And when I started meditating I was unconsciously plugging into bits of his belief system and expectations, which of course, are about a thousand years out of date. During this visit, and also those of March and May 2000, you seemed inordinately pleased with my progress. Finally you insisted that I not be either surprised at your presence or bashful at your praise. I understood I was to let all that go. Which I did, or tried to do. More recently, during this early winter of 2000, when doing the early morning light meditation, I was repeatedly asked/told not to express humility or piety at being 'selected' for this 'honor' of being the receptacle for this light energy, as many around the globe were giving themselves as assistants in this process of raising the physical level vibration toward that of the astral. In fact, as I now understand it,

The process is cosmic in origin, and has been ongoing for quite some 'time', and our efforts are more in the way of stabilizing the grounding the energy flow, humanize it as it were.

So that's me giving up my humility. I guess I was afraid I'd get arrogant with the seeming power of it all.

H.S.: But you're much too wise to be arrogant now.

Gordon: I've been through that one before, right?

H.S.: And in that all-time-is-now level of consciousness you're going through it right now.

Gordon: Yes, I was afraid you'd say that.

H.S.: Why afraid my friend?

Gordon: Well it's a figure of speech really. But I get your point: I should be ready for this by now.

H.S.: Okay, focus on the energy vortex and feel.

Gordon: Okay I got several images quickly. (1) Someone in the european christian bureaucratic hierarchy righteously enforcing his will on parishioners and colleagues, (2) the philosopher in heated debate, insisting, (3) the chinese trader shouting and slapping his wife, (4) the celtic chieftain loudly berating his men, not for lack of courage, but lack of forethought and insight, qualities that he alone maintains, (5) the druid righteously condemning the christians, and (6) the primitive ragged wife in ancient tribal times, planning and then executing the murder of her cruel husband, eviscerating him as he slept, all the while planning to shack up with his rival. That enough for now?

H.S.: Yes, that's not all, but it's certainly sufficient.

Gordon: When did I learn to forego righteous anger?

H.S.: At different times you allowed its power to pass through you rather than take up residence. But certainly the king showed you that directing your humility to god and not to the nobles or clergy was by far the best solution to your problems, and the philosopher showed how to transpose every impulse with civility so that disagreements were dealt with kindly.

Gordon: I could listen to you for hours.

H.S.: The feeling's mutual, but let me assure you, it wasn't always that way. Many projections, if they got anywhere at all, only reached as far as the soul, and then only on rare occasions.

Gordon: Sounds like a classic case of no job satisfaction.

H.S.: You got that right. Holding the fort on your own is not nearly as much fun as flinging a party for all your friends.

Gordon: When I initiated contact this evening, I wanted to discuss the 'myth' of the higher self versus the 'myth' of Jesus/Buddha etc versus the 'myth' of class war and even the 'myth' of spiritualism, but now I'm moving into sleepy and don't have enough energy for it.

H.S.: That's fine. We'll get to it next time shall we?

Gordon: Thank you.

Friday Jan5/2001/Dialogue 7

Gordon: Many chores and seasonal responsibilities have gobbled up my time since we last spoke. I am glad a space has finally opened up.

H.S.: Seconds, hours, weeks, it's all the same to me. But yes, it's always gratifying to have our continuous energetic interchange manifest into words and concepts.

Gordon: I suppose it all must seem very slow to you, as I type out the words one by one and then correct the mistakes.

H.S.: Well, it's certainly a different rhythm than telepathy, but the challenge is something I enjoy rising to. Besides, as I'm sue you already suspect, I have other interactions to occupy my abilities.

Gordon: Other souls?

H.S.: Yes.

Gordon: Other souls in other epochs and societies?

H.S.: Yes.

Gordon: Past, present and future?

H.S.: If you so wish to indulge in the chocolate box of time.

Gordon: Nice metaphor H.S. Very seasonal.

H.S.: You should know, you gave it to me.

Gordon: I did?

H.S.: Quite specifically, on one of your nighttime visits, you mentioned all your Christmas boxes of chocolate and how much fun it would be to have a special one where the consumption of each chocolate would transport you to a different epoch and life. We vibrated in mutual amusement and I told you I would remind you again when you'd forgotten.

Gordon: If you knew about that then I guess you also know about this new literary project that's taken up much of my time, this Seven Fairly Lucid Dreams, where I'm trying to succinctly conceptualize the experiences of the spheres and the reincarnation cycle. I'll bet you even remember the day I got the idea.

H.S.: Of course, I was part of that. But not quite on your time schedule. On one of your visits here you'd been complaining about not recalling even one tenth of your astral adventures the next day, and I had suggested that you fictionalize it, because that would give your writerly talents free reign to use whatever your so-called imagination came up with.

Gordon: You should have seen me, I was driving my bus in the middle of Toronto, trying to scribble down lines at stoplights!

H.S.: I'll use my earth lives data bank on that one.

Gordon: Can we get back to that comparative thing I wanted to do last time, comparing the various myths?

H.S.: Fine with me. The myth of the higher self, want to start with that?

Gordon: Sure. First off, is it any different in effect than the myth of the soul, in that it gives you something to believe in other than this very limited ego personality?

H.S.: They are similar, but the myth of the higher self gives you a controlling interest in the actual dimensions of that eternity.

Gordon: Excellent, and I hope that it isn't too much for our readers to swallow.

H.S.: If they've come this far they can handle it.

Gordon: That's quite the concept though, a controlling interest in that eternity.

H.S.: Well, those who acknowledge the soul, feel its presence in their everyday lives, know that they are participating in a process that will not end with death, but they do not understand, but they do not understand that process in the post-mortem worlds to be directed at a distance by a being who is, in fact, them.

Gordon: Yes, that's it! Congratulations! I'm sure people will think this is a bit of mutual appreciation society, but you really have caught it there. I often now *feel* this process of the higher self slowly reeling in the soul like a baited fish through the spheres, the soul utterly amazed at all its wondrous experiences but not quite seeing it's being slowly pulled back home.

H.S.: And I don't *experience* it as a reeling in, more as a kind of irresistible magnetism, an inexorable and gradual dissolving of polarities which eventually results in unity, but very much a unity-in-diversity kind of unity.

Gordon: Once again I am reminded of the poet Leonard Cohen, who said somewhere "I am a hotel". A hotel is very unity-in-diversity, isn't it?

H.S.: Yes, all my dear souls staying together under one roof. In an earth sense it's a very appropriate image.

Gordon: I'm curious to hear now what your take is on the myth of Jesus.

H.S.: Am I to take it that you mean Jesus the man and not the Christ spirit which overshadowed him?

Gordon: In a word, yes.

H.S.: Well, certainly the myth of Jesus, by bringing down the divine experience down into the body of a confused carpenter from Galilee, helped man to feel his link to God. But by using the personality of Jesus as the only doorway to heaven, rather than the transcendent consciousness of which he was but a shining example, the church of the Christians caused a bottleneck in the spiritual evolution of this planet. In this, of course, there were not perhaps any worse than any other organized system of religion, where the bureaucratic priesthood seeks to solidify its powers over the populace by placing itself squarely between Man and God, but they certainly are as guilty as any. And as you know from your astral wanderings Gordon, the myth of Jesus takes most of its believers only as far as the upper astral, where they wait, in the blissful ignorance of what you call the typical religionist, for the salvation they know is coming. The ones who are burning with the fervor of their faith merge in ecstasy with the light and feel the process is complete, when in fact it is only another stage on an endless cycle.

Gordon: So would you say the Buddhist or the Hindu has an advantage there?

H.S.: That really depends on their evolutionary level. Lesser evolved souls do not *experience* the upper planes as such, they drift through them, *blissed out* as you say there, and when the desire for action overcomes them once more, down they go, losing their anonymity of bliss bit by bit until suddenly they're someone again, someone who may have subconscious knowledge of divine roots and evolutionary purpose, but who, on the surface of personality, is ripe for the next level of belief system to entrap them in some notion of 'who they are' and 'what they're capable of'. Now the advanced soul, coming out of say, a Buddhist or Hindu incarnation, has a small advantage over their Christian equivalent, in that they understand something of the reincarnation cycle, whereas the Christian or Muslim does not.

Gordon: I get the feeling that overall you find the myths of faith to be limiting for souls.

H.S.: They're like many experiences on your planet; useful for a certain level of growth, and limiting for another level.

Gordon: I can certainly understand that from my own lives.

H.S.: Good, I thought you might. Will your readers?

Gordon: Some will, and some will struggle with it, but I think as a whole my audience is ready for this sort of thing. As you said in your intro to *Eternal Life And How To Enjoy It*, I'm in touch with what a certain sector of the new age audience needs to hear.

H.S.: I'm so touched: you remembered.

Gordon: Keep working on that earth sense of humor and we'll have you down here in no time, having one of these incarnations you keep hearing so much about.

H.S.: That would be an interesting challenge.

Gordon: I know, I know, we can't get all of you into one body.

H.S.: You can't get all of me into ten bodies. I'm a transdimensional being don't you know.

Gordon: Tell me what it feels like…if you can put it into words.

H.S.: Once again I'm going to ask you to *feel*, and then use your own words.

Gordon: Ah, shift the burden to me, very clever. Okay: a seemingly large, soft, warm glowing white space that contains multitudes as it were; many forms and energies in potential. I could move around at will and felt welcome anywhere, and wherever I stopped I was suddenly at rest in the easiest of easy chairs, with any number of pleasant companions ready to manifest at my side, - long time lovers, favorite trees, social situations, any sentient being from any of my incarnate adventures, every slight desire manifested another bliss, added to the bliss of the surroundings, if you can call a featureless vacuum surroundings, and I felt an immediate closeness to the sun, as if that was where the highest consciousness dwells. And I felt conscious links with other galaxies and twigged to the fact that you have energetic deposits on other planets and perhaps always have had. You seemed completely at rest and yet bustling with energy, gorgeous ripples of which seemed so tantalizingly thrilling at every hint of a thought or reflex thereof. Wow, it was really something. And yes, you're right, we couldn't squeeze that into ten bodies.

H.S.: Not bad Gordon, not bad at all. Does that experience not give you an immediate understanding of why religious and political belief systems chain you to inferior heavens? That there is nothing quite so heavenly as your real self? That heaven is, indeed, in your mind?

Gordon: Yes. But can I communicate that to my readers? Maybe only if I encourage them to explore their own higher selves.

H.S.: Yes, lets hope this acts as a catalyst.

Gordon: So just to tie things up then. Are we saying that the myth of the higher self is, among other myths, the most liberating of all?

H.S.: Well, I don't know about you, but I am. Of course, as you're no doubt thinking, it's easy for me, I won't have to account for myself on some talk show, whereas you might. But let it be said, this is the myth that gains you admission to the blissful eternity that is nothing but your Self.

Gordon: Self as universe then.

H.S.: So be it: the word made flesh.

Gordon: Once again.

H.S.: Once again.

Following the hints in the last dialogue, the back cover of this little book, published in November 2001, proudly announced "*Being Watching Doing And Feeling Desirous*: that is one way to describe the urge to incarnate, the rhythmic impulse dignified by the term decision, which oft becomes the curse of the terminally vexed or lackadaisically perplexed. A finger pointing at the moon, is, of course, not the moon, but perhaps these exploratory dialogues between Gordon and his ever gracious cipher of gestation will serve as a pier from which to launch your own probe into the provocative advice of delight."

And despite that delight, a stroll through my notes from 2002 reveals little in the way of Higher Self communications; why that is I'm not exactly sure. Certainly retrievals and contacts continued, as did the slow composition of the novel *Seven Fairly Lucid Dreams*. Likely some local seminars in there too. But no specific attempts at dialoging till January 25, 2003. Despite the time lapse, I thought nothing of naming it

Dialogue8.

<u>Gordon:</u> It is wonderful to be with you're here again.

<u>H.S.:</u> Yes I welcome you and your readers. It is not only an honor, as you say on earth, but lots of fun to have you here.

<u>Gordon:</u> Yes, the pull is almost magnetic, and the desire to rest in your being is almost irresistible.

<u>H.S.:</u> Don't resist it, it's only love.

<u>Gordon:</u> But I have to be a recording secretary here, I can't just topple into bliss.

<u>H.S.:</u> Oh, just slip in for a moment and make yourself at home, and then we'll get back to the note taking.

<u>Gordon:</u> Okay. (a few minutes pass) Well, once again I can't tell where you stop and I begin.

<u>H.S.:</u> Neither can I when we're bonded like this. When you disconnect for earthly activities I can feel a lessening of pressure at the edges, as it were. An absence, a gap, a pause.

<u>Gordon:</u> When I first let go, as you suggested, I felt I had to swim through memories and experiences to get where I wanted to go.

<u>H.S.:</u> But I think you realize the memories and experiences are me, at least as much as anything else.

<u>Gordon:</u> Yes, I saw that there was nowhere to swim. I was there already, with you and the others in the group. All I had to do was widen my perceptions to include more.

<u>H.S.:</u> Ah yes, there's always more. More dust, more experience, more planets, more light.

<u>Gordon:</u> More belief systems too, I suppose.

<u>H.S.:</u> There will always be those.

<u>Gordon:</u> Until we remerge with God?

H.S.: Well yes, but you know you can remerge with god anytime you like. Sit down, relax, and move into the light; or the void as it's sometimes called.

Gordon: I know, lose my personality, forget Gordon and all his issues, float on the tides of the moment, whatever they are, and be as carefree as the wind. It's only my insistence on being separate from god that makes me suffer, right?

H.S.: Right.

Gordon: Do you gossip with the other Higher Selves in your neighborhood?

H.S.: Yes, as part of our multidimensionality, we radiate what you would call wiggly beams of light at each other. It's a sort of high level tickling. We're always devising ways of catching each other off guard.

Gordon: And it's just for fun?

H.S.: Almost everything here is. We're the clowns of the monadic plane, game-playing buffoons with enormous data banks of experience to draw on.

Gordon: As you said that, I was wondering if you might suddenly get serious if one of your energy projections onto the physical plane returned still suffering, but then I saw that the suffering would be shed, bit by bit, on the way up through the planes, and that they wouldn't get to you until it was all gone.

H.S.: Yes you're right, but more transcended than gone, in the way that the lines on old people's faces are said to represent the character formed by challenges and difficulties. But of course, no one returns to me whining and complaining, that's all dealt with on the astral and mental planes.

Gordon: This reminds me of the complaints that newage metaphysics takes the easy way out by not dealing with the social inequalities of most societies, the wars, the plagues, the poverty and cruelty.

H.S.: I sense you want me to answer this to somehow legitimize your own position, so that if people get angry at you, you can always say it was not you but your Higher Self that was talking.

Gordon: The pious prophet hiding behind his revelation?

Yeah, maybe you're right. Okay, I'll answer my own question. The metaphysical position is that every soul chooses its own experiences, from moment to moment, from day to day, from before every birth, and before any cycle of incarnations. But the incarnate personality is rarely aware of this state of affairs, and usually seeks to blame society and family, religion or god, for one or other of his misfortunes. And the density chosen for this planet was such that erroneous and just plain stupid belief systems were bound to arise from the murk of disconnection from the divine and grip souls in the desperate allure of their ignorance, creating a dependence that would take centuries to disassemble. And the other half of the position is, I guess, can you help the suffering to see their own mode of self-infliction? I would say, in most cases, no, that you cannot, although those that strive to do so invent many clever ways of seeing progress in the problem and congratulating themselves on their efforts. What seems to me to actually happen is that the energy for certain game playing bouts of ignorance eventually gets exhausted and the participants retreat to safer/higher/wiser ground to lick their wounds/count their blessings/plan another life.

H.S.: Then why do you strive to counsel, heal and retrieve?

Gordon: I should've known you'd say that. Because, I guess, of the few cases where a little well placed, well-timed nudge can boost the satellite out of its repetitive orbit and onto its original direction. And secondly, because I need something interesting and challenging to pass the time here, where the attractive illusions charm me into participating. Thirdly, I need to expand my sense of self and ability. And, oh yes, fourthly, accumulating information for your precious data banks back there on home base.

H.S.: Fine as far as you went, but you didn't say anything about dispelling darkness with light or investing matter with freedom.

Gordon: Well, what can I say, I got distracted, and my tummy's rumbling. But I sense that's correct, we are dispelling darkness with light. The darkness is the density we created all those millennia ago, when we stepped out of eternal nothingness and thought 'what devastatingly complex game can we create now?'

And then flipped over to this solar system and whipped up out of nothing a really dark dense planetary atmosphere where complete forgetfulness would be balanced with complete free will. We made the darkness and we channel the light, exactly the same way that we bring in the dirt on our shoes and then have to sweep the floor.

H.S.: And with that you'll retire to supper, all smug and self-satisfied?

Gordon: Not before I quote at least a little of the poem I 'wrote' upon waking from a nap the other day, a poem that I believe evokes at least some of your consciousness.

The Future Before
I am a spirit who spans the universe
Both known and ever so fortunately not;
I am also the tales that are endlessly told
Between the many takes of the script;
I am the completion of all strewn plot strands,
Boasting my status backwards through time
To the balloonists suspended in their own hot breath.

That spring saw the reopening of hostilities in Iraq. Notes for a meditation on March 20th reveal an attempt "to bring myself 'up' into the realm of love and understanding, away from the negative fearful war vibe we're living with. The day before I'd gotten quite cranky and irritable about the whole thing and didn't care for a repeat performance." Up through the focus levels past F26, where in "visions of crystal cathedrals and golden temples, the sort of highest refinement of the religious impulse in man, I feel much genuine heartfelt praise for the deity pouring from the structures."

After a quick visit to Shamballa, that mystical city of the spirit referred to in many esoteric teachings from many cultures, supposedly the place where the evolution of mankind is guided, where I seem to gain entry by turning myself into a photon, passing through the psychic barrier and reassembling inside, I head out for the "godhead/Brahman/absolute spirit level, where all the monads seem to hang out. A shining white sea of light with golden points twinkling like stars, and I know from previous visits that each point is a monad/higher self and that moving into any one of them can mean the unfolding of dozens of stories/lives." Then, greeting my 'own' higher self, I "float about inside as if it were a womb. HS agrees that that is one aspect of hir being. Quite lovely and blissful. After that I ask if he/she knows a war is going on. *Yes so I've heard* is the response, but it feels like a couldn't-careless shrug. *So what, there's always wars going on somewhere. It's an important part of the human experience.* He asks what part I'm playing and what I'm learning. I answer that I seem to be keeping the same philosophical attitude already developed in this incarnation. Which is? That there's sides with agendas and those agendas conflict. That each runs on fear and longs to gain or maintain power. And that aggression rises from the fear of losing power."

Then "we seem to share these ideas for a few moments and there's definitely a sense of 'me' patting myself on the back for being so smart. Then HS lets me feel how war activities of the other personality projections in the group are going on 'now' in HS's all-time-is-now perceptive abilities, and how "I", as another projection, am affected by them. I 'feel' swords, horses, bows and arrows, fire and all the hand-to-hand combat variations, duplicitous diplomacy and inventive use of poisons, paid seducers and aristocratic spies. A compact history lesson, complete with emotional and psychological reverberations.

Then it's almost time for me to go, so I bid farewell regretfully, as despite the action packed lesson, it's been a wonderful serene experience, a profound and calming meditation. Later I also recall that during it I was shown how each side in the conflict, including the peace protesters, are providing valuable life lessons for all those participating.

Then, on April 4th, whilst engaged on more exploration and retrieval activity I pause for a HS merge. It was in response to a request form a conversation board member concerning HS's thoughts on the inevitability of war. I notice that I also, split my astral self up, leaving one part to participate in the light projection exercises over the Middle East and letting the one merge with HS, whose response was as follows, -

"The fact of war means little or nothing to me, at least in the human sense. As a set of experiences its value is equal to all other sets of experiences. They all become useful information in my data banks. I have seen several physical plane civilizations rise and fall on this planet, each one a fresh experiment rising from the ashes of previous destruction, and I only use the word 'previous' to give a sense of familiarity to your accustomed linear sense of history. For me, if I choose to so focus, the fall of Atlantis is simultaneous with the heights of Ancient Egypt, or Europe being decimated by the black plague. The joys of a wedding day in classical Greece can be felt at the same time as the tragic death of a baby in renaissance Italy. The senate of Athens and the senate of Washington. I can tune into both and compare it to a meeting of tribal elders in pre-historic Siberia or Australia before the Europeans. The destruction of Atlantis, although stretched through centuries, can be compressed and compared to the bombing of Hiroshima and Nagasaki. The persecution of heretics by those who truly fear for the upsetting of their belief system, the torture of dissidents by the cynical and depraved, the repentance and forgiveness in the between-life state: they can all seem simultaneous to me. For you, if you choose to temporarily ascend and merge with your HS, it would be similar to watching, say, twenty or thirty equally engrossing movies all at once. And if not overwhelmed, you could focus in on any detail, or set of details, that caught your fancy. I am as interested in war as I am in peace, in fighting as much as nursing, in café arguments and barroom brawls. High-level diplomacy and sleazy back room deals. All forms of government and all forms of citizenship. The practice of power and the habits of submission."

I thanked HS for this and said I would do my best to remember and communicate it to the conversation board. HS asked that her love be passed to all on the board. That aspect of me moves back to the one hovering over Israel, remerges, and move son to Iraq for three sets of attempted retrievals. First a group of Kurdish fighters, who seem to sense what I'm up to and politely refuse, implying that they have much purposeful activity to pursue though deceased. Then a group of US soldiers, who radiate the usual suspicions and male pride, but eventually accede to my suggestion of a safe place for some R and R. That was it for that night, but let me just add an interesting experience from a few days later. Another group of Iraqis: I focus in more and they turn out to be all women, women forced into prostitution for the Baath party elite, women who tell me they can't go to heaven as is. A voice from the back shouts 'But we were forced into it!'. This gives me an in: I suggest that I know of a place that is half way to heaven and doesn't follow the normal rules. They gather together, I throw a circle of protective light around us and we're off to a reception area whose operatives will automatically cater to their specific needs. That's the great thing about astral organizations at reception areas. They always know just what to do and when to do it.

ETERNAL LIFE TIPS

(1) Don't take today so seriously: there's always tomorrow.

(2) Don't take this life so seriously: there's plenty of others.

(3) Every incarnation is a play: a play with actors, all of whom fancy themselves as directors.

(4) The plays are all tragicomedies, with equal measures of grief, joy, suffering and pleasure stirred into a pot of economics, politics, culture and religion.

(7) Nothing, on this physical plane, ultimately matters: it's all maya, illusion, a busy marketplace of thought and emotion, the play of light on shifting textures.

(8) This play, this surreally unpredictable courtly dance, exists to be danced, not judged.

(9) The part you have is likely the part you asked for, before being born. If you don't like it, you can always trade up or down.

(10) The parts you played before, and the parts you will play, can, and often do, influence you in the moment. If the subconscious drives and motivations of conventional psychology seem daunting, wait till you get a handle on this.

Final Note...

In response to your question, Gordon, the answer is Yes, it is possible for a soul to reincarnate without having first returned to merge with Higher Self. A variety of belief systems and unfulfilled desires lead souls back to earth without what is most desirable, that they dissolve their earth based personality in the all-forgiving, all-understanding light of the Higher Self. When souls choose, or are lead to do this, the "next' life is considered not so much a new incarnation as part two of the previous life, and is continued as such until the original life plan/goals are worked out to satisfaction. Thus people will take on lives which are very similar in, shall we say, set-up,....personality traits, family relationships, economic level and opportunity, so that lessons utterly failed or avoided can be encountered once more. Thus the murderer will be retempted to murder, the victim quickly confronted with the chance to be victimized, the brute the opportunity to be brutal, the cheat the chance to cheat. The fearful, the lustful, the timid, the controlling, the cruel, all are presented with many trap doors into their old ruts and habits. To see, of course, whether they can resist the easy way out and struggle to a higher level of being.

BOOKS

O books
O is a symbol of the world, of oneness and unity. In
different cultures it also means the "eye", symbolizing
knowledge and insight, and in Old English it means "place
of love or home". O books explores the many paths of
understanding which different traditions have developed
down the ages, particularly those today that express
respect for the planet and all of life.

For more information on the full list of over 300 titles
please visit our website
www.O-books.net

SOME RECENT O BOOKS

Earth Will Be Reborn
Marc Maramay and Val Lynch

An astounding contribution to channeled works - every page is filled with beauty and without repetition. This seasoned traveler who speaks so eloquently of new universes needs to be listened to with gratitude and respect. Its quality will be recognized by all those on the spiritual path.
Kay Mullin, PhD., author of *Wondrous Land*

1905047800 360pp £14.99 $29.95

The Good Remembering
Llyn Roberts

I stumbled into The Good Remembering and felt compelled to read it from cover to cover. Now I recommend it to anyone searching for insight into spiritual growth during these intense times. Responsibly and well-written, it is a magical, powerful little book that transcends words and speaks directly to soul.
Melody Beattie, New York Times Best Selling author of
Co-Dependent No More

1846940389 196pp £9.99 $19.95

Let the Standing Stones Speak
Natasha Hoffman

Destined to become an evergreen...a book that deserves to become a permanent point of reference for the serious seeker. This is a book not to be missed by anyone with either a heart, a mind, or a soul, let alone all three.
Ian Graham author of *God Is Never Late*

1903816793 288pp **£9.99 $14.95**

The Letters of Paul
A new interpretation for modern times
Sylvia Moss

Publication of The Letters of Paul, with revisions and commentary by the original author is an historic event. Above all, there emerges the universality of the teaching by the Christ, of love as the dictum for all ages to come. I was delighted and uplifted, and am pleased to commend the book to you.
Donald Keys, founder of SANE and co-founder of Planetary Citizen

1903816947 336pp 254x718 **£14.99 $24.95**

The Vision
Out of-body revelations of divine wisdom
Jaap Hiddinga

What a refreshing treasure I found this book to be. I felt like I had my own beliefs and intuition validated, and in others I felt challenged to look beyond my scope of comfort and to re-evaluate what I had come to know as true. This simple yet very insightful book can be a great help to many on their path to enlightenment.
StarzRainbowRose

1905047053 144pp £9.99 $14.95

The Art of Being Psychic
The power to free the artist within
June Elleni-Laine

A brilliant book for anyone wishing to develop their intuition, creativity and psychic ability. It is truly wonderful, one of the best books on psychic development that I have read. I have no hesitation in recommending this book, a must for every bookshelf.
Suzanna McInerney, former President, College of Psychic Studies

1905047541 160pp £12.99 $24.95

Journey Home
A true story of time and inter-dimensional travel
Tonika Rinar

2nd printing
A lifeline that has been tossed out from the universe to help tether those lost in the wake of recent world events. If you are willing to open your mind, Tonika will take you on a journey home, to a place that shines bright within each of us...... all you have to do is reach for it.
Amazon

1905047002 272pp **£11.99 $16.95**

Spirit Release
A practical handbook
Sue Allen

A comprehensive and definitive guide to psychic attack, curses, witchcraft, spirit attachment, possession, soul retrieval, haunting, soul rescue, deliverance and exorcism, and more. This book is the most comprehensive I have seen on the subject of spirit release. This book is a must for anyone working and dealing with people.
Becky Walsh, presenter of The Psychic Show on LBC

1846940338 256pp **£11.99 $24.95**

Spiritwalking
Poppy Palin

Drawing together the wild craft of the shamanic practitioner and the wise counsel of the medium or psychic, Spiritwalking takes the reader through a practical course in becoming an effective, empathic spiritwalker. In an era blighted by professional mystics, Poppy Palin is the real thing. You can trust her - and what she writes - completely.
Alan Richardson, author of *The Inner Guide to Egypt* and others

1846940311 320pp **£11.99 $24.95**

9 Days to Heaven
How to make everlasting meaning of your life
Teresa O'Driscoll

This book offers a tactile and tangible way to feel closer to God's world. The meditations are truly moving and inspiring. I highly recommend 9 Days to Heaven to anyone seeking to invite conscious contact with God at any level.
Reneé Killian-Dawson, author

1905047738 128pp **£9.99 $17.95**

Christianity in 10 Minutes
Brian Mountford

If you want to begin at the beginning with the Christian faith, I can't think of a better way than by sitting down and reading this little book through. Plain-spoken, straightforward, succinct, here is a fresh introduction to the essentials-what Christians believe, how and why they believe what they do, what difference it can all make. If you've been around churches all your life and never fully grasped what it's all about, this is a superb refresher. If Christian faith is brand new to you, what a helpful first step you're holding in your hands.
Rev. Dr. Sam Lloyd, Dean of the National Cathedral, Washington DC

1905047096 64pp **£4.99 $8.95**

Contemporary Creed
A mini-course in Christianity for today
John Morris

This is a great "little book" for study and personal devotions, reading during Advent and Lent, and as preparation for Holy Baptism and/or Confirmation.
Episcopal Life

Powerful, remarkable and thought-provoking. Don't miss it!
UKCBD

1905047371 176pp **£5.99 $14.95**

God at Eventide
A devotional diary
A. J. Russell

35th printing
This powerful sequel to God Calling has a message of hope and comfort forged out of adversity. It has touched the hearts of millions.

1903019419 260pp 135/95mm **£5.99 cl.** US rights sold

God in the Bath
Relaxing in the everywhere presence of God
Stephen Mitchell

This little book is destined to become a spiritual classic. The many spiritual pearls of wisdom found in this book connect the Christian journey of faith with the odyssey of life. A wonderfully refreshing and invigorating reading of Christianity.
Nigel Leaves, author of *Odyssey*

1905047657 112pp **£9.99 $19.95**

God's Space in You
Melvyn Matthews

2nd printing
A simply written but accessible book that will give inspiration
and help to those wishing to pray from within, in the business of
this world.

1842981013 96pp b/w illustrations 135/05mm **£4.99**
US rights sold

Keylines
Ann Henning Jocelyn

Anne Joycelin has been developing a following throughout the
country and, indeed, Europe, for her poetic reflections on love
and loss, growth and relationships. A book of hope and comfort
for all points of life's journey.

1846940435 160pp **£9.99 $19.95**

Other Temptations of Jesus
Lenten studies for adventurous Christians
John Henson

The Christian life is not about giving up, but taking up. The call of Jesus to discipleship is a positive one-love God and your neighbour. It's not about being serious, but happy and loving. Lenten studies for adventurous Christians. Recommended by the Archbishop of Canterbury, **Rowan Williams.**

1842981404 128pp £7.99

Other Communions of Jesus
Eating and drinking the good news way
John Henson

In these studies Christians are challenged to return to the mind of Jesus by allowing all the evidence of the gospels to be put into the balance. We have reversed his intentions. Communion should be a means of inclusion, not exclusion. Although the author's prime purpose is devotional, there are revolutionary implications. Should the churches take the contents of this book seriously, communion will never be the same again.

1905047495 220pp **£11.99 $24.95**

Perfect Freedom
Why liberal Christianity might be the faith you're looking for
Brian Mountford

2nd printing
*Wonderful, lively and robust explanation and defence of a more liberal
attitude to Christianity. If you want to know what liberal Christianity
is like in a few punchy sentences and a good deal of honesty from the
author then this book is for you.*
The Door

1905047185 108pp £9.99 $15.95

The Prophet of the New Millennium
Principles for an unprincipled age
Greg Dark

The Prophet of the New Millennium is not an alternative to
Gibran's book, it is a complement to it. Today's world is very
different to Gibran's. The political atlas has had to be modified
frequently. This provides the ethical equivalent. It does not seek
to define principles, or to provide answers, but it does seek to
help readers find their own questions.

1905047576 128pp £9.99 $16.95 cl.

Psalm
The world's finest soul poetry, told in a contemporary idiom
Peter Owen-Jones

Psalms are song lyrics, the poetry of the soul. Written around 2500-3500 years ago, they are part of our history, our consciousness. This selection, taking its inspiration from rap and country and western, brings the intent of the writers into the poetry and language of today.

1903816912 32pp 135/90mm **£4.99 $8.95**

True Stories

These inspiring true-life stories of faith, heroism and endurance, of suffering and humiliation, repentance and glory, trace the impact of the Christian faith down the ages and into the present day, into our own lives.

About the Bible 1905047347
About the Passion 1905047363
Of Conversion 1905047355

All illustrated, 128pp, **£5.99 $9.95**

The Wandering Sage
Timeless wisdom from our alternative teachers
Robert Van de Weyer

This collection of over 70 stories of Mulla Nasrudin captures the flavour of timeless wisdom and counter-cultural wit that is part of our Heritage. The stories are suitable for all ages, easy to remember, and once remembered never forgotten.

1903816653 128pp 205/130mm **£4.99 $7.95**

The Wise Fool's Guide to Leadership
Short spiritual stories for organisational and personal transformation
Peter Hawkins

This is a real gem of a book. Many readers will be familiar with the Sufi tales involving the holy fool Mulla Nasrudin. Here Peter Hawkins applies the Nasrudin treatment to management consultancy and the results are hilarious. Essential reading for anyone working in an organisation.
Scientific and Medical Network Review

1903816963 160pp **£7.99 $11.95**

Fairy World

This gentle introduction for children to the world of the elementals is a joy to behold with delicate illustrations to light up the pages. It takes young readers to an ancient land full of wonderful creatures. Fairies, elves, brownies, dwarves, gnomes, water fairies and pixies are all present and correct in this fluid, rhyming tale. the notion of karma is also explored so youngsters can learn from an early age that whatever you do will come back to you. Perfect bedtime reading.
Vision

24pp 155/135mm **£4.99 $7.95** cl

Fairy Lullabies 1903816769
Fairy Magic 190381684X
Fairy Secrets 1903816831
Fairy Spells 1903816823

Patrick and the Cat that Saw Beyond Time
Zoe d'Ay

This is a magical story. Truly inspired. It is itself a myth, a sacred story, which opens the heart to the other world which lies beyond and yet within this every day world. It is itself an initiation into that inner mystery.
Bede Griffiths
1903816661 128pp 210/140mm **£6.99 $9.95**

Relax Kids: Aladdin's Magic Carpet
And other fairytale meditations for children
Marneta Viegas

2nd printing

This is a marvellous idea for the younger generation. The perfect bedtime story as it relaxes the children and promotes happy, peaceful dreams. But it's not just for bedtime-it would also be an excellent aid for teachers in the classroom. Exquisitely illustrated with colourful illustrations to fuel the imagination. Such a simple yet effective idea-every parent should own one so youngsters can develop relaxation into the habit of a lifetime.
Vision

1903816661 128pp full colour throughout 210/140mm **£9.95 $14.95**

Relax Kids: The Wishing Star
52 meditations for children (5+)
Marneta Viegas

2nd printing

This is an enchanting and beautifully illustrated book for children, parents and even our inner child! Intense, sensory meditations containing images, actions, experiences, feelings, What a fun way to nurture your inner child, free your imagination and creativity, and build your own self-confidence and self-awareness.
ISIS talk

1903816777 128pp full colour throughout 210/140mm **£9.95 $14.95**